Curated

A Museum Love Story

Nellie Wilson

Contents

To Rust Belt women on SSRIs – we're built different.
And to anyone working to make a better future by
studying the past.

Author's Note

Hello -

Thanks for picking up Curated. It's my love letter to museums, historic research, found family in your 30s, defining success, living with anxiety, and finding happiness. It's inspired by my own time working in museums, my love for Colorado, and my work as a historian. There are a few things you should know before you head into it, just in case there are things in the content that could be upsetting to you.

This book contains:

Depictions of anxiety (Emmy, one of the main characters, is on SSRIs and is in therapy)

Open-door romance (multiple on-page sex scenes)

Alcohol consumption, references to marajuana

Use of the word "crazy" (addressed and corrected by characters).

I hope you enjoy.

Much love,

Nellie Wilson

1

Emmy

Of all the beautiful end-of-summer days, the universe had picked this specific one to fuck Emmy over.

Which was, honestly, expected. Things had been going too well for her recently.

It was supposed to be a typical day, nothing special, potentially better than average. It was the beginning of the end of summer – the heat was out of the air and the mountains sparkled, not yet capped by their winter hats of snow. Students hadn't yet returned to campus, so it was thankfully barren, only staff and graduate students slogging through extra classes and research.

Emmy sometimes missed her graduate school days. Almost, but not really. There was something liberating back then about being in her midtwenties and not having to worry about her career path and her life's legacy – just classes, part-time jobs, and cheap booze. Thirty-three was different, to say the least.

Before the Great Fucking-Over, Emmy had taken the bus to Vanberg University's campus as usual, holding a large cup of generic grocery store coffee in her hands and listening to a podcast to avoid anyone who wanted to make annoying small talk. Hopping off at the stop in front of the museum, Emmy took a giant sip of coffee, burned her mouth, swore to herself, and then crossed the street, avoiding the aggressive cyclists that tended to zip down the main street without looking for cars or pedestrians.

She looked up at the old house that held her home away from home — the Vanberg University Historical Center and Archival Collections (VUHCAC, which sounded less like a museum and more like an early 1940s supercomputer, so her friends referred to it as The House). The maroon brick building had a way of welcoming her in and helping her start her workdays. And keeping her company during late nights. And often weekends. The Queen Anne Victorian had been the home of the university's founding mother, Sara Jonesboro, and was located on the western boundary of VU's sprawling campus at the base of the Rocky Mountains.

Emmeline — Emmy — Bonaire was the lead curator there, a job she loved with all of her heart, even as it occasionally ripped that heart to shreds and stepped on the pieces. Her life's calling was to uncover and share the stories and secrets hidden in the museum's collection — the photos, the documents, the artifacts. Her current research, and what she had planned on spending her morning working on, was an exhibition that would convince visitors that Sara Jonesboro was not the reclusive, eccentric widow that conventional history had portrayed her as, but a progressive, proto-feminist who was responsible for the majority of the liberal sheen and welcoming atmosphere of the college town.

Unfortunately, that meant The House would have to *have* visitors to convince.

Emmy sighed and hoisted her messenger bag onto her shoulder again, shifting her coffee into her right hand to wrangle her keys out of a pocket with her left. She unlocked and pushed open the heavy oak door, and the bulky book-filled bag banged against her thigh, pressing on the bruise that hadn't gone away since her undergraduate days. She had been at The House more or less since she had moved to Vanberg to begin graduate school at twenty-four, where she had begun as a research assistant. Emmy had benefited from a series of retirements to move into the coveted role of *curator*, but she had also worked extra hard to get there. Campus rumor held that Sara haunted The House, though Emmy sometimes felt that *she* was actually the ghost. She had come to the building as a young woman and was doomed to spend her existence banging around the drafty building.

Emmy, for what it was worth, blamed the ghost sightings on the lack of funding to fix shitty old plumbing. Or heat exhaustion when the air conditioning didn't work.

Wiping the sweat from her forehead as she walked into the living room that functioned as a welcome center, Emmy tried to make sure that her bangs weren't permanently stuck to her forehead. *Why did I keep cutting these stupid bangs myself through lockdown?* she thought to herself. *I should have grown them out and not had to deal with any of this bullshit through the summer.* Huffing a stream of air onto her own face to cool herself down, Emmy waved to the graduate assistant managing the front desk and continued into a back hallway, walking up the former servants' staircase to her office, praying that the window air conditioner would decide to work today.

Unlocking the small room with her keys still dangling from her fingers, Emmy dumped her bag onto an empty chair and walked over to the window A/C unit to flip the switch. The machine sputtered, gave a groan, and refused to turn on.

"Fucker," Emmy spat at the unit. She opened the adjacent window to let in some of the cooler morning air before it warmed up too much. Slipping off her sandals and sitting in her creaking desk chair (which was missing half the padding on the left armrest), she slid over to her desk and shook her mouse to wake her computer and begin the daily task of sorting through her emails. She grabbed an old copy of last year's annual report (*History is Now!*) and was fanning herself, attempting to get her computer to connect to the internet, when there was a knock at her door. Swiveling around in her chair, adjusting her bangs, Emmy saw the museum director, Dr. Marshall Scholz.

Seeing Marshall (which was how Emmy referred to him in private – he always insisted on being referred to as "Dr. Scholz" in meetings) out of his office was a rare occurrence. A tall, gangly academic with curly red hair that could give 1960s Art Garfunkel a run for his money, Marshall rarely approached curatorial staff (and god forbid he would ever talk to public-facing staff). He preferred to spend his time working on translations of German legal documents (his research specialty), turfing grant applications to Emmy, or avoiding conversations with museum trustees (his other two specialties.)

"Dr. Scholz?" Emmy said, raising her eyebrows at him and sliding her chair a few inches toward the door. There wasn't much space in her office to roll, let alone to have a meeting with the director.

"Emmy. Lovely to see you," he mumbled. *You came into* my *office*, she thought. She blinked, waiting for him to continue his sentence and let her know why he was disturbing her morning email routine. "Meeting in the dining room. Ten a.m." With that loquacious announcement, he gave a curt nod and left her doorway. Emmy's eyes flicked to the time on her computer screen – 8:32 a.m. That gave her precisely one hour and twenty-eight minutes to figure out what the hell this meeting would be about.

Emmy didn't like surprises or unplanned events, and she especially hated knowing that *something* was going to happen without knowing what that something would entail. It was why her best friend, Phoebe, had learned never to just text her a *Can we talk*? and Jeremy, her other best friend, knew to let her know his plans for the entire evening when he invited her over to his house. It was why Emmy diligently read every agenda before heading into the meeting. And it was why her last attempt at a relationship had fallen apart. Ethan had gotten sick of her asking him what he was planning for every date.

He had also gotten sick of Emmy constantly asking him if he was mad at her. Turns out, doing that would make people mad, even if they weren't to begin with

Having generalized anxiety disorder made moving through the world a constant series of small disasters, always anticipating when the next one *could* happen and preparing for that outcome. A white noise of low-grade panic attacks. Emmy had been dealing with it since about the age of eleven, but that didn't make it any easier. It was just familiar.

Grunting at her computer, Emmy logged off and went in search of information. Meetings in the dining room of The House were rare and often meant big events – presentation of the annual report, meetings with the trustees, pitches to donors. The museum staff had a more casual environment throughout their offices, one that meant that most meetings were held in doorways or in the shared staff kitchen. Or in Emmy's ideal setting – one of the myriad bars or breweries in Vanberg to hash out ideas and disagreements. Emmy figured she would need a drink by the end of the day.

Leaving her office, Emmy went to find Phoebe. She checked the Education office (empty) and the kitchen (just a few graduate students eating leftover catering from last night's lecture on local archaeology). She finally found Phoebe eating her breakfast in the back garden.

Brushing up around five foot eleven with straight black hair and possessing a cynical outlook on life from her upbringing in a crumbling steel town, Emmy sometimes felt like the living embodiment of a storm cloud. Phoebe — five-two, curly brown hair, with an optimistic disposition — was in many ways Emmy's opposite, a ray of sunshine and positivity, always ready to provide a differing perspective when Emmy was going into one of her spirals. They had met when Phoebe had joined the museum as a graduate student, just one year after Emmy had graduated with her master's, and they had been inseparable ever since.

"Phoebes!" Emmy called, walking over to where her friend was seated on a bench. "Did Marshall talk to you?"

"About what?" she asked, popping a bite of blueberry muffin into her mouth. "About how we had over twenty people at last night's lecture?" Phoebe was the museum's education coordinator, which meant she oversaw all the programming for schools and summer camps. However, in the past two years, Marshall had also tasked Phoebe with "adult education" programs, which usually meant lectures on dry topics, served with even drier cookies. Phoebe, always a yes-woman, had agreed to the new tasks, even though she still wasn't a full-time employee. Emmy could empathize. Though she was a curator, she had finally arrived at the point where she didn't need to make some kind of money on the side while working full time, and that was just because of COVID relief money and student loan payment freezes. The joys of non-profit career choices, to be sure.

"I'm so proud of you, my dear," Emmy said dryly. "But I was talking about his cryptic announcement about this morning's meeting. It was *not* on my Google Calendar. I double checked."

"Yeah, he did say something when I saw him by the front desk as I walked in. Now that you mention it, it's suspicious as hell that he wasn't in his cave. He's never even been in the education office. Did his skin burn when he set foot into yours?"

"Right? Did you text Jer?"

"Not yet. I doubt he's even at work yet, so I'm sure he doesn't even know." Jeremy, the third member of their museum trio, was an exhibit designer who was perennially running late (except to happy hour) and had a habit of sneaking up the back stairs to his attic studio so no one would know exactly what time he arrived at work.

"Fair point," Emmy said, fiddling with her bangs. "It just gives me bad vibes."

"You think every meeting is about something terrible," Phoebe pointed out, crumpling up her muffin wrapper. "You have anxiety — it's sort of your thing, my dear."

"Fuck you," Emmy said with love.

Phoebe grinned and stood up, brushing a few crumbs off her pants and wrangling her hair into a bun. "I'm sure it will be fine. Just do a breathing exercise or go for a short walk. Then you'll feel better."

Emmy groaned in an exaggerated manner, following Phoebe back into The House. "*Fine*," she whined, elongating the word. "I'll go do my job and try to ignore the big, terrifying meeting that we have to attend."

"Proud of you!" Phoebe replied brightly, blowing Emmy a kiss and heading to the front desk. Emmy made her way back to the office, shooting a quick text to Jeremy to see if he knew anything, though it was probably a wasted effort. Jer, for all his artistic brilliance, never checked his cell phone.

It's probably nothing, Emmy told herself as she settled back into her desk chair. She looked down at her left hand and tried the activity her therapist had recommended. For every finger, she was supposed to think of a positive outcome instead of a negative.

Thumb: A big donation to a collection.

Pointer finger: Marshall came up with a new program idea.

Middle finger: Oh, fuck this.

Groaning, Emmy wiggled her mouse to wake up her computer and took in the collection of sticky notes that framed the screen. A bright blue one caught her eye, as it always did. *MAA Conference – April; Submission Deadline February*. Each year, Emmy attempted to get the courage to submit to the largest museum conference in the country, but she always chickened out at the last minute. She would end up submitting to smaller regional conferences where she knew her work would be accepted.

This was the year, she told herself, finally getting the computer to awaken. She was on to something with her research, and she had some great exhibit ideas. This was the year to make the national splash.

After she figured out what this meeting was about, anyway.

2

Emmy

After puttering through articles and emails, 9:45 had finally rolled around, and Emmy picked up her notebook and walked to the dining room. Emmy had a very "if you're on time, you're late" mentality, which had helped her get out of her shit hometown and had carried over to her professional life. This often set her apart from the other humanities academics she worked with.

From her office, Emmy headed downstairs, then through the living room and bedroom used as exhibition spaces, and then into the dining room. She was surprised to see it half-full of faces she didn't recognize. There was a large table in the middle (most visitors thought it was an artifact – Emmy took pride in reminding them it was a copy of the original because why would they allow a meeting with coffee to take place around an artifact?) that was crowded with people, so Emmy slid into a chair at an empty table to the side.

There was a woman dressed in a power suit at the front of the room. She looked vaguely familiar to Emmy, but she couldn't quite place her. Scanning the rest of the crowd, Emmy's attention snagged on a tall man with longer blond hair and intense green eyes behind thick, dark-rimmed glasses. He was wearing a standard light blue dress shirt, and he was looking at an iPad, making notes with an Apple Pencil. Emmy looked at her own battered notebook and free VU pen and felt technologically impaired.

Well, whoever *he* was, she wouldn't mind giving him a private tour of the museum later.

Phoebe showed up a few minutes later, dropping into the chair next to Emmy with an exaggerated sigh. "Seriously, what is going on? I have a million registration forms to process this morning because Marshall insists that schools still register through the mail."

"First off, I highly doubt you have a *million*," Emmy said dryly. Phoebe snorted in agreement. "Also, do you recognize any of these people? I feel like I've seen a few of them before, but I'm drawing a blank." Phoebe shrugged and opened her own notebook. It was covered in ridiculous stickers, most of them some type of pun. *Historians do it Chicago Style*, read the most recent addition.

"They're dressed so boringly," Phoebe commented, scanning her to-do list. Emmy had to agree – the majority of the unfamiliar faces in the conference room were in business casual, with gray, navy blue, and khaki being the dominant colors. The history museum's team tended toward "hipster" on a good day, "out-of-work art teacher" on an average day, and "struggling street busker" on a rough day, especially if there had been a happy hour the night before. Emmy looked over at Phoebe, who was wearing a bright yellow and black striped shirt that had embroidered bees over one shoulder.

"Agreed," Emmy said. "But I feel like I've seen some of them, maybe at a fundraiser or something?" She subtly pointed to the Ridiculously Attractive Man, who had pushed his glasses up into his hair and was spinning his Apple Pencil between his fingers. "I'd definitely remember being in a meeting with *him*."

"You're too much," Phoebe said. The clock turned to ten, and the woman at the front of the room with a severe bob and straight black hair cleared her throat and clicked on the projector.

"Fuck, a slideshow is never a good sign," Emmy muttered. The screen showed the Vanberg University logo and was themed in the college's colors of silver and purple.

"Good morning," the woman said with a clear, firm voice. "I am Sarah Tan, from the University's budget office."

Emmy's stomach dropped. Museums and budgets didn't have a good relationship on the best days, but issues were usually handled internally – or, more likely, by Emmy scrambling to shit out a grant application at the last minute. There was no way that this meeting, with these strangers, with this woman, could bode well.

See, Emmy thought to herself. *AnxietyBrain was right. This was going to be bad.* At that moment, Jeremy sauntered into the room with an apologetic wave.

"Lost track of time," he whispered, sitting next to Emmy. He flipped to a new page in his sketch pad and began to doodle, seemingly unaffected by being late and the presence of so many new faces. Sarah Tan, still at the front of the room, gave a sharp look to Jeremy and continued with her presentation. She clicked, and a new slide with a complicated graph flashed on the screen.

"As you may have heard, the state released its annual budget for the next year, along with the five-year projections for continued funding. Suffice it to say, it does not look good. This, combined with the residual fallout from shutdowns, the end of federal COVID relief money, and the decrease in tax revenue because of new laws, puts the future of your respective museums in jeopardy."

Fuck. Emmy's AnxietyBrain was in overdrive, and she tried to remind herself to slow her breathing, even though she felt her pulse begin to skyrocket. Sarah Tan clicked to another slide, and Emmy's leg started jiggling so aggressively that it wiggled the table. Emmy couldn't quite follow all the different graphs and figures that were flashing across the screen, her brain distracted by what it could all mean. Phoebe put her hand on Emmy's leg and mouthed *breathe*.

"Taking all of these factors into consideration, the university has made this decision for the long-term security of these institutions in fiscal terms." Emmy began to hate every word that came out of Sarah Tan's business-jargony mouth.

"The fuck does this mean?" Jeremy muttered, doodling a detailed middle finger at the corner of the page. The cold chill had turned to a series of pinpricks over Emmy's body, and she had started to chew on her thumbnail.

"That is to say," an older man with salt and pepper hair took over, "As of the fall semester, the Historical Center and Archival Collections and the Center for Science and Technology will be combined into one research center and museum."

"What?" The word rushed out of Emmy's mouth before she could stop herself. "How?" *What the fuck?* At least she didn't say that part out loud.

"Excellent question, Ms. Bonaire," said Sarah Motherfucking Tan – *How did she know her name?* – and clicked to another slide on the presentation. Emmy looked for Marshall, who was hiding in a corner of the room, pointedly not looking at any of the history museum's staff members. She wondered how long he had known about this upcoming change and how long he had hidden it. Emmy wondered (not for the first time) how Marshall had even found himself director of their museum when he seemed incapable of doing any actual administrative tasks. The next slide showed a timeline with a font so small, Emmy could barely read it. She squinted her eyes and tried to see what it while her stomach continued to churn.

"This seems like an aggressive timeline," Jeremy was saying. "When Fort Collins Museum of Discovery opened, it took years of planning."

"And that wonderful organization is the model for what we're hoping to achieve here at Vanberg University," Sarah Tan replied in a clipped tone. "However, budget restrictions and the university's strategic plan dictate that we must move at an aggressive pace in order to sustain the overall goals of the organization's metrics..." her speech meandered into incomprehensible bureaucratic talk, and Emmy's mind continued to spiral.

Emmy, worried about her job security, seethed with rage at Marshall. Sarah Motherfucking Tan continued to click through the slides with occasional input from the gray-haired man, who had revealed himself to be a Dr. Carter, the director for the Center for Science and Technology. Well, former director. Of a former museum. Emmy kept looking at Marshall to chime in or to say *anything* during the presentation.

Jeremy raised his hand, which was light years more polite than Emmy could imagine being. After receiving a nod of acknowledgment, he flipped through his notebook and asked, "What about our planned exhibition schedule? Events? I would assume that the CST also has a calendar they've worked on for some time." Emmy could tell Jeremy was doing his best to push down his frustration and assume a businesslike air to uncover more information, which was what he did best. He tended to soak up things in a casual way, a secret sponge for information.

"That's why we've brought you all together — to build the team that will figure that out," Dr. Carter said, smiling grimly. "Gathered in this room, we've got the essential staff members from both institutions. For the time being, this beautiful historic building will house all staff, and we will begin work on a plan to move exhibitions over to the CST's exhibition hall.

"However, we'll be in discussion about future plans for relocating staff and creating long-term shared space for collections and exhibitions. This will all be discussed in conjunction with the budgeting department, who will also be developing a fundraising campaign."

Sarah Tan cleared her throat again. "There are no plans for staff cuts at the moment, so it's important that we work together to support the mission of the new institution." Instead of being comforted by that statement, Emmy's brain hung on three key words — *at the moment*. That meant that there was a definite possibility of staff cuts in the future. Emmy had not busted her ass this long to have some high and mighty science curator swoop in and steal her hard-earned museum space and position. She felt her shoulders straighten, her face turn hard. This was war.

"New mission?" the Ridiculously Attractive Man asked, putting his glasses back on to look at the screen. "Isn't that usually done with input from the staff?" *Maybe he was one of the good ones*, Emmy thought. Were there even good ones at times like this?

"Circumstances being what they are, we decided it would benefit the combination if, from the get-go, there was one unifying mission to guide our work together," Dr. Carter said, pointing to himself and Marshall. Marshall, who still hadn't said anything. A new slide was revealed:

The Vanberg University Historical Center and Archival Collections and the Center for Science and Technology are joining to become the Center for Science, Technology, and History, where the community can experience the joy of learning through multiple disciplines.

Emmy had too many questions in her brain to truly process the flowery language of the new mission statement. Her breathing had gotten shallow, moving to the upper part of her lungs, and her eyes darted around the room. Every single unfamiliar face immediately became a threat — a threat to her institution, a threat to her job, and a threat to what she had been working toward for years. A threat to her future plans to make this museum mean something to the larger world. To make a legacy with her own research. She knew what happened when the humanities — especially history — went up against science and technology in academia.

History lost. Badly.

The university had been consistently cutting funding and staff from the departments of the Arts and Humanities for years now. Emmy had been able to afford her master's degree through fellowships that no longer existed. STEM fields, on the other hand, bloated their departments with grants and funding that pulled from both governmental and private donations. Emmy had always known, in the back of her mind, that VU was lucky to even have a museum devoted to history, knew how rare (and how useless, truth be told) a graduate program in museum studies was. But it was now being threatened, and Emmy didn't feel so lucky anymore. Her eyes cut over to Phoebe and Jeremy, a life raft of familiar faces in the sea of threats. Phoebe caught her eye and mouthed, *Drinks*? Emmy nodded, and Jer gave a curt nod of agreement.

As Sarah Tan and whatever his name was who directed the science museum kept talking about timelines and strategic plan developments, Emmy's mind went into survival mode. She started sizing up the people she didn't know. She figured she could write off anyone in a tailored business suit as working for the university's budgeting or HR department. Though it had been a while since she had worked with a scientist. Maybe in the 2020s they were able to afford better clothes than the ecology PhD student she had hooked up with during her first year of grad school. Maybe that evil corporate funding also came with a clothing budget.

The woman near the front of the room with pale brown hair and glasses? Emmy pegged her as a collections manager. The person next to her with hair that vaguely reminded Emmy of Bernie Sanders, who was scrambling and making notes on a yellow legal pad — probably a researcher of some kind. Not organized enough to be a curator (though, Emmy quickly considered her own desk and realized she didn't give off organizational vibes either). The sharply dressed woman with chunky glasses? Definitely in some type of design — exhibitions or marketing. The science center probably had their own social media manager, whereas the history museum's social media management fell to Emmy or Phoebe.

Emmy considered what she looked like to the other members of the room. Long, perennially straight black hair with a set of bangs. Tall enough that someone looking at her could tell even when she sat down that she was above average height. Gray eyes that tended to roll and a mouth that was usually contributing to her Resting Bitch Face. She had dressed for the end of summer today – a pair of loose khaki pants and a white blouse with a small, embroidered collar that, if you looked closely, was actually an intricate pattern of skulls and crossbones. The blouse was loose around her arms, which was nice, because Emmy was just getting out of a lifting program that had focused on her upper body, and her arm muscles had grown significantly and stretched tighter sleeves.

"Phoebe Whitford, education and public programs." Phoebe gave a small wave, then busied herself with wrangling her curly hair into a small bun at the base of her neck, which Emmy knew was her tell – she had decided to focus on something and give it her full attention.

"Jeremy Rinci, exhibitions." Jer – taller than Emmy, with the grace of a ballet dancer, gave another nod, his light blond curls tumbling over his forehead in an annoyingly fashionable way. His full lips gave a small smile as his glass-blue eyes swept over the room. Even though Jeremy would never be interested in Emmy, she still found herself getting nervous around him in meetings, his beauty stunning in a Renaissance painting sort of way.

Then, she realized, it was her turn. "Emmeline – Emmy – Bonaire. Archival Director and Curator at VUHCAC."

She knew, as soon as the words left her mouth, that the last part was a bitchy move. They were supposed to be one organization now — no one else was claiming themselves by their home team, but Emmy couldn't help herself. Everything felt like it was one second from slipping out of her grasp, and she was scrambling for any handhold she got.

Introductions continued, and Emmy's eyes continued to scan the room, not listening to the names, until she found herself looking at the Ridiculously Attractive Man. Emmy decided she needed a new name for him, since he was now known to be one of Them. She studied him for purely objective reasons, she told herself. His shoulders were broad, and his skin didn't have the paleness of someone who spent most of his time in a lab or a collection. His green eyes seemed to sparkle (ugh, of course they did), sweeping over the group of people in a lazy way, and his hair caught the sunlight in a way that reminded Emmy of illustrations of Adonis or Achilles. It only served to piss her off more.

Education, she guessed. Or public programs. She probably wouldn't have to deal with him that much — which was good, because Emmy became nervous around attractive people, and when she was nervous, she was sharp and short-tempered (even more than usual). Yeah, even marketing or PR would fit in. Or...

"Dr. Ryan Andersson. Geology Curator," he said with a rumble in his voice, eyes flickering around the room and a smile lighting up his face. He looked at her and gave a tiny wave. She glowered. Ridiculously Attractive Man was now Ridiculously Attractive Enemy #1.

Fuck.

3

Ryan

Ryan — Dr. Andersson, his mom would insist on calling him — had known something was off from the moment the meeting's invite had shown up on his Google Calendar yesterday. His director never called meetings out of their office space if he could help it, and he knew most of his staff avoided the Humanities Quad of campus out of fear of having to talk to new people. Ryan enjoyed eating his lunch at the park
there.

He looked down at his iPad, where he had scrawled a few notes, including the inane new mission statement, in his messy, all-caps writing.

Exhibitions? Curatorial priorities? Research funding? As curator — a role he had only started before shutdown and was now finally understanding in its full breadth — these were things he was supposed to know. Trained as a paleontologist, Ryan had made the decision early on in graduate school to spend less time in the field and more time in science communication, which had led him to working with various museums throughout his PhD.

Becoming a curator had seemed like a natural step, but there were a million different responsibilities he hadn't anticipated, and this was one more wrench in his plan.

"Dr. Ryan Andersson. Geology Curator," he said, looking around the room, trying to memorize all the new faces. Falling back on his Minnesota upbringing, he gave a grin that, in undergrad, he would have used to get a number at a bar. Now, however, it helped to win over new colleagues. His gaze, not for the first time during this meeting, caught on the woman seated at the round table in the corner. He widened his smile, gave a tiny wave – she had said she was a fellow curator, right? She met his eyes and gave a frown, and Ryan swore he could feel a chill that reminded him of playing pond hockey in St. Cloud.

"And, once again, I'm Dr. Carter – former director of the CST, and I will be assuming the role of interim director of the CSTH." Ryan had to remind himself that was the name of their new museum.

"Dr. Scholz and I have decided to reserve the rest of this meeting as an opportunity for you to get to know your new coworkers." I *guess that makes sense*, Ryan thought, his internal monologue in overdrive to process all this new information. Carter clicked a slide, and Ryan saw that each department from each museum had been combined, the science museum's staff names in Vanberg University purple, and the history center's names in VU silver. His eyes scanned the list, and found that, under curatorial, the department had been subdivided into two groups.

Collections managers — who, if Ryan had to be honest, did the real work of actually supervising and understanding the collection — were going to be meeting outside. Ryan, as a curator, was responsible for the overall direction of the collection and the way the museum used artifacts in exhibitions. Though he had probably been slacking there recently. Collections managers took care of the day-to-day, well, management of the collection: the preservation, thc intake of new items, the logistics of keeping everything safe and organized. There were three for the CST: Tim, in entomology, Satya, who helped him out in geology, and Jessi, who did something for engineering that Ryan didn't quite understand. The history center had two collections managers: one for artifacts, and one for archives, though Ryan honestly didn't know the difference.

For curators, that left him and — he scanned the list — a Ms. Emmeline Bonaire. That was *her*, right? They would be meeting in the kitchen. Ryan got up from the table, straightening out his dress shirt and ensuring his light gray slacks looked presentable after sitting through the meeting. He asked someone near him where the kitchen was and was directed into a small parlor that looked more like a sunroom than an actual kitchen. The woman who had frowned at his smile was already seated at the table, confirming that this was Ms. Emmeline Bonaire.

Her head was down over a notebook, and she was muttering to herself, her pen flying over the paper — writing, drawing circles, connecting those shapes with slashes and scribbles. Her black hair was over her face, but Ryan saw muscles in her back move with her writing and felt a wave of attraction.

Nope. Not here for that, he reminded his brain and other parts. Hooking up with coworkers was never a good idea. Ryan had learned that the hard way during his PhD in California. He gave a small cough to let her know he was in the room, and her head snapped up. Steely gray eyes met his, widened, then narrowed. Ryan tried Midwestern charm again.

"Doesn't look like much of a kitchen to me," he joked, looking around.

"That's because the rich people who owned this house didn't actually cook their own food. It's more formally known as a breakfast parlor, but everyone's called it a kitchen since I started here." She closed her notebook and stood, stretching her neck like she was getting ready to be on the starting block. "Hello, Dr. Andersson." She reached out her hand, and Ryan noticed that her nails were painted black but chipped near the top.

"Nice to meet you," he replied, shaking her hand, surprised to find a series of calluses on her palm. "And call me Ryan, please. There's no need for formal titles."

"Oh, okay," she said, pulling her hand away. "I'm Emmy. Just Emmy. No fancy PhD or anything."

"Hello, Just Emmy," he said, sitting at the table where she was. He opened his iPad, launched his note-taking app, and held his stylus between his fingers, twirling it as he watched Emmy sit back down and open her notebook. She seemed to take a moment to study the page she was working on, then huffed and turned to a blank sheet, smoothing her hand over the crease in the notebook.

"So," she began.

"So," he replied.

"Uh, we could talk about a collection overview. We're in the middle of an audit right now to see what we have. For years, people just shoved things in our collection without documenting them. We could talk about exhibition schedules or events, or we could talk about accessions priorities." Emmy tapped her pen on the table with each category she listed. "What's most pressing for you?"

Ryan leaned back in his chair and crossed one leg over the other. "Slow down. We're just getting to know each other." He cocked his head and looked at her. Her eyes flicked up and down, seeming to take in his entire body. She pursed her lips, considered him, then sat back and crossed her arms. Clearly, this was something she was passionate about and meant a lot to her, so he decided to go for what would be a safe topic. "I mean, I know your name, but I don't know a lot about the history collections and archives. What are your highlights? What are you excited about? What's your personal research?"

Her eyes lit up at the final questions, moving from a cold metallic color to a glittery silver. A-*ha*, Ryan thought, feeling like he'd just cracked the first bit of a code to Emmy.

"We're definitely not the State Historical Society. I'll tell you that," she laughed dismissively. "It's a nice little collection. We've got a lot on the history of the university, of course. And the papers of Sara Jonesboro, who funded the original college — that's primarily what I study. And a nice photographic collection of the town from the Victorian era." Emmy fiddled with her bangs, then clasped her hands together on the table, though they didn't stop moving. "I'd love to move the priorities to collect more on indigenous history and people of color in the area, but I'm knee deep in that collections audit. I need to figure out what we need to get rid of before we can add anything." As Emmy spoke, she continued to play with her fingers, constantly intertwining, lacing, and unlacing them, picking at her nails. Ryan had the desire to reach over and place his large hands over hers. He also quickly realized that the action would most likely result in him getting slapped.

"Plus," Emmy continued, oblivious to Ryan's thoughts about her hands, "our donors are old and boring and can be a bunch of assholes when you decide to advocate for the controversial opinion that white people have, historically, not been the best in the American West." She took a breath as Ryan chuckled. He was about to open his mouth to speak, but she cut him off with a question, "What are the science collections like?"

Ryan pushed his glasses up into his hair. "We're also not a very big museum collection. We've got a fair geology and paleontology collection — those are my areas of study — and a small entomology collection. But they don't have a curator; just a collections manager and a few grad students."

"A *few*," Emmy snorted sarcastically. "I've had to fight for every intern I've had in my years here, and it's usually an undergrad work-study position because we can't afford anything else." Ryan was just being truthful and honest, but he got the sense that something had turned in the conversation. It was like being back home and feeling the distinct chill that would roll in during a nice fall day that told you there would be snow in the evening.

Ryan tried to smile at Emmy again, which only made her lips press tighter together, their light pink turning almost white with the pressure. He decided to switch subjects slightly. "Anyway, over the past few years I've been here, the exhibitions have been focused a lot on the technology aspect. We work a lot with engineering professors and have been putting things together to demonstrate their research and the applicability of science."

She snorted again. Maybe this wasn't the right topic to switch to. "Lots of panels, few artifacts?" Ryan nodded. She rolled her eyes. "Let me guess – it was super easy for those to transition to online exhibitions during COVID, yeah?" Ryan nodded again, and this time, he felt the ice wave roll off Emmy.

"But funders like it, and we've had lots of luck getting grants."

"It must be nice that the National Science Foundation didn't exactly deal with the same pressures and cuts as the National Endowment for the Humanities," she shot back between gritted teeth. "What do the visitors think?"

"What?" Ryan didn't know what that had to do with the conversation.

"The visitors? You know, the people who actually come to the museum? The people the exhibitions are created for?" Ryan felt that chill grow somehow even colder and had visions of being six years old again and watching Arnold Schwarzenegger play Mr. Freeze. Did that make him Poison Ivy?

Ryan paused, ignoring his 90s movie related tangent, and thought for a second. "You know, I'm not sure," he said, hoping the vague statement could buy him time and goodwill with Emmy.

Her eyes widened. "You're *not sure*?" *Okay, so that plan backfired.*

"We've never asked them."

"You've *never asked them*? Dr. Andersson, let me ask you a question." Ryan could feel Emmy getting heated about something, the anger melting through her ice wall, like she was ready to blast him with a laser beam. He rewound the conversation in his head and tried to figure out where he had gone wrong. All he knew was that he didn't like feeling like they were enemies, and he really wanted Emmy to like him.

"It's Ryan," he gently corrected. "Please, go ahead."

"Well, thank you, Dr. Andersson," she continued, unabated. Her crisp bangs were shaking slightly, and her hands were opening and closing into tight fists over her notebook. "Do you really mean to tell me that you have been creating exhibitions without studying the visitors?"

Ryan backpedaled, not sure how he was supposed to respond or how this conversation had gotten so off track.

"I mean, people come to the Center, so I guess they like the exhibitions?"

"You *guess*?" Emmy nearly shrieked, then looked around the tiny room and lowered her voice to an intense whisper. Ryan would rather she'd have yelled. "You guess? Whoo, boy, we are very different, it seems." Ryan's heart sank. This was not how he expected the meeting to go. He tried a different tactic.

"Okay, okay. I guess we have some disagreements on that front. But I'm sure we can all learn from each other throughout this process." He gave her a half smile, something that tended to warm up people he worked with. Emmy remained tight-lipped, looking unconvinced. She had picked up her pen and begun to angrily scribble notes on the corner of a page. He tried again. "What exhibitions are on your timetable? What do you have in place? We just opened a new one a couple of months ago, so we can keep that one up when we merge into a new building."

"Wow," Emmy whispered. Ryan looked up from his iPad and pinched the bridge of his nose.

"What?"

"You assume that your exhibition will take priority?" Emmy's voice had gotten deadly quiet, and Ryan, once again, wanted her to yell at him instead. What kind of impulses was this woman creating in him? He wanted to reach over and rest his big hand over her frantically scribbling one, but he also wanted her to yell and scream at him instead of directing this poorly suppressed rage his way.

"That's not what I said. Please don't put words in my mouth," Ryan said sternly, uncrossing his legs and leaning forward.

"I'm sorry," Emmy said, though Ryan wasn't quite sure he believed it. He watched as Emmy closed her eyes for a second and took a deep breath in through her nose, held it for longer than was typical, and then released it through pursed lips. Lips that Ryan noticed, now that they weren't pressed together, were a bright pink color, which contrasted with her light skin and black hair. She shrugged her shoulders up to her ears and then dropped them. Her eyes opened, and Ryan was struck by how the cold gray had shifted to a softer color – the shade of clouds just before a spring rainstorm.

"I'm sorry," she repeated, her voice a bit softer. "This has been a pretty difficult day for me so far. Yes, our exhibits are a bit older, but we've been working on some new prototypes that have tested really well, and I found some great stuff from the archives that we were going to feature."

Ryan could work with this. "Excellent." He opened his iPad again. "What's the timeline?"

"We have a small staff, so it's when we can get things done that it works out. Probably in a couple of months, at best?"

"Our exhibitions are already done, so we can just move them to the new space when it opens so we have something," Ryan suggested, flipping to the notes page on his iPad to show Emmy the exhibition mockup they had presented to the grant committee. Couldn't she tell he was trying to be helpful?

"But what about our work?" Emmy replied, not even bothering to glance down at the iPad. She studied his face, and Ryan imagined she was taking in his open smile and brown-blond hair. "I don't want to throw it all away because your fancy posters are all in place. Plus the university has already cut so much funding and publicity for the humanities. This would just be another example of how, even though the university *says* it's a liberal arts university, it's that in name only." Emmy clenched her eyes tight and cleared her throat. She took another big breath. "Sorry."

"You're good. It's a weird day." He smiled at her again, watched her face harden again. *Okay, so smiling has the opposite effect on her that it does for most people.*

"I don't know," she said, running her fingers through her bangs, then dropping her hands in her lap. Ryan could see her forearm muscles moving, indicating she was still fidgeting with her hands. On another note — damn. She had nice arms.

"We can put a pin in it for now," Ryan said, and he noticed her shoulders relax, just a millimeter. "We can do a brainstorming session at some point to figure out how to make it all work or propose an exhibition that could showcase both collections or something." Ryan wasn't usually a rambler, but he wanted this meeting to end on some kind of positive note. This had already gone off the rails, and Ryan needed to rein it back in.

"That sounds...nice," Emmy said skeptically. She flipped her wrist up, looked at her watch. Ryan noticed it was a plain watch – just a standard Timex that looked like the one his mom had bought him in middle school when he started swimming. "What time is this meeting supposed to end? I know there was an agenda, but I couldn't really process all the information they were throwing at us after the announcement about the merger."

Ryan looked at his own Apple Watch. "We've got about five more minutes, then I think the Science Center people are heading back to pack up our offices."

"Where are you moving to?" Emmy said. She had missed *a lot* of the information, apparently.

"Uh." Ryan grimaced, unsure of how to break this news to her. "We're moving into your offices with your staff for a chunk of time until they can find more office spaces." Her eyes widened, then narrowed, that light gray sharpening to steel again. *Shit*. "Don't worry, though," Ryan said, flashing a grin. She frowned. "I don't have that much stuff. Basically just my iPad and my computer. I'll just need a table and a chair. Or just a chair."

"It's not your stuff I'm worried about," Emmy said, closing her notebook. "It's fine. I'll grab lunch with Phoebe and Jer and then head back and start to organize the office and make space for you." Ryan wanted to invite himself along for lunch to get to know her coworkers better – to get to know Emmy better – but he had a vision of his small and lovingly terrifying mother appearing from Minnesota in two seconds to chide him for forgetting his manners.

"Ryan Karl Andersson!" she'd say, her nasally accent and curly hair bobbing with each syllable, "You wait for someone to invite you along, and then you be the nicest boy ever so they invite you again!"

"It was nice to meet you, Emmy," he said, getting up and extending his hand to her. She stood up as well, dusting off her pants, and shook his hand gingerly, as if she wasn't sure what he was planning.

"Same to you, Dr. Andersson –"

"Ryan."

"Dr. Andersson," she repeated, letting go of his hand quickly. "I'm sure I'll see you in my – er, *our* – office soon. Does it pain you to be over on this side of campus? I've heard a rumor that you science people don't like to step foot near the Humanities Quad." She scoffed. "It might cost you grant funding." Ryan tried to ignore her bait. He got the sense she wanted him to argue. *You catch more flies with honey*, his mom's voice rang in his head.

"I'll be there in the next few days," he said. "Should I text you before I show up? I don't have your number."

"Just showing up is fine," Emmy said flintily. "If I'm not there, you'll figure it out." With that, she turned on her heel and left the small kitchen, exiting out the door and swiftly turning left. He heard heavy footsteps travel up the staircase above his head and tried to imagine Emmy stomping up them, trying to contain her frustration.

This was going to be an interesting semester.

4

Emmy

The lingering daylight disappeared the minute the three friends walked into Next Door after a day of work. Not that much actual work had been accomplished after the meeting, but still. Attempts were made. The bar, which also had no sign or easy to spot door, was a campus institution at VU, handed down from generation to generation of grad students as a place where the elderly students (read: late twenties, early thirties) could drink and complain in peace without twenty-two-year-old frat boys doing shots. Emmy had discovered it during grad school after an ill-fated date with a philosophy PhD student who spent the entire date talking about his own conception of reality while Emmy drank her way through the majority of a bottle of gin and ate seven slices of pizza. It was *next door* to a pizza joint, hence the name. Emmy had introduced Phoebe, and when Jeremy had started at the museum, they figured he was close enough to being a student that he could be let in on the secret.

It helped that the bar was just a block from the museum and wasn't crowded during the day. Emmy had lost track of the number of exhibits and programming ideas that the three of them had come up with at the bar in the six years they had worked together. It had been touch and go for the bar for a bit during the initial shutdowns, but a few well-marketed and well-timed GoFundMe campaigns had saved the bar for the foreseeable future.

"Okay, what in the actual fucking *fuck*?" Emmy asked, slumping down at the large wooden bar that took up the far quadrant of the space. There was a small dance floor, which tended to be where grad students got their freak on after nine p.m., and then a row of booths, each with their own green old-timey office lamp.

"Rough day?" Declan, the owner and usual weeknight bartender, said, walking over from where he was fiddling with one of the lamps.

"You have no idea," Emmy groaned. Declan's eyes moved over her slouched form, passed quickly over Jeremy, and landed, as they usually did, on Phoebe. She met his gaze, and he raised his eyebrows.

"I don't know if I can even get into it," she said, sitting in her usual spot. Without even ordering, Dec had started to make Phoebe her usual — a version of a Moscow mule with extra mint that he had invented the first time Phoebe had stepped foot in the bar.

"I'd love a gin and tonic," Emmy said, interrupting his drink making. Rewarded with Dec's usual scowl, Emmy grinned. Their standard drinks were placed on the bar —

Phoebe's mint-heavy mule, Emmy's G&T, Jeremy's glass of pinot noir.

"So what is it?" Declan said, slinging a bar towel over his shoulder and slouching against the bar near Phoebe.

"This is the most I've heard you talk in years," Emmy said sarcastically. She took a sip of her gin and tonic, the pine taste bringing her back to the present moment and reminding her that she wasn't here to berate the bartender, as fun as that was.

"Our museum is merging with another museum on campus," Jeremy said, swirling his glass of wine and taking a deep sniff. He took a sip, made a grimace, and then took a bigger sip.

"And it's an absolute hellscape," Emmy added.

"Really, it might not be that bad," Phoebe said, playing with her straw. Emmy shot her a death glare, and Phoebe held up her hands in surrender. "I mean, yes, it sucks. And the way the news was delivered was...not ideal. But the education people seem nice. They're just more excited about, like, lab experiments and old rocks than people. But I can work with that. And they've got way more resources at their disposal."

Emmy simmered and opened her mouth to correct Phoebe. *Those people are not helpful*, she thought. *They're here to take our jobs once they decide to phase out the history portion of the museum. They do not care about our work and what it means.*

Jeremy spoke first, however. "Their exhibitions team is"—he let out a dramatic sigh—"fine, I guess. They're boring as hell, and their ideas about what constitutes interesting design are basic, but they seem harmless."

Emmy boiled over. "Harmless?" Her hands flew in the air, almost knocking over her drink. Jeremy put a graceful hand over the top of his wineglass, and Declan moved Phoebe's drink behind the bar. "There is nothing harmless or nice about those people or this entire situation." She took an aggressive sip of her drink, breathing out through her nose. "I don't even know how I'm going to work with their main curator."

"What's his issue?" Phoebe asked, gingerly reaching over the bar to take her drink back.

"He's just..." she sputtered for a moment. "He assumes. He assumes that he knows what's best, and it's that damn science arrogance that I've always hated. It's the reason I left science in the first place." Emmy had started off her undergraduate degree as a chemistry major but had been bullied out of that path by a combination of unsupportive professors, cut-throat classmates, and her own mental health struggles. After what she preferred to characterize as a "miniature breakdown," she had switched majors to history and never looked back. "Did you know he just assumed their exhibitions would stay up when we combined?"

"Our stuff *is* kind of old and dusty," Phoebe admitted.

"But we're testing some badass new exhibitions! Oh, and that's another thing." Emmy sucked at her straw, frustrated to find that she had already reached the end of her drink. She eyed Declan and asked for another one.

He raised an eyebrow at Jeremy, who shook his head, and then at Phoebe, who shot him a grin and nodded.

"Anyway, that's the other thing," Emmy continued. "I asked him what visitors think about the exhibitions, and *he didn't know*." Emmy looked at Phoebe and Jeremy, waiting for their reactions to match her frustration. Phoebe rolled her eyes and Jeremy scoffed. "What?"

"Not everyone is as stoked about visitor studies as you are," Jeremy reminded her. "They also might test and evaluate in different ways."

"I don't trust him," Emmy said firmly. "Thanks, Dec," she said, grabbing her second drink and angrily squeezing her lime.

"Well, he's nice to look at," Jeremy offered. Emmy shot him a look.

"Which is even worse, because you know I get weird around attractive people," Emmy said. Before Emmy had realized that Jeremy was gay, she had been unable to advocate for her ideas in exhibition meetings, couldn't look him in the eye. It took Phoebe dragging her to Next Door and a deep dive of his Instagram for Emmy to realize that Jeremy would have no interest in her sexually, which opened a lovely door for them to become friends. She did always have a weakness for a tall, blond man. A memory of Dr. Andersson, his glasses pushed up into his caramel and gold curls, a half grin on his face, flashed into her mind. Emmy grumpily shut *that* mental image down.

"Em, let's be real here," Phoebe said, swiveling on her stool to face Emmy and Jeremy. "You're always looking for the worst outcome possible. What if — just for once — you were able to not anticipate the worst thing happening?"

"Uh, remember when I read the first news story about COVID and told you we were fucked?" Emmy said, pointing her straw at Phoebe. "And remember when I —"

"I'm not playing this game with you," Phoebe said definitively. "It's not helpful, and you know your therapist would say the same thing. Do you have therapy this week?"

"No, it's next week," Emmy replied. "I'm sure she's going to love hearing about this development." She tried to recall the basic reminders that a series of therapists had been telling her since she was nineteen.

Try mindfulness.

Focus on what you can control.

Breathe.

Emmy took a deep breath and pictured a familiar image. During her one and only half-marathon, at mile twelve, she had seen a sign that said *Remember why you started.* Dehydrated and exhausted, she had burst into uncharacteristic tears, and had taken to reminding herself of those four words when times were difficult.

When she moved away from her hometown to take a chance on this career.

When she had to take an extra barista job to afford the cost of Colorado living.

When she had to jump into a new position as curator and was terrified of failure.

When she had to tell a very wealthy and influential donor that they didn't need a collection of weird old clothes for the museum.

She had started on this path because it was important to leave a legacy through her work, to use history to make a better future. Yes, it was cheesy, and no, Emmy would never say those words out loud, but they were pinned to her mind.

The three of them — plus Declan — continued to chat about the upcoming changes to the museum. And at one point, Jeremy ran over to the pizza place and brought back a pepperoni roll for Phoebe, two slices of pepperoni for Emmy, and a calzone for himself — the same three things they always ordered.

"I don't know why you can't just split a pizza when all of you have some combination of cheese, sauce, and pepperoni," Declan said as he unpacked a box of bottles into the cooler for the evening crowd.

"Because it makes sense this way, Dec," Phoebe said, and Declan rolled his eyes at her. "It's just the way of the world, and you're going to have to accept that's how it is." Emmy had long thought there was *something* going on between the two of them, but every time Emmy had brought it up to Phoebe, she had laughed and shook her head.

The three continued to discuss what work would look like for the foreseeable future, with Phoebe and Jeremy batting down every disaster scenario that Emmy's brain could concoct. Eventually, Jeremy finished the remainder of his wine and closed his tab, with Phoebe and Emmy following suit.

"You're good to catch your bus?" Phoebe asked, to which Emmy replied with a nod.

"I'm fine. You don't need to drive me, little one," Emmy said, playfully ruffling Phoebe's hair. She sighed and looked up at the sun setting over the Foothills, took in the place that had become her home. "What are the two of you going to do at work tomorrow?"

"I had a little work to do on those mockups for the new living room exhibit, but I guess those are on the back burner, because we're not hosting exhibitions in our space anymore?" Jeremy said. "I guess I'll, I dunno, answer emails and start to figure out how to share the design space."

"At least you have a whole attic," Phoebe chuckled. "They've got three full-time educators and a bunch of part-time staff. I can maybe fit another desk in our space, but we're gonna have to share something. I think the part-time staff can all continue to share the flex office, but I might have to get copies of their schedules to organize it."

Emmy thought of her own office. It was definitely big enough for another desk, but that wasn't the point (and she would need to do a lot of cleaning and decluttering *for sure*). She didn't *want* to share her space. It had taken her long enough to get to the point where she a) wasn't sharing an office and b) wasn't working a second job and c) actually had some say in the type of work the museum was doing. And it was all going to be pulled out from under her in the course of one day.

"Em, do you need help organizing tomorrow?" Phoebe offered, looking through her keys. Phoebe was the most organized person she had ever met, though Phoebe had said that her brother's new girlfriend managed to out-organize her in some respects, which was impressive.

"I'm fine. I have a plan!" Emmy lied, pulling out her phone and navigating to a podcast. "Or, at least, I'll be developing a plan this evening."

"Okay. When you need help tomorrow, call me. And when you need reinforcements, I'll call June," Phoebe said, laughing as she headed in the direction of her car, leaving Jeremy and Emmy by themselves.

"Your space is already neat. You're fine," Emmy said, looking him up and down.

"Oh, I know," he said. "You've seen my house. I'm organized. *You* are not."

"Yes, my dear, but that's why I use this." Emmy dug around in her bag and pulled out a well-loved leather notebook that contained her weekly calendar and a running to-do list. She functioned exclusively with the benefits of those lists, Post-it note reminders, coffee, and gin. And a small handful of SSRIs she took each morning. After waving goodbye to Jeremy, who lived within walking distance, Emmy sat and began a new list in her notebook.

<u>Office Cleanup</u>

- Stack of books to review
- Desk Post-it notes

- Stack of books to return to the library
- Notebooks from grad school (need?)
- Stack of books I haven't read
- Take out trash
- Clean out minifridge
- Extra shoes under the desk
- Probably another stack of books somewhere

List making had been one of few useful things Emmy had gotten from therapy in her undergrad days. Her therapist in Youngstown had told her that she had a "pathological need to control things," and while Emmy thought he could have worked on his delivery a bit more (what else would be expected from an old steelworker who was in his second career as a therapist?), he was right. However, if she would have actually made a list that was honest, it would have looked like this:

<u>Life Clean Up</u>

- Talk to president about student loans
- Punch Marshall in the face for agreeing to this plan
- Talk to state senate about funding allocations
- Do laundry
- Publish research in a national journal
- Force Phoebe to talk to Declan
- Move into a new apartment
- Organize stacks of book in office
- Get a new office mate
- Apply for Museum Association of America session – <u>this year</u>

The arrival of her bus had Emmy closing her notebook and putting headphones in to drown out her thoughts on the thirty-minute ride back. Unlocking her apartment, she flopped onto her couch, opened up her notebook, and looked at the to-do list again.

"Fuck this," she said, tossing the notebook to the floor, where it landed next to a few dog-eared books on the Colorado silver rush. Emmy flipped on an old stand-up comedy special she had seen a thousand times, turned her brain off, and settled in to watch under a weighted blanket.

5

RYAN

A WEEK LATER, THE Center for Science and Technology had a new name ("the Philips Building") and two floors of freshly emptied offices. Its former staff were walking across campus in a single file line, carrying boxes and pulling carts of take-home exhibitions that the educational staff had created during lockdown. Ryan's box was not even a box. It was a few books that he could fit in his messenger bag, his computer, and his iPad. During grad school at UCSB, Ryan had been bitten by the environmental bug and had attempted to go as paperless as possible, and he only borrowed books from the library.

"You ready for this?" he asked Satya, his collections manager. Satya, who held a PhD from Oxford, had been indispensable to Ryan since the day he arrived. She had been his number one advocate when he applied for the open curatorial position and, he hoped, would help him out when he applied for tenure and a full professorship in a few years. If he stayed at VU. He had moved from Santa Barbara as a post-doc researcher and had ended up staying, finding Vanberg a comfortable fit for this portion of his career. But Ryan always had his eyes out for other opportunities at bigger museums with stronger collections, though he loved the way this smaller museum allowed him to get his hands dirty. He was still in the lab daily doing his own research, but he also got to help contribute to exhibitions. Pretty soon, if a few grants came through, things could be even smoother and more nationally recognized. He couldn't avoid that opportunity. Publish a few papers, curate an exhibition or two in the next few years, and then it was either tenure here or a huge opportunity somewhere else.

Curate an exhibition. Not for the first time over the past week, his soon-to-be office mate's frustrated face popped into his mind. He had always had an easy time getting people to like him, especially at work. Ryan knew he had a lot of pieces of privilege at work for him — he was tall, white, athletic, conventionally attractive, overly friendly. He knew he was not exactly what came to mind when most people thought of paleontologists.

Though, Ryan would always remind people that his sexual and academic awakening had happened when he saw Laura Dern in Jurassic Park, so biological paleontologists *were* sexy.

Ryan had always been able to win over people with a kind word or a big smile. But in his limited interactions with Emmy, that had not been the case. He cringed internally as he thought back to the email he had sent her the previous week as everyone else on staff was figuring out new office arrangements.

To: ebonaire@vu.edu

From: randersson@vu.edu

Subject: Office Warming Gift

Good morning, Emmy!

It looks like we'll be office mates starting on Monday. Is there a type of fancy coffee drink that I could bring you that day? Would you like to schedule a time to brainstorm some exhibition ideas?

Looking forward to it,

Ryan

To: randersson@vu.edu

From: ebonaire@vu.edu

Subject: Re: Office Warming Gift

Dr. Andersson -

I drink black coffee, and it's not worth it for you to buy that at the campus store. Plus, they over roast their beans there.

We can talk about an exhibition on Monday afternoon if that works for you.

Best,

Emmy Bonaire, M.S.

To: ebonaire@vu.edu

From: randersson@vu.edu

Subject: Office Warming Gift (Are you sure?)

Hi, Emmy!

Do you have a recommendation for a coffee shop with good beans? I'm happy to get some for you from there!

See you Monday!
Ryan

He hadn't received a reply to his second email.

"From what I hear, we're going to be able to keep our collections in the same building. It sounds like their archives are going to be moving over, which makes sense. I'd assume our temperature and humidity controls are better than you'd find in a drafty old building," Satya was saying. Ryan brought himself back from rethinking a simple email exchange and tried to fill in the gaps from when he hadn't been listening.

"That's going to be a huge pain in the ass for their curatorial staff," Ryan said.

Satya shrugged. "Moving fossils is way more intense from a weight standpoint. There are things in the collection that I know will never go on display, even if we wanted them to, because they're too damn heavy. Also, there's a reason that our collection is on the basement floor – you'd have to reinforce anything higher up, and I'm assuming the university definitely doesn't have space for that."

Ryan hummed his agreement, and their chatter turned to Satya's extensive knowledge of the scope of their collection. Ryan had been hired at VU in 2015 and had spent his initial year, and then two more, holed up in a lab to produce a publishable paper on the coprolite collection before his mentor, the old curator, had retired.

Stepping into the curatorial role made sense, but Ryan, with the added responsibilities of his new job, didn't have much time to learn the collection like Satya had. Then the collections had been closed off for the better part of two years. He had just started getting back into the swing of things when the museum merger was announced.

"It's definitely a more interesting place to work," Ryan said as the CST staff approached what had been known as the VUHCAC.

Satya snorted. "I still plan on spending most of my time in the collection, and I haven't moved my office from there. I'm just waiting until someone says something." Ryan knew that to be true. More often than not, he went searching for Satya to answer a research question or, more likely, to have someone to talk to when he was bored and going cross-eyed from trying to read a journal article on his iPad. "Good luck with your new roomie," she said, giving him a knowing look. Ryan had recounted how his initial meeting with Emmy went, asking for her advice. "I fuck women — it doesn't mean I know anything about working with them" was her terse reply.

"Welcome, welcome!" said the history center's director. Ryan couldn't remember his name. Something Germanic, he thought.

"Hi, thanks!" Ryan said, flashing a grin and shifting the bag in his right hand to his left so he could shake the man's hand. "I'm not sure where I'm heading, though."

"And you are?" he asked, mopping his large forehead with a handkerchief. The older building felt stuffier than his old office space, for sure.

"Ryan Andersson." A blank look. "Paleontology?" Still a blank look. "Geology?" Nothing. "I'm a curator?"

"Ah!" he said, reminding Ryan of a professor character in the 1980s Disney movies that his nephews loved to watch. "You'll be with Emmy!" He chuckled. "Have fun with that one! She's a firecracker!" Ryan gave a pleasant chuckle but had a hard time applying the word *firecracker* to someone who gave off the same vibes as a glacier. The director – former director – told Ryan to head up a back staircase and turn left once he reached the top.

Ryan walked through the living room, making a mental note to come back and look at the exhibits that were in place when he had time this week, and stepped through a door labeled Staff Only. He entered into a staircase that demonstrated the age of the building. It was clearly not built for men who were six four and had competed in butterfly since the age of ten, giving him extra wide shoulders. Ryan found he had to duck his head and shift sideways, crossing one foot over another, to make it up the stairwell. He emerged on the second floor, which was even warmer, and turned left, looking for Emmy's office.

"Emmy?" he called, poking his head into an open office.

"Next door," replied a short brunette with curly hair. "Good luck," she laughed. He kept going until he found her nameplate.

Emmeline Bonaire, M.S.
Lead Curator, Historical Center and Archives

He knocked on the door. "Emmy?"

"In here! Close the door quickly. Don't let the cool air out!" came her voice, along with a frantic shuffling of papers. He opened the door the smallest amount he could to slide his big body in and found Emmy under her desk, stacking a pile of books that looked to have just been knocked over.

A wave of cool air hit Ryan, and he had to swallow a groan at the sensation. "It feels so good in here" is what he said instead.

"Ha, yeah. I grew up with humidity and no air conditioning, so I don't play that shit anymore. Even though it's not even that humid here compared to where I grew up." She straightened from under the desk, adjusting her clothes as she went. She was wearing high-waisted black shorts that showed off her ample hips, paired with a loose white blouse and a collection of eclectic green and brown necklaces that rattled as she moved. Her black hair was pulled into a messy bun, but her bangs grazed her forehead and — Ryan noticed — were slightly stuck with a sheen of sweat. He did a double-take and noticed that her feet were bare, and she stood on a well-loved, ornate rug that was under her desk.

Ryan set his bag on the empty table he assumed would be his desk and ran a hand through his hair. "I know humidity, too. Minnesota summers are only made worse by the massive mosquitos that terrorize you there. Where did you grow up?"

"Ohio."

"What part?"

"Doesn't matter."

"Did you go to school there too?"

"Yeah."

"Cool!" Ryan said, filling in space. It was clear that Emmy wasn't an open book about her background, so Ryan turned around to the table he had set his bag on. "Is this for me?"

"Yeah." Emmy turned back to her desk and busied herself with organizing a stack of books. When she found the one she needed, Ryan watched her walk over to the tall bookshelf in the center of the small room and lift up onto her toes to slide the book onto the top shelf. He took in the muscles of her calves — defined, smooth — as she pulled another book off the shelf. Realizing that his gaze was going too high up her legs to be appropriate for a new office mate, Ryan turned around and looked at his desk. Just a plain wooden table with a single drawer on the side and a standard roller chair. Sparse. Simple. Luckily, Ryan didn't need much else. He unpacked his box — a small succulent that his sister Amanda had given him, the two books he had borrowed from the library, a small collection of pens and pencils. His laptop came next, along with the associated charging cords, then headphones and iPad and stylus.

Damn, he thought to himself. *I forgot Post-its*. For all of his embrace of paperless work habits, Ryan had never been able to find a suitable replacement for Post-it notes when it came to jotting down a quick idea or a list of things he needed to accomplish.

"Uh, Emmy?" he asked, turning around. She had been watching him, her head cocked to one side while she leaned against her own desk. It was covered in stacks of books, a few notebooks and notepads, and – Ryan noticed with delight – Post-it notes in various colors stuck to almost every item.

"Yes, Dr. Andersson?" she said, clearing her throat.

"First off, seriously, it's Ryan. You're not a student in a class I TA'ed, and we're coworkers, so please call me Ryan."

Emmy sighed. "Sorry, it was pounded into my brain by a teacher in high school that if someone worked hard enough to get a PhD, you referred to them by their title."

"The only people who call me Dr. Andersson, besides the freshmen in my Geology 101 course, are my mom and my aunts," Ryan chuckled. "Seriously, Ryan is fine, especially since we're roomies."

"Yay. Fun times," Emmy deadpanned. "I hope you're better than my freshman year roommate who had her stomach pumped within two months of starting college."

"I can hold my booze," Ryan cracked. "Anyway, I was wondering if you had a stack of Post-its I could borrow. Or a supply room I could raid."

Emmy snorted. "Supply room? More like what we can manage to wrangle in the copy room. It's on the bottom floor, by the way, behind the living room. Good luck fighting with Bertha if you have to make copies, though."

"Is that a person? Like an office assistant?"

"No, that's our printer. It's so old it should be its own exhibition." Ryan felt the tiniest thaw in Emmy's chill with that small joke. He decided to press, to see if he could encourage her to melt a little.

"How do you like to work? Do you have a set schedule for when you're in the office? Do you play music?" Ryan preferred to work with music and tended to spend his mornings in his collection and his afternoons in the office if he could manage it.

"I like music," Emmy admitted. "But it has to be without lyrics. I have headphones, though. I like to run the A/C in the summer, but when fall rolls around, there's a nice breeze in this office if you open a window. I tend to spend most of my days in the office — I really do love this building — and I've been trying to digitize what I need for my research so I'm not in the archives, because it's really stuffy."

"Probably why you're moving those over to our collections building," Ryan said, absentmindedly recalling what Satya had told him. Ryan watched Emmy process his sentence, her spine growing rigid, her lips pursing. Apparently, this was news to her.

"Excuse me?" she said, her eyebrows shooting up into her bangs.

"That's what my collections manager told me — something about keeping everything in one place — and the archives are easy to move."

"There you go, assuming again," she muttered.

"We've got great temperature control," Ryan added. "The entomology collection has — ironically — great pest control. Someone told me that you've had a problem with insects. This could be a solution!"

Emmy took a deep breath and began to flex her hands in and out of fists, which reminded Ryan of their initial meeting. "We had a *minor* dermestid infestation that we caught early — with no damage — and that was during

COVID when no one was on campus. While I agree that we could use better monitoring, I'm nervous about the assumption that moving our archives and artifacts will be *easier*." Emmy pronounced the last word with deadly precision. "Why would that be?"

I was just asking for a Post-it, Ryan thought. "Well, there are a lot of small specimens in entomology, and the insects are sensitive to temperature changes. And our geology collection has a lot of huge specimens that are really heavy and bulky to move."

Emmy paused for a second, seeming to think over what he had just said. "So your insects, if I'm not mistaken, are mostly preserved, yeah? Dried out or wet collections in jars?" Ryan nodded. "Right. Our archival documents are incredibly sensitive to light and temperature. Even moving them across campus is going to be an ordeal, not to mention the issues with moving some of the older preserved items." Emmy tapped her fingers on her desk. "We have a lot of old furs and clothing that were preserved before the 1930s, and you know what that means." Ryan looked at her – he had been trained as a geologist, then specialized in paleontology. Even when he did work with larger natural history museums, the collections that he worked with were all millions of years old and didn't contain organic matter.

"They're...delicate?" Ryan guessed.

Emmy sighed and looked at him as if this was an obvious piece of information. "It means they were most likely preserved with arsenic, which is going to be a biohazard clusterfuck to move."

"There are no strict plans yet —" Ryan backpedaled.

"Then why are you talking as if there are?" Emmy said in a cutting tone. "Also, I would think that as a curator, I would get some say in this entire situation. Did you get to contribute to this plan?"

"No! It's just something my collection manager mentioned today," Ryan said, unsure of how his request for a Post-it had spiraled into a quiz on collections policies and procedures. "I'm sorry if I freaked you out."

"It's fine," Emmy said, shaking her head and giving the impression that it wasn't fine at all. "Here," she said, picking up a Post-it packet and tossing it to him. "I'm heading to the collection this afternoon, anyway, so you'll have time and space to settle in." She began to gather her belongings, reaching for three books, a notebook, and a notepad, along with a pencil pouch. Angrily shoving them all into a battered messenger bag, she slung it onto her shoulder and grabbed a pair of sunglasses from her desk. Ryan noticed there were three pairs still remaining.

"Okay, well, bye," Ryan said, unsure of how to let her go after this meeting. "Will you be around this afternoon?"

"Probably not," Emmy said, beginning to walk out of the office.

"Wait," he said, standing up and reaching out. He wanted to grab her wrist but knew that would be too forward. How had this conversation gone completely off the rails in a matter of minutes? Ryan felt like he was scrambling, slipping on ice and trying to regain his balance.

"What?"

"Is there a time we could schedule to talk about exhibitions?" Ryan offered. "Tomorrow? I can do some work in the collection, give you space, and we can shift this planning meeting to another day that works better for you."

"Fine," Emmy said, shrugging her bag back on her shoulder and moving to turn out of the room again. He'd try to kill her with kindness. Again.

"Can I bring you coffee?"

"It's fine. Don't worry about it," she said. Looking over her shoulder at his desk, she turned her head and studied it. "Is that everything you brought?" Ryan nodded, and Emmy made a noncommittal noise. He couldn't tell if she approved or not as she swept out of the office with a final goodbye.

Puzzling himself over how every interaction with Emmy confused him and left him feeling off-balance, Ryan resorted to what any good scientist would do. Research. Opening up his laptop, he googled "Emmeline Bonaire Vanberg University" and looked at the results.

The first was her staff bio, followed by a series of articles she had written for the museum's blog during COVID, then a playlist of YouTube videos produced by Emmy and two other staff members of the museum — a Jeremy and Phoebe, it looked like. The videos apparently took viewers behind the scenes of the museum when visitors were still not allowed. He clicked on her staff bio and read.

Ms. Emmeline Bonaire studies the history of science in the American West with a specific focus on the ways in which female benefactors facilitated research in the post-silver rush era. Her work has been published in Colorado Historian, Science Studies Monthly *and more. She has presented sessions at the Mountain West Museum Association and the Western Visitor Studies Association Conferences. She has curated or co-curated exhibitions for VUHCAC, History Colorado, and the Buffalo Bill Museum & Grave. When not working on historical research, Ms. Bonaire enjoys weightlifting, hiking, and skiing.*

B.A. History – Youngstown State University

M.S. Museum Studies – Vanberg University

Ryan continued to scroll through her blog posts and articles, even diving into one of her academic papers entitled "Revealing the Archival Process to the Visitor: A Proposal for an Exhibition" that he got a few pages into before realizing he was out of his depth. Ryan knew paleontology and his own research and collection well. Emmy knew the museum *experience*, in addition to her own research. Her articles and blogs bounced from the importance of looking for gaps in a history collection to understanding why a variety of people visited museums. He saved a pdf of one of her articles to his iPad, then opened one of the videos, this one of Emmy walking the viewer through an exhibition at the center.

After a few minutes, Ryan realized three things:

#1) Emmy was a brilliant historian who had the ability to distill complex topics to a simple, quick-witted summary.

#2) Emmy was gut-wrenchingly attractive, especially when she was talking about the work she was doing at the museum.

#3) Emmy was not being her full self with him.

The first point didn't surprise Ryan, and neither did the second. Ryan's eyes had snagged on Emmy during that first meeting. She was a gorgeous woman, no doubt, but hearing her talk about her research was something else. He hadn't had a serious girlfriend since he broke up with Amelia in California, but he had enjoyed the occasional date and the more frequent fling since moving to Vanberg. When he imagined a woman he wanted to spend time with, he wanted someone whose mind was attractive, as well as her body. It was point three that was annoying him. Ryan had always had an easy time getting people to like him, but for some reason, Emmy was putting up shields and walls and blockades against him.

Chewing on his lip, Ryan doodled in the corner of a Post-it note. Operation Get Emmy to Like Him would be put into motion with their brainstorming meeting tomorrow.

For the good of their professional collaboration, of course.

Ryan was making a list of things to work on during the afternoon when he realized that the video of Emmy in the museum was still playing. He looked up to see her laughing at something the videographer had said.

Operation Get Emmy to Smile at Him Like That.

6

Ryan

Ryan, if he was honest, had spent too much time the previous evening planning how he was going to win Emmy over during their meeting this morning.

Coffee? Check.

Protocol for exhibition planning? Check.

New stack of Post-its? Check.

Midwestern charm? Check.

Ideas for exhibition? Check.

Ryan balanced the two cups of coffee in his arm as he walked into The House, already feeling the familiar wave of musty warmth greeting him as the older air conditioner struggled to life. Ryan considered himself an early riser, liked to swim in the morning, liked to get places on time, so he was surprised to find Emmy already in the office when he walked in.

He quickly shut the door behind him and studied her. The air conditioner was already on, but Emmy hadn't noticed him walk into the office. She was chewing on her fingernails – they had been repainted a dark red color — and looking closely at her computer screen, which contained a series of black and white images. She was wearing a green dress that had some sort of tiny flower pattern on it, and Ryan tried — he really did — not to notice the way the short sleeves fluttered around the muscles of her shoulders and upper arms. He was reminded of the reconnaissance research he had done on her. She liked weightlifting, so her muscular physique made sense. Her legs were tucked up into her chest, feet not on the floor, but if Ryan had to guess, he would bet on her being barefoot. She had AirPods in her ears and was rocking her head back and forth to the beat of her music.

"C'mon, c'mon, baby," she said to her computer screen, zooming in on an image and searching for some unknown detail. She looked closer at the screen, her nose almost touching the image, and Ryan laughed to himself. He was sure he had a similar intensity when he was at his microscope.

"Good morning," he said, walking over and setting a cup of coffee on her desk. She jumped and looked up at him, her black hair shaking with the movement.

"Sorry, didn't notice you there," she said.

"S'all good. That's for you," he said, indicating the coffee and taking a sip of his own drink. "I hope the beans are okay." She opened the lid, took a tentative sniff, and then took a sip.

"They're good," she said softly. "Thanks."

"What were you working on?" He nodded at the computer screen, which was zoomed in on a photo of an ornately dressed woman receiving some sort of award at what looked to be the Vanberg town hall.

"A bit of my personal research. This" — she pointed to the woman on the screen — "Is Sara Jonesboro, who donated most of the money and land to start the college in her will. We're actually in her house right now. Anyway, we know she received a few commendations from the mayor for her 'sponsorship of science' before she passed, but the actual text of commendations has been lost, so I'm looking at photos and seeing if I can read it on them." She rubbed her eyes and took another sip of coffee. Opening her eyes, she met Ryan's, and he saw that spark of academic excitement he had seen in the videos from the museum.

"Any luck?"

"Not really." She pushed away from her desk and turned to face him, her legs crossed under the skirt of her dress. Considering him for a moment, she asked, "What do you study?"

Ryan took this opportunity to create a little mystery about himself, to have fun with her. Smirking, he replied, "Coprolites."

Emmy rolled her eyes. "What are those?"

"You can google it."

"Or you could just tell me."

"Nah, it's more fun this way."

"I hate surprises," she said.

"It's not technically a surprise, because you could find the answer at any time."

"Are you always this difficult, or am I special?" Ryan ignored the way his stomach flipped when Emmy called herself special.

"It's just how I am." He grinned and sipped his own iced vanilla latte. "Ready to brainstorm?"

"All right, Doc, let's do this," she said, rolling her chair an inch closer to him, revealing a bare foot that had been tucked up under her seat. *Okay, Doc was a step up from Dr. Andersson*, he decided.

7

Emmy

Emmy didn't know how to process Ryan, who waltzed into her office — her space — with his big body and big smiles and big, overwhelming, positive energy. To be honest, Emmy didn't trust outgoing and positive people. Her history had led her to believe that they were overcompensating at best and hiding some deep, dark secret at the worst. However, the coffee he brought her today *had* actually been good. That was a point for him. Emmy had worked as a barista throughout undergrad and grad school, and for a few years into her professional life, which had left her with a tendency to wake up early and a taste for perfectly roasted coffee beans.

Studying Ryan, she tried to figure him out. He was wearing jeans that had no business hugging his thighs in *that way* this early in the morning, paired with a simple short-sleeved button-down that had some sort of small print on it. Emmy looked closer, tried to keep her cool, and had to stop herself from rolling her eyes when she saw that there were tiny triceratopses all over his shirt.

His slightly curly hair was damp still, more brown than blond, and he had his thick-framed glasses pushed up into his hair. They fogged up, Emmy noticed, when he walked into the cool office. She watched Ryan as he got ready for their brainstorming meeting, which, Emmy hadn't had the heart to admit to him, she found absolutely ridiculous.

The best brainstorming sessions weren't planned and organized. Instead, they came from colleagues who knew and liked each other getting drinks and rambling about their research passions. They did not come from sterile "meetings" with people who were more than likely on their way to stealing not just your office but your entire job.

They'd probably start with phasing out her curatorial responsibilities. But Emmy had quite literally written the book on her collection and was in the middle of that collections audit and deaccessioning unnecessary items, so they couldn't say she wasn't necessary. What did they need to keep, what did they need to give away — that's what kept her up at night, at least when she wasn't reliving the worst moments in her life.

Then they'd cite a "lack of funding" or a "lack of interest" in historical collections. But Emmy had four years of grants that proved a sustainable funding model (which was a far cry from the in-debt collection she had taken over), and she had a series of studies that proved that the local community *was* interested in historical exhibitions about the town, even if they wanted to see things the collection didn't reflect. But Emmy had plans for that too — a new proposed collections mission and scope that she had been working on since she started the collections audit.

This was how Emmy operated. Find all the things that could go wrong and then work twice as hard as everyone else to make sure all the options were covered. Yeah, it was exhausting, and yes, Emmy's mind was constantly making up scenarios she hadn't anticipated yet, but it had allowed her to be successful. To get out of her shitty hometown and graduate from college when no one in her family had done that. To move across the country on a graduate assistantship and make a life for herself in Vanberg. No one — not her family and not her professional peers — could look at Emmy Bonaire's life and say that she didn't bust her ass to make sure that everything went right.

Emmy was snapped back from her anxiety spiral when Ryan walked over to her desk and handed her a crisp sheet of paper. Emmy glanced at it and felt her stomach drop. *Oh no.* This was final proof that the two of them could never work together in a productive way.

It was a Brainstorming Protocol.

Emmy had first been exposed to these in grad school, in a museum education class that was run by someone who had never actually taught children. It was a series of predetermined questions meant to develop a specific outcome instead of a free-flowing conversation. Emmy believed that the materials in a collection had a story to tell, that it was her job to bring those stories out and share them with the world. Questions that looked to make money and create safe exhibits? No thank you. Actually, fuck them.

Emmy took a deep breath. “What’s this?” she asked, attempting to keep her voice light and forcing a smile on her face.

“It’s a protocol!” Ryan’s earnest excitement made this even worse.

“For what?”

“Exhibit idea development.”

Emmy cleared her throat. “Do we really need this?”

“I’ve found it to be really helpful in our exhibit process —”

“For your posters?” Emmy couldn’t keep the electricity out of her voice. She glanced down at the protocol, noticing that it started with a question about curatorial research and continued on to questions about collection strengths and finished up with questions about corporate funding opportunities. This was worse than she had originally anticipated.

“I’m getting the sense that something is off,” Ryan said, leaning back against his desk and crossing his legs at the ankles. No one — especially not a paleontology curator — had any business looking this casual and attractive in Emmy’s office this early in the morning. In fact, where attractive men usually made her nervous, Ryan’s presence this morning served to piss her off.

“Yeah, something is off,” Emmy said, waving the piece of paper in the air. “This is bullshit.”

“Wow, tell me how you really feel.”

"This has nothing to do with the visitor! This has nothing to do with relevancy or unlocking a new understanding of history or science for people who come to the museum. This," — she poked at the paper again — "Is a way to get funding."

"So?" Ryan said, and Emmy felt something in his demeanor shift, felt him move into a defensive mode. *Yes,* she thought. *Argue with me. I knew your niceness was all a facade.*

"So? This is cold and stale."

"That seems like something you'd like," he shot back.

"What in the hell is that supposed to mean?" Emmy stood up from her chair and crossed her arms.

"You haven't exactly been welcoming through this entire process."

"Oh, I'm supposed to roll out the red carpet for you all to storm in here and take over our museum?"

"We're not doing that."

"You nearly have double the staff we do!"

"Our old offices were needed for other staff."

Emmy snorted again. "Let me guess. More petroleum engineers whose positions at the university are funded by oil companies? Or are they *climate researchers*" — she put air quotes around those words — "whose research conveniently supports the idea that there can be clean coal, even though those people have never stepped foot in Appalachia?"

"Dammit, I don't know."

"Let's get one thing clear, Dr. Andersson," Emmy said, gritting her teeth.

“Ryan.”

“Okay, *Ryan*. I know that we — historians, humanities scholars — are the underdogs here. But I am not going down without a fight, and I will advocate for my staff and my collection.” She breathed deeply through her nose.

“We’re just brainstorming!” Ryan said.

“Not with this protocol.” Emmy threw it in the recycling. “Because this protocol ends with a boring, safe, bland exhibition, and that’s not why I do this work.” She whirled around, shoved her feet into her slides, and gathered her essentials — notebook, headphones, phone, Post-it notes — and shoved them all into her bag. “I’m heading to the archives for the rest of the day. Enjoy the office. Shut the A/C off when you leave. Thank you for the coffee.” Emmy took a final sip of the coffee and aggressively — probably too aggressively if she was being honest — threw the cup in the trash.

Ryan pinched the bridge of his nose, walked over to the A/C unit, and shut it off. “I’m heading to my lab today, anyway. You can have the office.”

“It’s yours, Doc. Enjoy.”

“I insist, Emmy.”

8

RYAN

OPERATION GET EMMY TO Smile at Ryan had been readjusted time and time again. By the end of the month, it had become Operation Get Emmy to Tolerate Ryan. First, it was a day where his Bluetooth on his computer had struggled to work, and he ended up playing his music (with lyrics!), which had interrupted Emmy's focus. Then there was the day his duffel bag containing his wet swimsuit had leaked and soaked a book she had on loan from the library.

To be fair, Emmy wasn't innocent either. Her books were always scattered around her, including on the floor. He had also found her snooping around his desk, trying to look at what he had scribbled on the Post-its, and she had backpedaled and flushed a dark red. Another morning she had ended up behind him in line when he ordered his morning vanilla latte, which one barista always rang up as a black coffee, and Emmy had rolled her eyes and mumbled something about "white male privilege" and blown off his offer to buy her coffee. Then she had complained that Ryan had "too much stuff" in their office, to which he had simply counted the number of piles of books around her desk. At one point, he had even considered putting a line of masking tape down the center of the room and agreeing which side of the room they could be on, just like his sisters had done in middle school.

Following that, he had sent a series of emails that he had thought to be friendly, proposing ideas for exhibitions, and she had responded to each of them with three- or four-word sentences.

Finally, when he had decided to apologize to her with another coffee from the shop she liked, he had spilled it all over a paper she was editing. And then made the comment about needing to red pen papers like his high school English teacher without thinking. That day had ended with Emmy accusing him of judging her work style and both of them agreeing to work in their respective collections.

Presently, a discussion that had begun about potential grants they could apply for that would benefit both collections had turned into an argument about who should be doing the actual writing and submission of the applications.

"I should write them," Emmy was saying. "I write grants all the time, plus we have to do way more writing in the humanities than in science."

"If you haven't noticed, I've also published papers," he shot back. "And I've worked on exhibit text, too. I know how to write."

"But can you write with feeling? Can you make the grant committee believe in your research? That it matters?"

"Can you? I've read your emails."

"What is that supposed to mean?"

"Why are your emails so cold?" Ryan said. "Would it kill you to personalize them a bit and add some emotion to them? It feels like I'm reading a corporate memo."

Emmy snorted, and Ryan steeled himself and began to prepare for what he had gotten used to — the dissolution of any civil conversation between the two of them when he inevitably put his foot in his mouth. Ryan knew he was a smooth talker, was a charmer, but something about Emmy always made him say the wrong thing, and there was a way that she would flick her eyes over him, and he just *knew* that he had fucked up.

Emmy made Ryan feel like he was a freshman at his first homecoming dance in St. Cloud. Too nervous to ask any girls out, he had shown up alone, and his older sister Jennifer had encouraged him to ask her best friend to dance. However, Ryan hadn't wanted to wear his glasses because he thought they made him look like a nerd, so he ended up asking another junior girl. One who hadn't been prepped to say yes to Ryan, whose biggest achievement in their high school was making the varsity relay swim team and starting a science club. One glance at Ryan with his long limbs that he hadn't grown into and she looked down her nose at him and snorted.

Just like Emmy had done now. "What now?" he asked, frustrated.

"Do you know what it's like for professional women?" she asked, pulling her feet up under her. "If I used as many exclamation points as you, people would tell me that I'm unprofessional and immature and that I shouldn't write emails like it's my high school diary. Phoebe once included a smiley face — not even an emoji, but like an AIM smiley face — in an email to a principal, and he called the museum to tell Marshall how no one would take his education *girl* seriously if she wrote like that."

"Oh" was all Ryan could say. He thought it benefited him to seem approachable and down-to-earth. But a lot of things benefited him.

"Yeah, and let's talk about makeup. If one of us doesn't wear our base level makeup to work, people will walk up to us and ask us if we're tired or sick." Ryan didn't even realize Emmy was wearing makeup, but he figured that wasn't the right thing to say at this time. Or ever.

His sisters were going to kick his ass.

"So yeah, we have to get up before our male counterparts do so our hair looks nice and our makeup is done. And god forbid we wear a T-shirt to work." She looked pointedly at the short-sleeved V-neck Ryan wore. *I thought it made my arms look good*, he thought. "Because then it tells people that we don't take our jobs seriously."

"Uh," he said, desperate for Emmy to know that he had heard her, was trying to be an active participant in the conversation.

"Right. *Uh*." She snorted. "I'm going to go to the archives and work on the digitization project." Picking up her bag, she slid her feet back into her shoes and walked out of the office in a huff. Ryan caught a whiff of her distinctive scent as she left: grapefruit, the sweetness with that tang that fit her personality.

9

EMMY

"I CANNOT BELIEVE WE have to fucking do this," Emmy said, getting into Phoebe's car — an old green Camry that held a lot of dents from last winter's hailstorm. "I have a million things to be doing and zero ideas for a new collaborative exhibition, but I have to spend the day at a fucking summer camp."

"Hey!" Phoebe replied, handing Emmy a dirty chai to soothe her grumpy mood. "It's my *brother's* summer camp."

"I know, I know, and it'll be great to see Colin and June again, but I am not a team-building person." Emmy hated the forced bullshit bonding that happened at these types of retreats. During her freshman year orientation at YSU, she had been forced to play a game that involved telling two truths and a lie, and after hearing seven people tell some variation of "I broke my *arm* not my leg," Emmy faked a migraine and spent the rest of the day wandering around campus by herself, which she much preferred. Having to do this as a professional — she had a master's degree, for fuck's sake — was her idea of hell. Having to do it with the science center's staff was even worse.

She immediately got a premonition of Ryan's smiling face, his stupid blond curls probably glimmering in the sun up in the mountains. Something hot and...interesting...simmered in her stomach at that image. Annoyance, she figured.

Emmy had been furious for the past two weeks. Ever since Carter had announced the team-building retreat to "create a collective group of brilliant professionals" and Jeremy had kicked Emmy under the table so she didn't yell out her frustration. She was already sharing an office with Ryan. Though in reality, one of them ended up leaving in a huff most days. Did she really need to be out here attempting to share all this bullshit with people she already knew or didn't even want to know? This was taking away time that she could be using on her research, on telling Sara's story. One evening when she couldn't sleep, she had begun looking over a set of scanned diary entries from Sara that she hadn't looked at since grad school. There was something there that Emmy felt close to discovering.

"You know, you should at least be grateful we're not doing an overnight retreat," Phoebe said, sipping coffee that Emmy knew contained at least 35 percent creamer. Taking a generous gulp of her own drink and enjoying the extra spice and burn from the ginger, Emmy considered that. "I have friends who work in university admissions, and they go overnight to the camp every year. Sometimes with their undergrad employees."

"That is, what, the sixth circle of Dante's Inferno?"

"For you, yes," Phoebe snarked as she pulled into Jeremy's driveway. Compared to the two of them, Jeremy's house was positively palatial. He lived in an old craftsman bungalow that was immaculately clean and decorated, and Emmy always felt a surge of jealousy when she looked at it. Emmy liked her apartment, yes, but having a house would be different. And something that was going to be out of her price range for years. Phoebe, who had a similar living situation, plus two jobs (not counting the extra random shifts she picked up at her brother's camp), heard Emmy's envious groan and turned and glared at her.

"Stop," she hissed quietly as Jeremy walked out of the house holding a sleek steel thermos that Emmy knew contained some type of uniquely flavored tea. "Yes, his house is gorgeous, but you know how he got it, and you wouldn't want that to happen." Jeremy's parents had both died within two months of each other when he was in undergrad. As an only child, it left him with their entire inheritance, which Emmy had been led to believe was significant. He bought the house when he moved to Vanberg and had been working on the interior design ever since.

"I know, I know," Emmy replied, waving to Jer as he opened the back door.

"I hate the woods," Jeremy said as he buckled his seat belt.

"We know, love," Emmy said, patting his knee in a faux-sympathetic way. "Which is why we're all still baffled that you're here and not in New York or LA."

"Both of you hush," Phoebe scolded, sounding every inch the educator she was. "If we have to do this, we should at least go in with a positive attitude. Plus, it brings in money for Col's camp, and I haven't seen him in a few weeks." Phoebe loved her brother, idolized him, and, Emmy knew, envied him after he had recently found the love of his life. For all her logic and level-headed advice, Phoebe was a romantic at heart.

"I just don't know why we have to do it with *them*," Emmy said.

"Because we work with *them*," Jeremy contributed from the back seat.

"I mean, the education people aren't that bad," Phoebe said, turning onto the highway that led out of Vanberg and into the mountains. Emmy was looking forward to the cooler temperatures that came with higher elevation at least. "Remember, they're nerds like we are, but nerds about, like, rocks and bugs instead of old, dead people."

"But old, dead people are cool," Emmy whined. "Better than whatever boring-ass old rocks or whatever Ryan studies."

"Have you not talked about your research with him?" Jeremy asked. Emmy shook her head. "God, he's lucky. You never shut up about that shit with us."

Emmy glowered. "We've talked about Sara, of course. And he told me what he studies, but it's a word I don't know, and I'm too stubborn to look it up. I'd rather continue thinking that it's something very stupid."

"You know, I went down to their collections the other day," Jeremy said conversationally. Emmy gaped at this small betrayal. "What? It was a professional curiosity. They're cold, yeah, but the climate control seems to be awesome, and there are a lot of things that would be really fun to make mounts for. Though I will say their geology collections manager is about as positive as you are, Em."

"Perhaps that's my friend-in-waiting," Emmy deadpanned.

"You're being an ass this morning," Phoebe said, passing a semitruck. "Did you sleep well last night? Did you have any special visitors?" Emmy shoved Phoebe in the arm. "I'm driving!" she laughed.

"Please, that bed has been occupied by only me since lockdown ended," Emmy replied. She considered for a second. "Well, most nights, at least."

They drove on, making casual conversation as the car wound along the highway and continued up in elevation, trees and rock formations replacing buildings and billboards as they headed farther away from Vanberg. Emmy had been to Camp Peek-n-See before, accompanying Phoebe occasionally on the days she worked at camp to make some extra income. Emmy opened her phone, and for the thousandth time, flipped through the agenda that had been emailed last week.

Emmy told a lot of people that she hated surprises, which was true, but what Emmy actually hated was being unprepared, being caught with a situation that she hadn't had the time to analyze and understand from a thousand different angles. She skimmed the schedule, and her eyes landed, as they always did, on the event after lunch.

12:30 – 2:30: High Ropes Course

Emmy's stomach dropped when she read the words, even though she had read them every time she looked at the email. She hated heights. Hated observation decks on tall towers, hated flying, even hated the experience of standing at the edge of the Grand Canyon. It was much too easy for Emmy's mind to progress to what, to her, was a logical outcome: one slip, one tiny failure, and she was dead. Shit, she didn't even like walkways through atriums or convention centers after reading about the collapse of a series of walkways in a hotel in Kansas City in the 1980s.

Emmy planned on faking a migraine, her go-to move, after lunch and asking Colin, Phoebe's brother, if she could hide in the dining hall and use their wi-fi to catch up on emails. Her planning was cut short when Phoebe took a highway exit and, soon enough, pulled up the gravel driveway that led to camp, driving under an arch that said CAMP PEEK-N-SEE 1914.

Emmy got out of the car and took a deep breath in, loving the crisp air and the lack of humidity. Phoebe spotted her brother, his hair up in a tiny bun, talking to his fiancée, a shorter woman with curly red hair and an animated manner of speaking.

"I'm gonna go say hi to Col and June," she said, walking away. Jeremy got out of the car, grumbling and spritzing bug spray over his long limbs. Emmy looked around, reacquainting herself with her surroundings. She hadn't been up here since the first few months of COVID, when she and Jer and Phoebes had rented a cabin from Colin and had a debaucherous week when they thought the world was ending. The camp was a little slice of paradise, tucked at the base of a mountain — a ring of cabins set around a lake, with a climbing wall, firepits, and a dining hall that was original to when the camp opened in 1914. Her gaze went over the scenery, and then she spotted Ryan. He was looking at her and smiling.

She groaned to herself. *Of course he was in a good mood*, she thought. He was probably one of those freaks of nature who loved team building, probably got hard from small talk. Her brain caught on that last phrase. And then, of course, she found herself thinking about Ryan's dick. Ugh.

Not only was he in a good mood, but he looked good. He was wearing black running shorts that hugged his quads — *good lord, look at those quads* — and stopped just above his knee, which was borderline indecent on him. He wore a baseball tee that had some type of beer logo on it, and a well-loved baseball cap was on his head, his curls spilling out the sides. Emmy ignored the flip in her stomach as he began to walk over to her.

10

Ryan

He couldn't help but notice her. It had become a bad habit that Ryan had tried to break over the past few weeks, but his eyes and attention were drawn to Emmy as soon as he walked into any space she was in. Shit, he knew the minute the car she was in pulled into camp, and this was a wide-open camp. He tried – he *really* tried – not to spend too much time looking at her body as he walked over to her, but he failed. Almost as badly as he failed organic chemistry sophomore year of college (which was pretty damn bad).

Emmy was wearing a dark green racerback tank top that showed off her defined shoulder muscles and had a sweatshirt tied around her waist in a way that reminded him of the girls he'd had crushes on in high school. Her black hair was up in a high ponytail, and her legs were clad in mid-length leggings. Ryan sent a quiet note of thanks to whoever had reintroduced skin-tight leggings to women's fashion, especially when the women had legs like Emmy's.

Be nice, he scolded himself. Though being nice was second nature, at least in public. Emmy's pale skin flushed slightly, and she looked away when she caught his eye, and that spark of attraction in his chest flared again. Could it be that she was also intrigued by him? Yes, she was an ice queen and built up frozen walls that belonged in *Game of Thrones* during meetings and in the office, but Ryan couldn't help but get the sense that something fiery ran under the surface. Like one of those volcanoes in Iceland with a thousand letters in its name. He took a deep breath – *thank god for swimming* – and walked over to her.

"Good morning, Emmy," he said, hands in his pockets. Definitely not to hold his shorts out a few inches to disguise the effect she had on his lower body. Nope.

"Doc," she replied curtly, eyes darting around the entire group, around the camp, anywhere but his face. He nodded to Jeremy, wished him good morning as well.

"You know what I don't understand?" Emmy asked, not to Ryan, but not *not* to Ryan. This could mark the first occasion she had almost begun a conversation with him, initiated that connection, and Ryan was going to pursue it.

"Yes?"

"We're apparently under so much of a budget cut that we have to combine museums and exhibitions, share offices like they're childhood bedrooms, but we can pay for the entire staff to go play in the woods for a day?" Emmy huffed and blew a stream of air up at her bangs, ruffling the straight black hair.

"Good morning to you, too, Sunshine," said a tall man who was walking over to the three of them, his hair up in a tiny bun. Phoebe was following close behind, chatting to a woman with curly red hair and hips that gave Emmy's a run for their money.

"Col, I can't even deal with your energy right now," Emmy grumbled as the man wrapped his arms around her and pressed a goofy kiss to the top of her head. *Who the fuck was this guy*? Ryan thought. The two laughed and joked like they had some previous connection, and Ryan found himself jealous of how the man needled Emmy about her moods and attitude in a way that Ryan could never get away with.

"Ah, Em. You love it out here," the man said, wrapping one arm around Emmy's shoulders and showing off the rest of the camp with his arm. Ryan, who had a very distinct urge to wrench the man's arm off Emmy's body, began sizing the slimmer man up in a way that his dad had tried to teach him to do when he was playing bantam hockey.

"Trees? Yes. Mountains? Yes." Emmy shrugged out of his grip – *victory* – and crossed her forearms and cocked her hip in a way that Ryan really didn't need to see. He already spent too much time avoiding looking at her lower body in the office. "Talking about my favorite flavor of ice cream and my *feelings*? Playing icebreaker games? Ugh." She snorted again. Her eyes moved, caught Ryan's, and he steeled himself for one of their typical sniping arguments. Her eyes turned flinty, the sun reflecting on her hair. "I bet you love icebreakers, huh?"

Sometimes it was annoying how well Emmy knew him, had a sense of his personality that she had sized up in their initial meetings and found lacking. Ryan did love icebreakers, but Ryan liked any activity that allowed him to get to know people better. He looked forward to getting to know Emmy today. *For work collaboration reasons*, he reminded himself. But he also liked to use the personal connections he made during these activities and small talk to connect with his colleagues. He grinned over at Emmy, took his baseball cap off, and placed it back on his head. "Yeah, I do," he admitted. "I like getting to know people."

"I totally agree!" the mystery man said. He put out his hand to shake Ryan's. Ryan wanted to slap it away and fight the man for putting his hands on Emmy. Which was totally not an appropriate feminist impulse. "I'm Colin."

Ryan did what a nice boy from Minnesota should do and shook the man's hand. "Ryan."

"I'm June," said the woman. Ryan knew these people didn't work at the museum, but they seemed to be close to Phoebe, Jeremy, and Emmy, so he would be nice. Did they work at the camp? "I also hate icebreakers," she continued, smiling at him softly. "I had to do too many at my old job, and I had to beg Col here to promise I'd never have to facilitate them when I'm helping out at camp."

"I think she's going to make me write it in our vows," Colin cracked. The woman blushed red and rolled her eyes a bit, though she shot a look at Colin that was full of lust.

As if noticing his slightly hidden confusion, Phoebe stepped next to Colin and pointed between him and herself. "Ryan, this is my brother. June is his fiancée, and she lives here with him." Her eyes darted between Ryan and Emmy, floated over Colin and June, and she sighed. Understanding settled in his mind, and Phoebe turned on Emmy. "Colin was nice enough to give us a group discount for coming up today, and he and June are working for free to bring down the rate even more, so quit being an ass." June laughed, and Emmy rolled her eyes.

"Yeah, she's a real straight talker when she wants to be," June said, noticing Ryan's surprised expression. While Ryan had chatted with Phoebe in the occasional meeting or when she stopped by to distract Emmy when she got overly stressed, he had always thought her to just be a perfectly nice and, if anything, slightly bland coworker.

"I hate nature," Jeremy said, slapping at a bug on his leg, breaking the slight tension between the others in the group. "It's beautiful out here, Colin, no offense, but I would rather be inside. Or in the city. With a nice glass of wine. And a nice man. All of those are difficult to find out here."

"You'd be surprised," June said, slinking her arm around Colin's and kissing his shoulder. It hit Ryan then, how obvious it was that these two were in love. They barely had eyes for other people around them for a conversation, let alone for any type of romantic interest. Something inside Ryan calmed and settled.

"Should we help him?" June said, pointing to where Marshall was attempting to get the attention of the group. Not only was the man dressed like a bargain 1970s camp counselor, high white socks included, but his voice could barely be heard in meetings in the museum, let alone in front of the entire staff outside. Ryan, without thinking, put two fingers to his lips and blew a loud whistle, a trick he had known how to do since he was a little boy.

"Jesus Christ; that was loud," Emmy said, dramatically putting her fingers in her ears and looking at him. "Next time, give some warning, 'kay?"

"Sorry," Ryan grimaced. "Thought I'd help Marshall out."

"God knows he needs it," Emmy joked. "I could use you in meetings with donors." Ryan's whistle had worked, cutting off the rest of their conversation as the assembled crowd of collections managers, designers, exhibitions staff, and assorted employees ambled together, a mix of people who looked genuinely excited to be outside and people who looked like they avoided sunlight at all costs. It would be an interesting day, for sure.

"Good morning, good morning," Marshall said, waving his hands at everyone. Dr. Carter stepped in, assuming his position of authority with a simple wave of his hand.

Ryan liked Dr. Carter, who had hired him at the museum, even though the man could be a bit brusque and businesslike at times. He thought Carter had put their museum in a good financial position, even if Ryan had definitely begun to agree with Emmy that perhaps their collections and exhibitions had skewed toward what donors wanted rather than what science dictated. "Good morning, staff. Thank you for being here."

"As if we had a choice," Emmy mumbled under her breath. She had shifted her position to face where the two men were speaking and, in doing so, maneuvered herself next to Ryan's side. He looked down at her, and she met his eyes, her gray irises shining silver in the morning sun. He chuckled softly. The right side of her mouth tipped up in a sarcastic grin, and she playfully shushed him. "Focus, Doc."

Carter continued. "We've brought you all here today to foster interdepartmental collaboration and to break down the silos that have existed between and internal to our respective institutions."

"Does this man ever speak like a human, or hasn't the new software downloaded yet?" Emmy whispered to Ryan. He warmed at her close contact, at this small lifeline of connection between them, felt the hair on the back of his neck stand up.

"Not really," he whispered back, leaning down slightly to speak into her ear. She flicked her gaze up at him, and the corner of her mouth kicked up again. Ryan decided that he could refer to that as a smile — no, *two* smiles. She'd given him two smiles today. Small victories.

"We will participate in a variety of team-building activities as a whole staff and small groups in the morning, break for lunch in departments, and then return outside in the afternoon for the high ropes course. Ideally, this will help us to foster trust and collaboration that we can bring back to the CSTH starting tomorrow." Carter looked pleased with his speech, though Ryan felt like he was just listening to someone recite a marketing brochure. "We will be led by a variety of members of the camp staff, including the camp director, Colin Whitford, who has graciously donated his time and the reservation today." Colin waved bashfully at the crowd, then turned his gaze back to June. The way they looked at each other was so heated — so full of love, yes, but also full of lust — that Ryan felt like he was intruding on something.

"Phoebe probably begged him to rent us the camp so her brother would take a break from nonstop fucking June," Emmy snarked. Ryan had to bite his lip to stop from laughing. Carter continued, and Ryan felt Emmy roll her eyes next to him.

"We will begin our morning with some small-group facilitated outdoor connection activities and icebreakers. I *do* expect you all to participate to the best of your ability," Carter finished. From behind him, Ryan heard Jeremy groan, and Emmy grumbled something to herself.

He looked at her, decided to needle her and play with her for a bit. He got the sense — no, he directly knew from experience over the past few weeks — that Emmy was the exception to the adage *you catch more flies with honey*. "What? You don't want to know people's favorite flavor of ice cream?" In a bold move, he let his eyes drift slowly down to her lips. An image of Emmy eating an ice cream cone — slowly, seductively, but with a sarcastic undertone he knew she would carry into anything — popped into his head, temporarily scrambling his thoughts. He looked up and met her eyes, noticing how her pupils widened and a light blush dusted across her cheekbones. “My favorite flavor of ice cream is strawberry, for the record.”

11

Ryan

So far, the highlights of the morning had been the moment Emmy touched his arm, then when he made her laugh, then when he caught her staring at his lips. Sure, it had been great to get to connect with coworkers. Even his fellow scientists had started to come out of their shells, and Ryan had the chance to chat with a few other support staff who were hired when the Center was fully remote.

But it was that small spark of connection with Emmy, who had lowered her walls a centimeter at best, that had Ryan's smile buzzing. He did his best not to watch her during the group team-building activities, and he tried not to always find himself next to her when groupings were being made. He spent a lot of time reminding himself that this was about getting to know all the staff members, not just a certain sassy historian. He did want to help create better exhibitions, better science; it would help to promote the museum, to promote his own career.

But, somehow, he always came back to Emmy's sarcastic comments, her wry smile, and – good lord – her legs.

The entire staff had balanced on a large seesaw of some kind, lined up by birthdays without talking, and completed a maze blindfolded with a partner giving directions, among other activities. Each activity was led by camp staff or Phoebe's brother, who, after their initial interaction, Ryan had taken a liking to. Ryan had always wanted to go to summer camp growing up, but with three sisters and himself and only one working parent, it wasn't in the cards financially. Sure, he spent a lot of time out in nature – it was hard not to in Minnesota, what with the ten thousand lakes and all that – but Ryan liked doing activities with people. He had spent a lot of time with other boys his age, gallivanting through the wilderness. Which is where he had discovered his first fossil, just an impression of a leaf on the bottom of a stone in a creek that turned over after a spring rainstorm.

"Lunch will be from eleven thirty to twelve fifteen. Feel free to grab food from the dining hall and take it anywhere you'd like around camp," Colin said, winding a length of climbing rope around his arm as they closed the last team-building activity. "There's the porch off the dining hall, the common open space, even the dock at the lake." Ryan noticed that his cheeks pinked slightly when he mentioned that last location, and he wondered what significance it held for him. "Just be back in front of the dining hall at quarter past noon. And please make sure to clean up all of your trash and bring back your dishes and silverware."

"And separate your compost!" Phoebe added. "Col gets really excited about how much the worms can eat!" Colin rolled his eyes, and Phoebe stuck her tongue out at him. Ryan was reminded of his relationship with his sisters. He should probably call them on the drive back down from the camp.

Ryan walked in and grabbed a perfectly reasonable camp lunch of a cold cut sandwich, chips, a pickle, and a can of seltzer, then walked outside, looking around the open space. He decided to walk outside to the deck and eat where he could see the lake. That way, he would still be close to where he needed to be. He was surprised to find Emmy out there already, perched on an Adirondack chair, unwrapping her sandwich and looking out over the lake.

"Mind if I join you?" he asked, lingering near the edge of a chair. *If she needs alone time, I can find somewhere else.*

Emmy huffed a sigh, then seemed to be having a debate with herself in her mind. Finally, she gave her head a small shake and said, "Sure." Ryan sat down in the chair, stretched his long legs out, and unwrapped his sandwich — turkey and cheddar. He picked up the extra packets of mayonnaise and began to spread it between the cheese and meat.

"Do you even have any sandwich left at the end?" Emmy said. He looked up and was pleasantly surprised to find that she was watching him, that half smile on her face. Ryan grinned back sheepishly.

"I'm a Midwesterner," he said, shrugging, as if that explained it. If he wanted to go further, he would talk about how his mom only bought Miracle Whip growing up, a combination of her perennial attempts to lose weight and to save money, so he always jumped at the chance to eat mayo. But he and Emmy weren't like that yet. *Yet.*

"So am I," Emmy replied, slipping a chip between her lips. "But I use condiments like a normal person."

"Ohio, right?" Ryan remembered asking her that on the first day they shared an office and how badly it had gone. Well, he couldn't take back the attempt at small talk now.

She sighed, and he could almost hear her talking to herself in her mind. "Youngstown," she said. "Famous for steel mills, corrupt politicians with bad toupees, and for having the highest murder rate in the country as I was growing up." She munched on another chip. "Oh, and it was recently named the poorest city in Ohio." She gave a few fake cheerleading moves.

Ryan wasn't sure if he was supposed to laugh or not. "I take it you don't go home very often?"

"Home is Vanberg," she replied seriously. "Youngstown is where I grew up. I haven't been back since I graduated from college." She nodded at his baseball cap. "Minnesota, huh?"

"Yep," he replied. "St. Cloud. Uff-da and all that." Emmy returned a blank look. "It's a Minnesota thing," Ryan explained. "Like an 'oh well' type of vibe. My mom is, like, seventh generation Minnesotan, so she has the whole

Midwestern mom thing down — hot dishes and bowling leagues and the Fargo accent."

"You don't have much of an accent," Emmy observed.

"Not many of our generation does. I mean, do you sound like a steelworker?" Emmy pulled a face. "Exactly."

Emmy didn't expand on the conversation, and Ryan was going to try this new thing where he didn't push her to connect with him, didn't force the small talk. It almost physically pained him. They returned to eating their lunches in silence, the only sound chips being eaten and seltzer water quietly fizzing.

After about five minutes, Ryan couldn't handle the silence. He had seen Emmy with her friends, knew she was a talker when she wanted to be. "I always wanted to go to summer camp," he tried. "Did you go?"

"Did you miss the part where I said 'poorest city in Ohio'?"

"Fair point."

"To answer, no. Where would I have gone? Lake Erie? The rivers leading up to it caught on fire like seven times. It was so polluted when I was growing up that we couldn't eat fish from it." She looked thoughtful for a second. "Are the lakes in Minnesota as gorgeous as everyone says?"

Ryan smiled, thinking of the ponds that spotted the land around St. Cloud. "Yeah, they're pretty amazing."

"You're lucky," she said quietly. Ryan knew there was more there, an undercurrent of her relationship with her hometown and home state, but he was nice enough to know when not to push.

Well, sometimes.

"Yeah," he acknowledged. "But I definitely prefer living in the mountains."

"Oh yeah." Emmy lit up. "I like to spend all my weekends out here, hiking or skiing."

"I've never been downhill skiing," Ryan admitted. "Cross-country, yeah, but never downhill." *You could teach me*, was what he wanted to say, but that would be way too forward.

"It's the best. You feel so free and in touch with nature. Plus, the après ski drinks make all that effort worth it!" The image of Emmy sipping a hot toddy in front of a fireplace appeared in Ryan's head. He shifted suddenly, trying to adjust the compostable paper plate on his lap to hide how much he liked the image of her outside of work, relaxed, the smile he'd seen her give her friends reserved for him.

"Maybe our next staff bonding retreat can be at a ski resort," Ryan said without thinking. Emmy laughed.

"Yeah, and they can rent out Aspen for us and shower us all with private chalets." Emmy finished her sandwich, folding the wax paper wrapping into a neat square and organizing her trash into the cardboard box it had come in. It was so different from how Ryan had seen her at work. There, she was all chaotic piles, Post-its on top of other Post-its, and scribbles in her notebook. He liked seeing a different side of her.

"Are you excited about this afternoon?" he asked, trying to find a topic to continue their conversation.

"Hell no." The words rushed out of Emmy's mouth.

"Why?"

"I, uh..." she stuttered, grew quiet. Which, again, was unusual in the way that he had come to expect Emmy to speak to him – usually she was keeping a leash on her anger or trying not to shout her frustration when he said something that inadvertently offended her – but he had never seen her like this. Guarded, like a timid dog. "I don't like heights," she finished abruptly, as if to communicate that it was the end of the conversation and that she didn't want him pursuing it further.

Ryan, for once in his difficult and frustrating and annoyingly arousing relationship with Emmy, took the hint and didn't press her.

12

Emmy

A DINING BELL OF some kind rang out, signaling it was time to head back inside and regroup. Emmy was annoyed at herself for a lot of reasons as she and Ryan cleaned up and headed back inside. She was annoyed that she'd had a full conversation with Ryan. She was annoyed that she had admitted to herself how attractive he was. She was annoyed that she had revealed things about her background. She was annoyed that his charming demeanor had worked on her, which caused her to reveal said things. And she was annoyed that she had almost revealed her fear of heights to
him.

When Emmy said she didn't like heights, she was selling herself and her constant anxiety short. Emmy didn't feel things in halves. A previous boyfriend had broken up with her after he had gotten frustrated with her need to have a strong opinion on every topic he brought up. Emmy didn't dislike things – she hated them. Dreaded them. Was terrified of them.

Especially heights. Especially heights that were connected to things that were out of her control.

She barely noticed Ryan take a seat on the bench next to her, where she had plopped down next to Phoebe, as she tried to remember everything she had read about high ropes courses last night. She learned they were tested regularly by the companies to make sure their investment and brand reputation were sound. She had looked up the American Camping Association's standards to ensure that there was regular maintenance and training. She had been a few seconds from calling Colin and asking him to send her the maintenance history, along with the brands of harnesses he used and the company that had installed the course. But even she knew that was taking it a bit too far. Plus, the less people knew about how seriously Emmy's brain spiraled, the more she could pretend to her friends that she was normal.

Because a normal person didn't have multiple tabs of safety ratings of harnesses up on their phone so she could quickly double-check what brand she was about to put on her body against a few different models.

Because a normal person didn't scour OSHA reports for *climbing injuries.*

The skills that made Emmy a great historian — she wasn't shy there; she was a badass historian — also allowed her anxiety to take over her mind. She was excellent at researching, was a quick reader who was able to skim multi-page reports for the stats and information she needed. But AnxietyBrain also did that for her fears, and she didn't need that information bouncing around. LogicBrain knew that but had been in a losing battle against AnxietyBrain for over twenty years and still didn't have a winning strategy.

"Em." Jeremy said, poking her in the shoulder, shaking her out of her thought process.

"Huh?" she asked eloquently, looking around to see whether she had missed a huge announcement.

"I saw your brain going," he said softly. "Wanted to bring you back to the group before you had to go do something else this afternoon." *My brain is always going.*

"Thanks, love," she said, blowing him a kiss. He caught it and crossed his legs, sipping a mug of tea he had managed to charm Colin into getting for him.

"Um, hello again," came a wiry voice, and Emmy groaned. Marshall, still with his high socks, plus a new pair of pit stains, was standing in front of the room, attempting to get the group's attention.

"Hey," she whispered, poking Ryan in the ribs. *Don't think about the fact that you touched his ribs.* He turned toward her, and his eyes widened slightly behind his glasses, flicked up and down her body before returning to her face.

"What?"

"Can you do that whistle thing again?" Emmy mimed putting her fingers to her mouth and blowing. *Don't think about putting your fingers in his mouth.* "Help the poor man out. He shouldn't be out of the museum this much. It's too much Vitamin D for him."

Ryan chuckled a healthy breath that sent tingles down Emmy's spine, then put his fingers to his lips and blew a whistle. *Don't look at his lips.*

"Thank you, Dr. Andersson," Carter said, taking the lead from Marshall, who looked relieved. Ryan tipped his baseball cap to him in a joking gesture. "We've all bonded as a full staff and eaten a delicious lunch. Now we'll embark on some smaller group work with a focus on the partnerships we believe will be most advantageous to our success as the new CSTH. We ask that you approach this afternoon's high ropes course with a positive attitude and ethic of collaboration with your partner." He cleared his throat and looked over the crowd. Emmy thought she was imagining it, but she felt like Carter's eyes had landed on her for a second longer than anyone else. *Fuck.*

"Partner pairings are on the whiteboard by the door," came Colin's voice from the background, where he was already wearing a climbing harness. *Dork*, she thought as she usually did about Phoebe's brother.

Emmy got up and picked up her drawstring backpack containing sunscreen, ibuprofen, anti-chafe cream (a girl with her thighs had to be prepared), and a water bottle, slinging it over her back. She readjusted her high ponytail and stretched her shoulders as she walked over to the pairings. The staff was gathered around it like it was the announcement of the cast list for a high school musical. Emmy had never participated, preferring to spend her time working part-time jobs to save money or taking community college classes. She waited for the crowd to clear and scanned the list quickly.

Team 23: Emmy Bonaire - Ryan Andersson

Of course. They shared an office. They were supposed to be developing a brand-new exhibit to present to the board that would anchor the new museum, whenever that would be built. Of course they were going to be partners.

Dammit, AnxietyBrain. Why couldn't you have anticipated this *outcome*? It was really unfair how Emmy couldn't direct her anxiety toward things that would actually be useful in her life.

"Ready to *Free Solo* this thing?" Ryan asked, coming up next to her and grinning.

Fuck.

About fifteen minutes later, Emmy's brain hadn't moved on. *Fuck. Fuck. Fuck. Fuck. Fuck.* The single curse word bounced around her mind as she finished strapping on her harness, cinching it as tight as she could around her waist. She had only had to readjust the leg straps three times to get them over her quads, but then she struggled to deal with the extra webbing around her waist. Whose bodies were these harnesses made for, anyway?

Emmy tried to channel LogicBrain as she braided her hair quickly down her back in order to place the red turtle shell-shaped helmet on her head and clip it under her chin. *High ropes are safe. You planned for this.* She had planned for it, yes, but had forgotten how tiny the wires would be. Not to mention that it was a wooden structure. Were there termites in this part of Colorado? Was the wood treated? She should pull out her phone right now and text Colin. Or she could google *termite range Colorado Rockies + elevation* and take a quick look at some maps...

"Whoo!" came a voice from above her, and Emmy's neck snapped back so she could watch Jeremy — reserved, cultured, metropolitan Jeremy — cheer with joy as he went careening down a zip line. Good lord, what horrors did this have if Jeremy was enjoying himself? Up was down and down was up. SpongeBob was Squidward. Ryan was actually nice...

"Ready partner?" Ryan asked, coming up behind her, his arrival heralded by the sound of webbing slipping along his running shorts. Emmy tightened her waist belt again so it nearly cut into her hipbone and turned.

The man was attractive in the office — Emmy had finally admitted that to herself. But good god; Ryan in a climbing harness was obscene. Harnesses were not supposed to be attractive on people, she thought. She glanced around at her coworkers. Everyone looked slightly awkward, squished and squeezed into the bright blue webbing. But *fucking Dr. Ryan Andersson* had to look attractive. His quads were only emphasized by the leg straps, and Emmy had to scramble in her backpack for her water bottle when she looked at the bulge between his thighs that the harness didn't help but put on display like the centerpiece of an exhibition.

Seriously. Obscene.

"Sure," Emmy said warily, holding up two lame thumbs. Ryan made a move like he was about to put his hands over hers but seemed to stop himself at the last minute.

They got in line where the partnerships were lining up. Phoebe turned around and waved, partnered with a fellow education facilitator from the science center who seemed, well, perfectly nice and boring.

Emmy snuck a glance out of the corner of her eye at Ryan, who was studying the ropes course, his chin turned up to the sun and his eyes darting around. He swallowed, and Emmy watched his Adam's apple move. *Fuck.*

"What are you studying?" she asked, trying to get her mind off his body or the fact that she would soon be — what was it? Seven stories? — up in the air.

"Just trying to figure out the best path for working through everything," he replied, cocking his head, causing a curl to flop out of his helmet. He even made that stupid thing look good. Asshole.

"Why would we want to do everything?" Emmy asked. "Can't we just get up there, go to one of those little bird nest thingies, and then make our way back down the ladder?"

Ryan's laugh surprised Emmy, full of excitement and joy. "And waste free ropes course time like this? Nah, we have to do it all. Also, you can't just climb down." He nudged her shoulder and tipped his head to where another straight-laced museum staff member was grinning at the top of a pole and clipping into the zip line. "Watch Satya over there." He pointed past her, and Emmy noticed his arm muscles. "See? At the end, you zip down, and then you're back on the ground."

Emmy's thighs began to tremble, a sure sign that her body had finally begun to pick up on the anxiety in her mind. Her panic attacks always began in her muscles, progressing to her bloodstream when the adrenaline caused her heart rate to spike.

Breathe. Breathe. It's safe. You're fine, she repeated to herself as a makeshift mantra. There was only one group ahead of them. She could do this.

"Do you want to go first?" Ryan asked, stepping back and gesturing in front of her, toward the ladder and the rope that was being staffed by a guy who looked like a younger version of Phoebe's brother.

"Sure," Emmy said quickly, trying to get it out of the way. She walked over, closing and opening her hands to try to get them to stop trembling, praying to whatever spirits lived in the forest that Ryan wouldn't notice. When people (other than Jer and Phoebe) had picked up on her anxiety before, it always made Emmy feel like they thought she was weak or they pitied her. And those were emotions she had no time for, especially not with Ryan.

She was clipped into a rope and a lot of instructions were given to her, but only a few landed in her ears. *Step up the ladder, move the rope, get to the top* were the ones that mattered, and Emmy kept repeating them to herself as she put one foot on the ladder.

Victory.

Second foot, second rung.

Fuck yes.

Another step, third rung. Move the rope. Keep looking up.

Okay. She could do this.

Fourth step, her hand moving up another rung. It looked like just six or seven more, so Emmy could just count down and —

"Yeah, Emmy!" came Ryan's voice from below her, causing her to make a critical error.

She looked down.

Suddenly, the ground that she swore had *been right there* zoomed away, like a tunnel perspective in a *Looney Tunes* cartoon. Emmy became hyperaware of every sensation — the slight shake of the ladder when she moved, the absurdly small rung her foot was on, the fact that the rope didn't look like it could hold her — she knew that last bulk cycle wasn't worth the deadlift PR, dammit.

Her eyes wide, she whipped her head around, gripping the ladder so hard her knuckles turned white. Looking down again, she made direct contact with Ryan's green eyes. Where she had expected to find judgment or pity, she found a different emotion — compassion.

Huh, that was new was the last thought to flit through Emmy's head before the overwhelming panic set in and her entire body and mind froze up.

13

Ryan

When Emmy had said she didn't like heights, Ryan had brushed off the statement, categorizing it with the way people said they didn't like spiders or snakes. Something that gave them the heebie-jeebies, as his mom would say. A shiver of unease that could easily be pushed through with an eye roll and a laugh.

What Emmy was exhibiting right now was certainly not a case of the heebie-jeebies.

Ryan had a good sense of noticing detail, but he usually put those skills to use behind a microscope. Unfortunately, it also meant that he knew how Emmy moved and how her body showed her true emotions before her mouth did (not that she could ever really hold her tongue for long). When she was with her friends, her muscles were relaxed and flowing. When she was in meetings, she was strong lines and a broad posture, like a predator approaching a larger beast. When she talked to him, her muscles almost crackled with the electricity from holding herself still.

Right now, Emmy was rigid. Color had drained from her face, and Ryan caught small twitches of movement in her hands and legs.

Emmy wasn't nervous. Emmy wasn't a little afraid of heights.

Emmy was *terrified.*

He hadn't meant to catch her off guard, only wanted to encourage her and show support – *as a colleague*. But the moment she looked down and locked eyes with him, Ryan had realized his mistake. She wasn't ignoring everyone on the ground; she was focusing on the path above her so she didn't look down.

Oh shit.

Taking a broad stride over to the staff member, Ryan asked if he could quickly get clipped in. When told that he needed to wait until Emmy was at least two rungs higher, Ryan gave him a steely glare and muttered, "She's freaked out. Let me get up there and talk her through it." The staff member hesitated, and Ryan tried again. "I don't want to clog up the line, and I think that it will make her even more nervous if more attention is on her. I promise I'll keep six rungs between us as soon as she starts climbing again." The man nodded, and Ryan was clipped in. He put his hand on the ladder but noticed that it shook.

"Emmy," he called up. "I'm coming up, so the ladder might shake a bit." She kept holding on to the ladder with a death grip, her body unmoving, but Ryan caught a quick nod of her head.

As he moved up the ladder slowly, Ryan tried to channel any bit of grace he had gathered from learning how to glide through the water for decades, trying to minimize the movements as much as possible.

He also tried to not stare at Emmy's ass as he climbed up. In the middle of her having a crisis was not the appropriate time to be ogling her; he knew that. But he was only human, so maybe he allowed himself a quick peek.

When he got up right under her — *not like that*, he told his dick — he reached up and tapped her on the ankle.

"Emmy, I'm right here," he said. "You're gonna be fine. We're just gonna get up to the top of this platform, and then we're gonna reevaluate the entire situation. You'll feel better when you get up to the platform. It looks super stable." She turned her head to look at him, and he *tsked* at her, tapping her ankle again. "Nope, don't look at me. Eyes up, Em."

He watched her take a deep breath and let it out, her body shaking as she did so.

"You've got this. I'm right here," he said softly. "Do you want me to distract you?"

"Yes," she squeaked. "Anything."

"Well, I'll tell you about my research, even though it might legitimately put you to sleep. I study coprolites, right? That's fossilized dinosaur shit." He breathed a sigh of relief as she let out a tiny laugh. It was unsteady at first, but then it blossomed into what he could feasibly categorize as a chuckle. He continued, "Yeah, yeah. Make all the jokes about it. I only started because we had a collection at UCSB. It seemed like it was going to be an easy topic to research and get my dissertation while doing so. Turns out, you can understand so much about not only the diet of dinosaurs — that makes sense, of course — but also the prehistoric environment if you slice the coprolites really thin. Like see-through thin."

Emmy had begun to climb again, making her way steadily up another rung. Conveniently forgetting what he had told the staff member on the ground, he followed closely behind her, still trying to move as gingerly as he could. He continued rambling about his research, pulling out conclusions from his PhD he hadn't thought about since that paper had gotten accepted and published. Finally, Emmy clambered up onto the platform, throwing her chest on the wood and scooting her ass up to follow. Ryan waited on the ladder below her until she was able to stand up fully, hugging her body to the telephone pole that stabilized the platform.

Ryan pulled himself up onto the small deck and tried to give her room. He really did, but the space was only so big, and Emmy was tall and broad, and Ryan was...well, also tall and broad. His body crowded close to hers, and he had a heightened awareness of her — a slight tang of outdoors and sweat mixed with grapefruit. Biting the inside of his cheek to suppress a groan, he lifted his hand up to Emmy.

"Thanks," she said, giving the world's most half-hearted high five. She peered around at the other groups on the ground, then muttered "shit" and lightly tapped her head against the pole.

"What?" Ryan asked, confused. She should be so proud of how she did. She made it to the top, she conquered her fears.

"It's so embarrassing," she muttered. Ryan continued to give her a quizzical look, which was typical. Emmy took another deep breath, and he waited, giving her time to clear her thoughts. "My anxiety makes me look weak and stupid. And now everyone we work with saw that I can't even climb up a fucking ladder without losing my shit. Without someone having to come and rescue me." She looked at Ryan, and he saw another new emotion — defeat.

"Uh, that's bullshit," Ryan said, swiveling around on the platform and looking across the course. "You just did a badass thing and pushed through. I was there talking to you, but you had to do the climbing."

He waited a minute again for Emmy to think, to chew over what had just happened. And then she rolled her shoulders back. "Okay," she said, as if she had made up her mind. "Okay, let's fucking do this."

"Do what?"

"This whole damn course," Emmy said, tentatively taking one hand off the pole to gesture around. "I'm not wasting that near-panic attack by only doing one of these things."

"Okay," Ryan said, unsure of where this new energy had come from. "I was looking, and there are seven platforms — eight if you count the one we're standing on. Let's pick them off one by one."

"Like a to-do list," Emmy said, meeting his eye and lifting one corner of her mouth in a small smile.

"Exactly." Ryan couldn't resist the urge to make one tiny joke. "Do you have a Post-it note up here?"

Emmy laughed this time. A full, joyous laugh. Not even with her usual sarcasm or skepticism. "I do have some in my bag on the ground, in my notebook."

"No!"

"You never know when a good idea is going to strike you," she defended.

"I'll take your word for it, Em," he said, pointing to the next set of obstacles. A simple bridge made of wooden planks with rope handholds along the side. "Let's start with that one. It seems like the least intimidating." Emmy nodded and walked off the platform, grabbing the ropes and sliding her hands along each one.

They worked surprisingly smoothly together, navigating the bridge and a series of swinging platforms that were placed a few feet away from each other. Ryan would offer suggestions sometimes, and Emmy would take them occasionally, but never without some biting jab back at him. He found that he liked it when they were being playfully prickly with each other, working toward finishing this larger goal.

This was what had been missing from their working relationship. Something where they weren't both automatically on the defensive. Something they could work toward together that didn't threaten the hard work Emmy had put into the museum for years.

Ryan watched Emmy as she gripped a knotted rope above her head to maintain her balance, a sliver of a yellow sports bra peeking out from her tank top. Her back muscles rippled, and Ryan was once again drawn to staring at her shoulders and trying very, *very* hard not to think about how her muscles would stretch and contract as she lifted or as she did...other things.

His mind was still distracted, reining in his attraction to Emmy, thinking of the next witty quip he could toss her way for her to bat down, when he mis-stepped, missing the next platform. He grabbed for the rope but only caught air, and then he was falling.

14

Emmy

"Geez, Doc. Are you a brontosaurus with how much noise you're making behind me?" Emmy was particularly proud of being able to give Ryan shit *and* recall a specific dinosaur name. She turned her head and looked over her shoulder to take in his reaction but was confused when she didn't see

him.

"Fuck!" came Ryan's voice from below her. Emmy looked down to see him dangling a few feet below the middle platform, evidently having slipped off.

Thank god these harnesses are approved for people his size, she thought, her eyes quickly scanning his body to see if he had any injuries. Was he hurt? All the straps and carabiners looked safe and connected. She didn't see any blood, and his chest was rising and falling. He had sworn, too, so he wasn't unconscious.

"Ryan!" she shouted, maneuvering herself over to him. "Jesus, are you okay?"

"I'm fine, I'm fine," he said, kicking his feet in a lazy manner. "My pride is hurt, but that's kind of typical around you." Emmy rolled her eyes and scoffed. She looked around to find a staff member, and her eyes caught on Colin, who was watching the scene from a nearby platform with a fascinated smirk on his face.

"Colin! What the hell are we supposed to do?" she demanded.

"You're partners," he said nonchalantly. "Help each other up."

"Goddamn unhelpful smart-ass camp fuck," Emmy muttered, turning around and making her way over to Ryan. She looked down, where he swung slightly, not even fazed in the slightest. She looked over her shoulder at Colin. "Now what?"

"Reach down," he replied, "and pull him up."

"Pull him up? He's enormous!" Emmy said, then mentally slapped herself at those words.

"Thanks, Em," Ryan said, letting out a sarcastic laugh below her.

"Oh, you know what I mean," she hissed. "You fill every damn doorway in the museum with your linebacker shoulders."

"They're from swimming, thank you very much."

"I'm going to leave you down there."

"Aw, c'mon. Do what the dork says and help me."

"You know I can hear you, right?" Colin called, faking offense. "I'm your best friend's older brother. You have to be nice to me."

"I don't have to do shit, Col," Emmy said, laughing.

"If you're not nice to me, I'll sic June on you."

"Ugh, fine," Emmy said. "But only because Phoebe likes you." She looked down, then groaned again. "Seriously, what am I supposed to do?"

"Kneel down and hold on to the rope to steady yourself. Reach down with your dominant hand and grasp on to his wrist. Once he gets a hold of you, he can reach up and grab a rope," Colin explained. Emmy followed instructions and kneeled, reaching her left hand down.

"Here," she said, wiggling her hand at Ryan. He reached up and slipped his hand around her forearm, gripping tight. Emmy gripped back, and for a moment, it seemed like they were in a competition to see who could squeeze the other's arm the hardest.

Emmy counted it as a win when Ryan said softly, "You're strong as hell."

"Sure," Emmy said, waving away the compliment and engaging her back muscles and quads to begin to get him closer to where he could grab the platform she was on. "*Don't* tip me over," she warned.

"I won't," Ryan replied, placing both hands on the platform and, in a positively impressive feat of strength, pulling himself up next to Emmy.

"That was..." Her voice trailed off as her mouth went dry. *I'm dehydrated*, she reasoned.

"No different from pulling myself out of a pool, and I've been doing that for three decades," Ryan replied. And, damn him, now her brain was full of images of wet muscles, Speedos, and other thoughts that had inhabited her brain during the 2000 Sydney Olympics when she was in love with Ian Thorpe.

Emmy brought her attention back to the present moment. To getting off this stupid platform and to this stupid retreat and to slamming a not-stupid gin & tonic as soon as she could. She took in their current situation. Ryan and Emmy were both on their knees, which were touching, on a small slightly swaying platform.

"Okay, let's finish this," she muttered. "I'm gonna —"

"Wait, I'll —"

Both Emmy and Ryan attempted to stand at the same time, legs, hips, and torsos colliding and sliding against each other. Emmy heard Ryan take a quick inhale of breath as Emmy's hand briefly grabbed on to his hip to steady herself. And she was sure she made some uncomfortable noise as Ryan's hand grazed her shoulder as he righted himself. Emmy stood up — finally — and found herself chest to chest with Ryan, eye level with the hollow of his throat. She took a few moments, fascinated by his Adam's apple bobbing as he swallowed slowly and the way she could see his pulse flutter just below it. She was overcome with the urge to lick her way up his throat, then bite at that crisp jawline that was usually tight with frustration around her.

Shit.

"Want to finish?" Ryan asked, nodding toward where Colin was still on the platform. He had taken out his phone and was texting. Emmy had a sinking feeling that he was texting June or Phoebe (or both) about this interaction.

Emmy answered Ryan's question by making her way off the platform, using every bit of strength left to reach

Colin. He was clipped to the center pole, and he pocketed his phone as she reached the platform.

"Well, that was fascinating," he said, lips pursed.

"I will push you off this platform," she muttered.

"Workplace crush?" he teased.

"More like workplace nemesis."

"Mm-hmm, sure," he said, unconvinced. "I know a thing or two about pretending to ignore someone."

Emmy looked at him with raised eyebrows. "Didn't you two get together in, like, six hours?"

"Felt like forever," he replied, his eyes going soft.

Emmy made a puking noise.

Ryan followed close behind her, and the two of them maneuvered their way to the final element, which was the zip line down to the ground. The sweet, sacred, glorious ground that Emmy might kneel down and kiss when she got there.

She had put on a good facade for most of this, buoyed by the rush of adrenaline and pride she had gotten from managing to get up to the first platform (*with Ryan's help*, AnxietyBrain reminded her). But that was fading, and she just wanted all of this to be done.

"Do you want to go first or second?" Ryan said, pointing to where a stocky guy with lots of tattoos waited, carabiners and other zip line equipment in hand.

"I…" she began. "You go first," she said. She could prove to herself that she could wait a bit longer. What had one therapist called it? Exposure therapy?

You're safe, you're safe, you're safe, she repeated in her mind.

Ryan got clipped into the zip line in a few seconds, making casual conversation with the camp staff, finding out the man was from Seattle and loved baseball. Ryan turned around and gave Emmy the widest grin she had ever seen, then winked at her. “See you on the ground, Em.” And with that, he launched himself off the platform with a yelp.

Emmy counted how long it took for Ryan’s feet to touch the ground — ten seconds — and reminded herself that people had been going down this zip line all day. It was safe.

But what if you’re the straw that breaks the zip line’s back?

It was never a good sign when her anxiety started to mix metaphors. Deciding to rip off the bandage, Emmy stepped up to the staff member and held out the loop on her harness’s waistband. “I’m ready,” she said, probably more rudely than she intended.

She half listened as he explained the instructions, scanning the length of the zip line and the small crowd waiting on the ground below.

“You’ve got this, Em!” Ryan called, clapping. He put his fingers to his mouth and whistled again, and Emmy felt her whole body flush.

“I’ve got this,” she muttered to herself, walking to the edge. “It’s ten seconds.”

She’d go on the count of three.

One.

Two.

Fuck.

Three.

Emmy left the platform and prepared herself to slam into the ground below, but the zip line worked and pulled her down, the whir of the connector sliding. This was not terrible. It was actually...fun? Exhilarating? Exciting?

Emmy's feet were on the ground before she could even remember to start her ten-second countdown. She had done it. A smile spread across her face as she unclipped her harness with shaking hands and turned around, looking for someone to celebrate with.

Ryan was the first person there, and he was smiling wide, too. Like he was happy for her, like he was proud of her, like he gave a shit about the fact that she had overcome her stupid anxiety.

"I did it!" she said, like a small child who had just learned how to ride a bike, throwing her hands in the air. "I did it!"

"Yeah, you did!" Ryan said, stepping over to her and wrapping his arms around her in a hug.

Oh.

Oh.

Ryan's body was big and hard and enveloped her. It was not a phenomenon Emmy was used to at five eleven with the ability to deadlift over three hundred pounds. His arms were strong and – oh, *fuck* – she had unconsciously wrapped her own arms around his torso, which she was also noticing was lean and chiseled underneath his T-shirt. He smelled *clean*, like the outdoors, but with a distinctive chemical undertone she had caught in the office.

As if he realized what he had done at the same time that Emmy did, Ryan released her suddenly and looked down at her, hands on hips. She returned his gaze and mimicked his gesture. And something inside her shifted, flipped, resettled.

"Truce," she said.

"Huh?"

"Truce. I'll stop looking for everything you do wrong if you will occasionally listen to me."

"I don't know if that's how a truce works," he said, taking his helmet off and mussing a hand through his hair, curls catching the glint of the sunlight.

Emmy rolled her eyes. "Okay, I'll also be open to some new ideas and not just..." She stopped, took a deep breath, then groaned. "I won't just write them off because you come from *that* museum." He smiled at her again, this time a bit softer and less giddy.

"Truce," he said, putting out his hand so she could shake it. "Now, I'm getting this harness off before it impedes my ability to have the children I do not want." With that odd comment, Ryan was off.

"Nemesis?" said a skeptical voice behind her. Emmy whirled around to find Colin there, June and Phoebe surrounding him.

"Shut up," Emmy said, unable to come up with a wittier retort.

"Really great, Em. Ten out of ten response," Phoebe said. "Come on, clean up your stuff so we can go get drinks and dinner with these two lovebirds." Emmy looked to the couple, where Colin's hand had slipped under the back of June's shirt and she was attempting – and failing – not to show how it affected her.

"Keep it in your pants, Col," Emmy said, and June turned even redder.

15

Emmy

Emmy spent the weekend as she normally would. A few beers with Phoebe and Jeremy. A hike. A lifting session. An hour or so on Sunday night where she sat down with a planner and her running to-do list and organized her week, making sure that everything that had popped up on her digital calendar was transferred to her paper calendar. Monday morning came too soon, as it usually did. And Emmy bounced around her apartment, making coffee, packing her lunch, double-checking that her gym bag was packed. Pulling out an outfit that brought to mind autumn in the Midwest — all oranges, reds, and browns — she swiped on makeup. After all that, she still ended up being ten minutes early for her bus, so she sipped her coffee in the chill of the morning while she waited.

How was she supposed to approach the workday after the — breakthrough? Is that what one would call it? — with Ryan at the camp? She had ignored the way Colin had tried to get her to open up about the events of the day by turning the conversation to June every chance she got. God bless his lovestruck heart, he took the bait every time. Which allowed her to avoid sharing too much with Phoebe or Jeremy. Jer, who had only wanted his standard one glass of wine, was lovingly coerced into a second glass by Phoebe and had slept the entire ride home, snoring so loudly it was difficult for Phoebe and Emmy to hold a conversation. Another potential pitfall avoided.

Emmy was happy to see that the office was empty when she arrived, giving her time to settle in. She slipped off her clogs and began to unpack her bag, opening her planner and logging on to her computer (god knows that would take a lot of time). She poked around in her bag, then, rolling her eyes at herself, walked over to Ryan's desk and placed a small package on top of his closed laptop.

She had just started to sort through her weekend emails when Ryan opened the door. Professional Ryan was back, all tight sweaters and form-fitting pants and distractingly cool sneakers. With that ensemble, Emmy thought he would fit in better in a tech startup down in Boulder than he would in a dusty old museum in Vanberg.

"Morning, Doc," she said, swiveling in her chair to face him.

"Happy Monday, Emmy," he replied, sitting in his seat. Emmy watched him notice the package and look skeptically at her. "Should I trust this?"

"If I was going to poison you, I'd be a lot stealthier than *that.*"

"Hey, it could have been a 'hiding in plain sight' type of situation," Ryan said, nimble fingers opening the box. He looked confused, then laughed out loud. "Post-its?"

"You're always borrowing mine," Emmy said, annoyed that she had to explain her gift. "So, in the interest of our truce, here is a gift."

"I get it, Em," he said, smiling. "Thank you. And now I feel like an ass for not getting you a gift."

"Give me the gift of listening to my ideas and accepting that my emails are cold," she said. He began to open his mouth, probably to try to dig himself out of that hole again, before she laughed. "I'm kidding, Doc. What's your schedule like today?"

"Catch up on emails, figure out what to do about an issue in the collection," he replied. "You — oh." His computer, assigned to him by the science museum, had booted up their shared email server faster than Emmy's.

"Oh?"

"There's an all-staff meeting scheduled for one." He looked at her. "Did you know about this?" Emmy scanned her planner, sure that she had checked everything off yesterday.

"No." She groaned. "Fuck."

"What's wrong?"

"The last time we had an all-staff meeting, we ended up in this Museum Brady Bunch situation, so I don't exactly have the most faith in how this is going to go."

"You're crazy," Ryan said, laughing.

And there went all the good vibes and talk of new working relationships. She could have handled a lot of comments — *you're a goofball* or *you're a fool*, something like that. But that word — *crazy* — had been lobbed at her for years. Often in fights in the heat of the moment.

By her parents when she would have panic attacks about homework assignments in high school. "Why are you so crazy? It's just school."

By her so-called friends in undergrad when she had her breakdown sophomore year and was unable to get out of bed for a week. "Why are you so crazy? Just get up and shower."

By a boyfriend when she had been shouting at him to just fucking tell her where they were going so she could plan ahead. "Why are you so crazy? Just go with the flow."

"I'm not fucking crazy," she spat at Ryan. "How dare you sit there with your attitude and judge me?"

Ryan's eyebrows stitched together. He looked so confused, Emmy almost felt bad for him. But no, everything came easily to him. No one had seen him express perfectly typical emotions and then jump to conclusions about his ability to do a job or go to school or be a friend or a lover. "I didn't — it was just a joke, Emmy."

"Real funny, Ryan, ha ha." The walls were all of a sudden close, and he was *there*, and she just needed to get out.

Remember why you started. She willed herself to recall what she said to herself on the bus this morning. That she was going to turn over a new leaf, break new ground, have a clean slate — some other corny phrase Ryan would probably use.

She slammed her eyes closed, took a deep breath. Shrugged her shoulders up, relaxed them. *Ugh, fine.*

"Okay, Ryan," she said, opening her eyes and staring him down. "In the interest of our truce, I'm going to stay and talk this through."

16

Ryan

Ryan sat in his chair watching Emmy engage in a series of stretches and breathing that seemed important. He felt unable to move, trying to rewind the footage in his brain, unsure of what had transpired over the past five minutes. One moment, they had been talking like he had always wanted. The next, she had grown heated and frustrated. Usually, he could figure out why, but he was at a loss here.

"What you said is pretty ableist," Emmy said. "Like, historically, *crazy* is a term that's been used to discount ideas. Not to mention the way that women have been put in asylums when they're unconventional. And then we'd have to get into lobotomies and Rosemary Kennedy and" — she took a breath, gathered her thoughts again — "it's just not cool."

"Huh?" Ryan didn't understand anything that had happened since he arrived at the museum this morning. Maybe he should head outside, turn around three times, spit, then come back inside. "I was just making a joke, but I didn't mean it seriously."

Emmy breathed deeply through her nose, then fixed him with her cold, steel-gray eyes. "Yeah, that's a really sensitive word for me. Also, you should probably just cut it out of your vocabulary in general."

Ryan nodded but was afraid to ask questions for fear he would say the wrong thing. Again.

She continued, "If you haven't seen it in the office, I'm sure that the ropes course made you realize that my brain doesn't work like yours. And not just because I've got a great memory and am fantastic at bar trivia." Emmy pulled her hands into fists, then stretched her fingers out wide, her nail polish purple and chipped. "I've got anxiety. Like clinically diagnosed, take medication-for-it anxiety. Technically, Generalized Anxiety Disorder with a touch of obsessive tendencies." She gave him a few seconds to piece it together, and a lightbulb went on in his head.

"Shit," he whispered.

Emmy raised her eyebrows and gave him a grim smirk. "Yeah, your casual joke is actually one of my biggest worries about meeting new people. Just because my brain works differently doesn't mean I'm unable to do my job."

"You can do your job. I didn't —"

Emmy held up her hand to stop him. "I know you didn't *mean* it, but that's how it can be *perceived*." She sniffed her now-cold cup of coffee, wrinkled her nose. "All of these things — I *know* they're not true, but what I *know* and what I *feel* can cross those wires."

"I'm sorry," Ryan said.

Emmy shrugged. "It's fine. But now you know."

“I think I’m still trying to apologize for our first meeting,” Ryan said, grimacing.

“Talking me through the ropes course made progress there.”

“So we’re good?”

Emmy gave a sharp laugh, a welcome change in her attitude. “We’re working on it. Consider yourself lucky. I’m still furious at the girl who accused me of cheating in third grade.”

“I’d never accuse you of academic misconduct!”

“You better not.” She smirked. “I’m off to visit Jeremy to talk about some designs he sent over. I’ll see you at the meeting.” With that, she was out of the office with a lingering grapefruit scent. Ryan looked at the Post-its she had given him, tossed them from one hand to the other, then turned back to his email and attempted to get work done.

Ryan was unsurprised to see Emmy already in the dining room for the meeting when he arrived, her head close to Phoebe’s, whispering and pointing to something in her notebook. Ryan took a seat on the other side of the room, next to Satya, and busied himself by flipping his stylus between his fingers.

Marshall was standing at the head of the room, but the meeting started when Carter walked in and called everyone to attention. As usual, Jeremy slid in a few minutes late, grinning an apology to the group and sitting next to Emmy and Phoebe. What he wouldn’t give to have work friends like that. To have a group of people in the city who understood what he did and the nuances of his work but would also be down for drinks or hikes or whatever those three did outside of the museum.

Ryan was half listening to Carter's presentation. It was the same dry format he always used, full of complicated graphs and charts that contained colors that were too close together and font that was too small to read. Something about the budget, something about fundraising for –

"A new building? Already?" Emmy's voice interrupted Carter's smooth presentation. Ryan's head snapped to where she was. She was half standing, and Phoebe had a hand on her arm, looking like she was trying to pull her back down. Jeremy was shaking his head.

"Yes, Ms. Bonaire. Our plan is to open a new building for the combined exhibition space, as the CST will be repurposed in the next one to two years for different departments for the university."

"But we have buildings!" she said, still incredulous. "And they're fine!"

"The board has agreed on this as a future path for the combined collections," Carter said, his tone growing a bit harder. "It is advantageous for the entire staff to get behind the fundraising efforts to show the local Vanberg community the importance of our research and collections so they can support us."

"And the exhibits," Jeremy said, clearing his throat, which surprised Ryan. Usually, the taller man – even taller than Ryan – was a quiet observer.

"And educational programs," Phoebe added, still trying to get Emmy to sit down.

"Those, too," Carter said, though Ryan knew he was patronizing them. Something hot and acidic blossomed in Ryan's stomach at the way their director so casually dismissed the programs that had brought so many eyes to the museum and – *oh, fuck.*

He had done the same thing to Emmy when they first met, assumed that the science programs and collections would – *oh.*

It took all Ryan's self-control not to drop his head into his hands and groan. He had been *such* a damn idiot.

The rest of the meeting was an overview of a planned fundraising gala the board had put together quickly and planned to put on in a few weeks' time, figuring that the sooner they could begin the fundraising campaign, the better. Plus, it was almost the holiday season, so the board thought they could use Giving Tuesday to encourage more donations. Emmy snorted and rolled her eyes. And he found that he had basically the same reaction.

Everything in his body felt mixed up: his emotions, his reactions, his thoughts. There was only one thing he could do to clear his head and regain some control when he felt this dysregulated. He was heading to the pool for at least a mile swim as soon as he could this afternoon.

17

Emmy

Emmy slung her gym bag into the locker at the on-campus gym with more force than was necessary. First she'd had to deal with everything from this damn museum merger, and now the new admin team decided that the most important thing to do was to host a fundraising gala? And at the Science Center?

Grabbing her water bottle and notebook, Emmy trudged into the weight room, praying that she wouldn't have to fight some undergrad frat boy for a squat rack. She needed to be alone right now, to not talk to anyone, to just move the weights and use that pain and pressure in her body to process her emotions. Or more accurately, not process her emotions.

There was a rack open — thank god — and Emmy got under the bar quickly, warming up and falling into the familiar pattern of a squat. She needed more plates, so after her warm-up, she walked over to the rack on the other side of the room to grab one. When she came back, a guy with obnoxious over ear headphones was under *her* bar. Doing curls. In the squat rack.

"Dude," she said, setting the plates down. "I was here."

"I'm working in," he replied, barely looking at her.

"I'm not done. And you didn't ask."

"I saw you put the bar back and figured you were done," he said, finally turning around and lifting one earpiece.

"I literally just finished my warm-up and went to get plates," Emmy said, indicating the stack of iron at his feet. "It's my workout."

"I need it more," he said.

"Why?"

"'Cause I'm a guy." And that was it. That set Emmy off.

"You all think you can just walk in and take over everything! You're an asshole, and your form is shit. You're compensating with your low back and are gonna blow a disc one day." Emmy's voice had gotten louder, and the kid, to his credit, backed off and found somewhere else to do bicep curls.

Emmy let herself be loud, be obnoxious, during her lifts, grunting like she usually hated people doing. It had felt so therapeutic to get this anger and frustration out instead of keeping it bottled up or drowning it with a gin and tonic. She couldn't be this angry around Phoebe or Jeremy, with their positivity and go-with-the-flow attitudes. She couldn't yell at Marshall for selling out the museum. She couldn't say what she thought in meetings with Ryan, couldn't process the fact that he was annoyingly helpful and understanding and wouldn't fight with her the way she needed. These emotions were getting in the way of what she needed to focus on — her museum, her research, her legacy here.

Finally done with her workout, she put her plates back and decided to treat herself to a few minutes in the sauna. She'd turn her mind off for a moment, focus on the way the heat wrapped around her muscles, and allow herself to grow loose. Calm. Blank.

Emmy had to walk through the pool to get to the sauna, where she enjoyed a refilled bottle of cold water and took her shirt off, leaving her in her sports bra and leggings as she sweated out the last bit of tension.

Emmy's mind was able to remain blank for roughly two minutes before she began to consider her job, attempting to take a bird's-eye view of the situation, which had been recommended to her by her therapist in their session last week.

The work itself was wonderful. She was making a difference, bringing a forgotten woman's legacy to light, leaving her own legacy through her research. That mattered. That was the reason she had first pursued history.

Remember why you started.

A college English professor had made her class read *My Antonia* and talked about how the most important legacy that someone could leave was their children. Emmy had decided early on in life — at maybe thirteen or fourteen, sometime after she had been confirmed and promptly left the Catholic Church — that she wasn't cut out to be a mother. She had left that class fuming, and her next class was public history.

History for average people.

History that anyone could see.

History that left a legacy.

That was the moment Emmy had decided what she was going to pursue, how she was going to bust her ass to get out of her town. Not just to get a degree, but to do something that mattered. All the late nights in the library, the early mornings opening coffee shops, the Google searches for "how to get into graduate school" and "how to write grant applications." They had all led her to her curatorial role. A place where she had found the legacy of Sara Jonesboro and was going to bring it out to the world. People deserved to know that the person everyone could have written off as a bitter old woman could be understood as the key to the town's liberal, inclusive, and scientific reputation.

Her work fucking mattered.

Her life in Vanberg mattered.

She had made a home here, carved out a life all on her own. One she loved. With people she loved.

She was a damn badass.

Feeling confident and loose, Emmy gulped the last of her water, turned off the sauna, and walked out of the tiny wooden room, enjoying the way the cool air of the pool swirled around her body, caused goose bumps to spring up on her arms, her nipples to pull to hard points under her neon green sports bra. She rolled her shoulders and stepped across the pool deck until someone got in her way.

Who the fuck…?

Then she realized the shape of those shoulders. The way that the body was broader and taller than hers. The wet curls that stuck to a forehead.

Fuck.

"Em?"

Emmy grimaced, then arranged her face in a smile. "Ryan?" *Don't look down, don't look down.* "What are you doing here?"

He smiled and shook his hair out, giving Emmy the distinct impression of a golden retriever that had just gone swimming in a pond. "I was doing laps after work. I usually end up swimming a few miles a week, but I try to fit them in before work." He shook his head again, trying to get water out of his ear, and grinned. "I slept in, and then I had a pretty rough morning." He gave her a pointed look. "And then I had this stupid meeting where this ridiculous fundraiser was brought up. So I hit up the pool to work off some steam." His eyes, with rings around them from his goggles, traveled up and down her body, and Emmy was suddenly reminded of the fact that she had taken off her shirt in the sauna. She was just in a sports bra, and it was probably an old one that had stains. His eyes found hers again, and his face flushed.

Ridiculous, indeed.

"I was lifting," she replied lamely and finally gave into temptation and let her gaze travel down his body. Ryan's shoulders were capped with defined muscles that slipped down to triceps and biceps Emmy would give her left foot to dig her teeth into. Scanning his body quickly, she took in smooth pecs with a trail of hair between them that dipped between annoyingly defined abs down farther to — Emmy forced herself to stop her perusal at the waistband of his swim shorts. She definitely noticed he had that damn vee of muscle at his hips because *of course* he fucking did.

"Oh?" Ryan said.

"Yeah. Moving weights up and down? It's a pretty simple concept." Emmy wanted to run away, back to the locker room to change and then back to her house so she could open up her bedside drawer and take care of all of this annoying sexual tension in her body and scream into a pillow.

"I know what lifting is," Ryan said.

"All right, bye," Emmy said, moving to walk around him, to put this awkward interaction behind them. That was stopped when Ryan placed a hand on her shoulder. A big hand. A big, cool hand that touched Emmy's overheated skin.

"Em?" She looked at him, ignoring the way his hand felt on her, still pissed at what he had said earlier, at all the shit that had been thrown at her today. "I'm sorry."

"What?" These were words she wasn't used to hearing. She was used to saying them herself.

"Uh, well." He fidgeted with the swim cap and goggles in his hands, switching them from one hand to the other. "I'm sorry for giving you the wrong impression about the museum merger when we first met. For assuming things. For not listening."

"Oh," she replied, taken aback. "Oh, okay. Um, thanks. I appreciate that." She looked at him, tried to see if he was genuine or just saying this to get on with things, but she took in his body language and realized that, yeah, he was sorry. “Thanks,” she repeated.

“Great. Also, if you ever wanted to catch a ride to the gym together or anything...” he offered, gently pulling her body toward his.

“I’m good,” she replied curtly. “See you at the museum,” she said, and basically ran to the locker room to take an incredibly cold shower.

18

Ryan

When Ryan came into the office the next morning, Emmy was curled up on her chair, shoes off, as usual, her long limbs contorted so she fit in her rolling chair. Her computer glasses were on, which caused his stomach to flip, and she was looking at the screen, reading a document that was written in elaborate cursive. Her lips were moving as her eyes scanned the text, and the bun on top of her head swayed from side to side as she bobbed her head to the music in her headphones.

Ryan came up behind her chair and looked over her shoulder. "What are you reading?" She jumped, startled by his words.

"Christ, do you always sneak up behind women like that?" Emmy said, tugging her headphones out of her ears and tossing them onto her desk. Ryan grinned an apology and used his chin to indicate the screen.

"What's that?"

"A new journal entry I found that mentions something I haven't seen before," Emmy said.

"About Sara?" Ryan found it endearing the way that Emmy called her research subject by her first name, like they were friends. He caught her talking to Phoebe and Jeremy about her a lot. *Sara would do this*, or *Sara would love it if we*...Like she still existed in the house or sat on the board.

"Yeah," Emmy said, smiling slightly. "One of the undergrad work-study students was scanning in a journal. This entry caught their eye, and they sent it over to me." She pointed at the screen with one chipped fingernail. "See here?"

"Yeah?"

"I've read Sara's journals so many times I could probably recite them in my sleep, but this is a journal of one of the first professors at Vanberg. It was Vanberg College then and was primarily a liberal arts school." Emmy shifted a bit, took her glasses off, and turned to face Ryan. "This line right here mentions something about a donation ceremony happening the following month, underwritten by, quote, a strange, wealthy woman." She laughed. "If that doesn't sound like my girl, then I don't know who it is." Emmy rolled her neck and squeezed her eyes shut. Then she opened them wide. "I was going to head down to the archives and check on the rest of the journal, see if I could find another entry that would explicitly name Sara." Emmy stretched out her legs and slipped them into her ankle-high boots that, of course, she had kicked off while working at her desk.

Don't think about her saying "explicitly." Don't think about her bare feet.

"Can I come with you?" Ryan asked, surprising himself with the boldness of his request. He had expected Emmy to say no immediately, to avoid spending more time with him. But she shrugged her shoulders and said, "I don't see why not." Ryan felt a surge of victory, but forced his face to remain calm, not to smile.

He followed her out of the building and across the western quad of campus, to a small, square three-story brick building. Opening one of the metal doors, Emmy turned and headed down a small hallway toward a desk, where a bored-looking undergrad was flipping through their phone.

"Sage?" Emmy said, interrupting the scroll.

"Hi, Emmy!" the student said, fumbling as they put down their phone.

"You know it's fine. No one actually comes here, anyway. You can use your phone as long as" — Emmy cocked her head — "you've finished the scans for the day?" Sage nodded, and Emmy smiled. "Sage, this is Dr. Andersson. He works with me over at the combo-museum."

"Hi, I'm Sage." An awkward shift. "Uh, they/them, if you could." Ryan nodded. He hadn't ever introduced himself with pronouns until he had begun working with more people in the humanities.

"You can call me Ryan," he said, putting out his hand. "He/him." He looked at Emmy. "Did I do that right?" he stage whispered. She gave a small eye roll and an even smaller smile.

"Yeah, Doc. You're woke now. Don't tell the oil executives."

He shoved her shoulder playfully. "I assume the rules are pretty similar down here? Keep everything where it is. Don't touch what you shouldn't?" He had meant to make a joke about collections procedures, but his eyes slipped to the skin of Emmy's bare shoulder. *Don't touch things you shouldn't.* Emmy turned to Sage, clearly giving the student the spotlight to explain things.

Sage, realizing what Emmy meant, coughed and referred to a piece of paper taped to the desk. "No pens or any other marking materials, just pencils. No tape, just Post-its. No eating or drinking or smoking or anything fun." Sage smiled at Ryan.

"Do I get to wear fancy gloves?" Ryan wiggled his fingers as he followed Sage and Emmy back toward the archives.

"Not anymore," Emmy said. "They used to recommend that – even when I was going through school – because they thought that the oils on your skin could damage papers. Which, yeah, they do. But everyone who has ever touched these documents put their fingerprints on them. But gloves dull your sense of touch." Emmy held out her own hands. This time, her nails were dark red but still a bit chipped on the thumbs. "You need to be able to feel how the papers move, how the pages turn, and it allows you to examine them more fully."

Ryan loved when Emmy slipped into talking about her work. Her eyes paled and gleamed, turned the gray of a shiny coin. And her face lit up, the corners of her mouth always smiling, even if she was making a joke or giving him shit. She was softer in those moments, her guard momentarily let down as she shared her vast amounts of knowledge.

They had entered into a small room that reminded Ryan of the study corrals he had used as an undergrad in Minnesota, hunched over textbooks, trying to memorize scientific formulas. A small box of documents had been laid out already, along with pencils and pieces of scrap paper. Emmy sat at the desk while Ryan hovered behind her, unsure of where to go.

"Don't just creep behind me," she said and nodded to the heavy wooden chair next to her. "Grab a seat." He slid in next to her and adjusted his glasses on his nose. Sage waved goodbye and told Emmy to text them if she needed anything.

"Okay," Emmy said, tying up her hair in a tighter bun. She shuffled through the old books on the table, found the one that had a large plastic divider next to it. "A-ha. This is the one Sage marked today."

"Why were they going through it?"

"We're in the process of trying to digitize most of this collection before a grant runs out," she said. She pointed toward a machine in the corner, which had the base of a copier and a large lamp or fume hood above it. "That's an archival quality scanner. Sage's job is to scan every page in, and then anyone can access the collection from anywhere."

"Sounds boring."

"It's an easy work-study job. They can listen to music or podcasts or whatever, and it gets them experience in the archives. Plus they get paid for it, which is rare. One of my first grad assistant jobs was going through a database and looking for duplicate entries. It was boring, but I got a feel for the breadth of the collection." A look of annoyance flashed over Emmy's face. "So much of our side of museums relies on unpaid labor and 'internships' that only rich people can afford to do. A big part of what I've tried to do at The House is find ways to pay people for their work. It's one of the biggest ways we can bring different types of people into museums so it's not just —"

"Straight white guys like me," Ryan laughed. "I know, I know."

"You're not so bad, I guess," Emmy said, mostly to herself, and Ryan wanted to run victory laps around the tiny collections space. She shook her head slightly, then opened the journal, finding a few pieces of torn scrap paper tucked into specific pages. "These are the entries Sage marked." Emmy flipped to one, and her eyes began to scan the page.

"You can read that?" Ryan said. He, like most of the people he worked with, wrote in some version of all capital letters or block print. He had learned cursive in Minnesota a lifetime ago but could only sign his name on official documents.

"Yeah, Ry, I can read that. Don't get Phoebe too angry, or she'll start ranting about how the fact that kids aren't taught cursive means they can't read primary source documents anymore," she laughed. Ryan did, too, only understanding about 60 percent of that joke. "Were you taught cursive?" she asked conversationally.

Ryan nodded. "We even had handwriting competitions in second grade."

"I bet you did *not* do well."

"Why would you say that?"

Emmy flicked her eyes to him, laughed again. "I've tried to read your chicken scratch, Doc. You hide it on your fancy iPad, but I think you could have had an excellent career as a medical doctor." Something hot pooled in his belly at the way she had seen small peeks of him and had saved what she learned to tease him. "Even if you did learn cursive, it was probably Palmer Cursive. This is Spencerian, which is a bit more tricky to read."

"How did you learn?" he asked, leaning over her shoulder. He watched her finger trace over the written words on the page, caught a whiff of that tangy grapefruit scent that followed her everywhere she went.

She turned her head, registered how close he had gotten, but didn't pull away. "I took a paleography class one summer at the National Archives in DC." Ryan shaped his lips around that word, pulled from what he remembered from learning about root words in high school.

"Old writing class?" He laughed. "You took a class on old writing?"

Emmy smiled. "You study old shit. You have no ground to stand on."

"What are you looking for?" He wanted to know how every gear in her brain turned, how she grappled with information and put it together to make something new. He wanted to know what sound she made when she discovered something new, how her face would change with that revelation. He wanted to know what the skin of her neck tasted like, if she was tart like that damn grapefruit scent or if she was sweet.

He wanted.

"I'm looking for mentions of Sara, then I can cross references those dates with donation records in the University Archives." Emmy's voice broke him out of his spiral of desire. "She wrote in her own journal how most of her donations were anonymous, because the college administration didn't want to be seen as relying on a woman for their new academic project."

"That's dumb. Money is money."

"You'd think," Emmy said flatly. With a small huff of laughter, she turned back to the journal and began to scan pages, much in the same way Ryan saw her doing in the office, where her nose was almost pressed to her computer screen.

Ryan leaned a bit closer, trying to hear the words she was whispering to herself. He tried to follow the words on the page, but he kept getting distracted by the fact that her neck was long and elegant and *right there.*

Emmy's body stilled momentarily, and Ryan looked closer at her face. Her bottom lip had slipped between her teeth, and her eyes moved all over the page. "Fuck yes," she whispered. Then again, "Fuck yes. Here it is."

"Show me." He followed where her finger was pointing and did his best to make out the loopy script.

This damned woman will not leave us alone with her ideas. The Widow Jonesboro does have some excellent ideas, but we cannot accept those. We can, however, accept her money.

"Asshole," he said without thinking.

"Welcome to doing history through a gendered lens." She laughed, then looked over her shoulder again, her gray eyes meeting his. He had the impulse to move his glasses up into his hair. Emmy took a long breath, and he watched as her eyes left his, slid down to his mouth, then made a quick path back up. A sharper breath this time, and now his own eyes watched hers. He saw the light indentation from where she had been biting her lip, saw the way her lips were slightly parted, shallower breaths moving through.

"Em," he whispered, leaning forward a centimeter. She matched the lean with her own, and *fuck yes*, he was going to get to kiss her, he was going to get to touch her shoulder, he was going to get to pull her body against his —

"We're closing for lunch," came Sage's voice from the hallway. Emmy's eyes widened, and she launched herself back, her chair scooting across the floor so she was suddenly an arm's length away from him instead of almost pressed against him.

"Great, Sage," Emmy said, louder than she usually talked. "I'm going to mark a few pages that I'd like scanned and sent over to me. I'll also email you some dates to check in the donation records of the university, if that's okay." Her sentences were rushed, as were her movements, as she began to shove slips of paper with pencil notations on them into the journals.

Goddamn undergrads and their need to obey rules, Ryan cursed. He moved back from the table, giving Emmy the space she needed to do work, as well as give his body time to cool down from that...

Moment?

Collaboration?

Almost kiss?

Whatever it was, he could tell it unsettled Emmy as much as it did him. She rushed out of the archive with him trailing behind her, a pencil stuck through her bun. She didn't make any comments, didn't give him shit for almost leaving his keys at the front desk with Sage. She almost stomped up the stairs and out of the building, where she whirled around and faced him.

"Doc," she said. *Okay, we're going to talk about it and set some boundaries. And I'll apologize and pretend that I don't go wild thinking about her legs and her feet when she slips off her shoes every day.*

"Yeah?"

"I think I'm on the verge of something big. I'm gonna be in the office all afternoon, and I could really use the time to focus. Could you head to your collection today?" She looked around him, he noticed – at the trees behind him, at the undergrads crossing the path behind him, at a scooter that zoomed next to her. But not at him.

On the verge of something big, indeed.

"Sure," he said, nodding. "I'll swing back to The House and grab my stuff and then get out of your hair for the afternoon."

19

Emmy

EMMY NEEDED DISTANCE. SHE needed perspective and distance from the museum. Phoebe and Jeremy were her family, yes, but they were also her coworkers, so it was time for a new approach. Hear from someone who didn't think about collections and exhibitions on the daily. It was exactly what she would have done in her historical research – get a new set of voices from a different source to add to the narrative she was crafting from the archive. Luckily, she had just the place, and it was only about a fifteen-minute bus ride outside of town.

Mountain Friend wasn't the only brewery in Vanberg, but it was the most popular, due to the variety of events the brewery hosted and, frankly, the phenomenal beer. On Wednesdays, Foster, one of two siblings who owned Mountain Friend, hosted a trivia night that Emmy had started attending in graduate school. While she wasn't a regular attendee anymore, she still dropped in from time to time. Drinking a few beers and slam dunking on grad students at trivia sounded like a great distraction.

And, if she and Foster got to talking afterward, hearing a platonic straight friend's perspective could be helpful for her to sort out her feelings about Ryan.

Hopping off the bus, Emmy slipped a sweatshirt over her head. Then, she walked the few blocks to the brewery, housed in a business park on the outskirts of Vanberg. She walked in and waved to Flo, the brewer, who helped out behind the bar on busier evenings.

"Hey, Foster," Emmy said, finding the shorter man with light brown hair behind the bar. He managed the business end of the brewery, which also involved organizing events and occasionally bartending. "Can I have a glass of Nattural Dark?" Each beer that Mountain Friend brewed had a name that was some kind of subtle homage to Vanberg's Swedish forefathers (Flo told Emmy that *natt* meant night, which made it perfect for a stout). Emmy loved the idea, though she had been nudging Flo to do a collaboration beer with the local tribe for months.

He nodded and returned quickly with a glass of the stout – one of the few beers that Emmy actually liked. She took a sip and caught Foster up quickly on the situation with the museum merger, to which he acted appropriately (appropriately being that he was upset on Emmy's behalf). Though about halfway through her explanation, she got the sense that he wasn't really listening, in the way you would if someone was telling you a story you had already heard before.

"That sucks, Em. Want to talk more after trivia? I had a lot of friends text me that they're planning on being here tonight, so I want to get set up." Emmy nodded and waved him off, and he headed toward the microphone stand. Emmy played with her phone for a bit, switching between scrolling through social media and reading some Wikipedia entries she had saved. She liked to play trivia solo, enjoyed hanging on the outskirts of the brewery and then giving a bashful wave when she placed. She had just launched the website to submit answers when she heard a familiar laugh.

No. Not here. Not *her* brewery. Not after he had invaded *her* museum and *her* mind.

She must be imagining things. Ryan was in her head enough during the day. She clearly hadn't had enough time away from the museum. That or she hadn't been drinking her beer fast enough. Emmy had unlocked her phone again and was preparing to enter her solo team name (Fresh Princess of Bonaire) when she heard that laugh again, closer this time. She looked down the bar and saw Doctor Ryan *Fucking* Andersson taking a beer from Flo. And grinning at Flo like he knew her.

And — oh *fuck*, seriously? — then Foster walked over and gave him that stupid back-slapping-hug that every straight man knew how to do. Emmy slouched, willed her bangs to grow even longer and hide her face, and buried her head in her phone.

It didn't work.

"Emmy?" She rolled her shoulders back, pulled her sweatshirt down over her knuckles, and turned around on her barstool.

"Hey, Ryan," she said, gritting her teeth. "What are you doing here?"

Ryan nodded over his shoulder to a group of people that looked vaguely familiar from whole-staff meetings and the retreat. “A gang of us play trivia most weeks. I’ve never seen you here.”

“It’s been a while since I played,” Emmy replied. *Be nice*, she reminded herself. “What’s your team name?”

“Don’t Be a Dino-Sore Loser.” He smirked, and Emmy wrinkled her nose. She hated bad puns, which made being friends with Phoebe and Colin difficult.

“That’s...something,” she said and made to turn back to her phone, but Ryan put a hand on her shoulder.

“Do you want to join our team?”

Emmy held up her phone. “I play solo.” Ryan pressed his lips together and nodded once.

“Oh well. Maybe next time,” he said. “Good luck, Em. We get pretty competitive.” *You have no idea.* The one perk of growing up where Emmy did was that she got two different broadcasts of *Jeopardy!* each night, and she would watch them both to try to remember the questions she missed the first time.

“Welcome, welcome!” came Foster’s voice over the speakers, and Emmy sipped her beer, got ready.

Ryan had no idea *she* was competitive, too.

—

Emmy had gone through another two beers by the final round, a sports round (*dammit*), which led to her tying for second place with the science museum, both of them losing to a group of mountain bikers in town for a race. Emmy tried to slip out and was putting her bag on her shoulder when Foster shouted her name from across the bar.

“Where are you going? You promised me a hangout!”

“Fine,” Emmy said, turning around and walking over to him. Most of her new coworkers had left, but Ryan was still chatting with Satya.

“Foster!” Ryan called, slightly louder than normal. “Y’know Emmy?”

“Of course,” Foster replied, slinging an arm around Emmy. “She’s been coming here for years!” Emmy gave a weak wave, smooshed into Foster’s side. He was an overly affectionate friend, which Emmy tended to hate, but Foster had the goofy younger-brother vibe that meant he could get away with anything.

“Why didn’t you tell me about her?” Ryan said, continuing to speak loudly, swaying slightly. He narrowed his eyes at Foster. “Are you keeping her a secret?”

“Ha, like anyone could keep *her* a secret,” Foster said, reaching up to pat Emmy on the head. She pushed away and rolled her eyes, looking between the two men.

“She’s so smart,” Ryan continued, unabated. Emmy looked at Satya, the collections manager, who mouthed *he’s drunk*. “She’s bold, too. Not afraid to call out bullshit. She’s cool.” He turned to Emmy, his eyes glazed. “You’re cool.”

“All right, Ryan,” Satya said, taking him by the arm. “Let’s go. I’m driving you home. Again.”

“How come all these men put their arms around her?” Ryan asked Satya as she hustled him out of the bar and into her car. Foster and Emmy watched the two leave, and then she slumped into a chair.

"*Ugh*," she groaned.

"Talk to Uncle Foster," he said, sitting down with one of his custom mugs.

"What are you drinking?" Emmy said, trying to distract him.

"One of Flo's newest experimental beers," he replied, taking a sip. "She added juniper to this sour, which you might like because of your gin obsession and – don't distract me. I know your ways."

"Dammit."

"You forget that I've known you longer than anyone else in town, even if Phoebe did sweep in to steal you as a best friend."

"Why didn't you tell me you knew Ryan?" she asked, sipping a glass of water Flo had brought her.

"I honestly didn't think it would come up," Foster replied. "He was in a different friend sphere than you, didn't think you'd ever know each other. He's a good guy, comes in a lot with his coworkers. He and I have hung out a few times, but I get the sense he's busy with work a lot." He looked at her, toyed with his short beard. "In that sense, he's a lot like you. Get him drunk enough, and he usually starts talking about science communication or how the new *Jurassic Park* movies don't include enough actual paleontology."

"That's nothing like me," Emmy scoffed.

"I've listened to you complain about every single historical film I've ever brought up," he responded.

"Not every one. I told you that *Lincoln* —"

"Yes, yes, I know. Made a vote on the constitution interesting. I've heard it." He looked into his beer, seemed to consider his next choice of words. "It's funny that I never thought of introducing you two. It makes sense, though. I can't believe I didn't see it before."

"See what?"

"You make a nice pair."

Emmy made a noise somewhere between a shout and a snort.

"Why not?"

Emmy sputtered. "Because!"

Foster hummed a knowing noise. "He's talked about you before, you know." Emmy made another noise of disbelief, but a current of electricity zinged through her.

Not wanting to sound too much like she was at a slumber party in high school, she played it casual. "Oh?"

"Nice try, Emmy. He didn't mention you by name, but he's come in and talked about this new coworker he can't get to like him." Foster drained his beer. "He does always talk about how smart you are, though. And one time, he let it drop that he found this coworker, and I quote, 'distractingly attractive and intimidating.'"

"That's on my business card," Emmy quipped, trying to not let it show how much those words warmed her insides. He got up and got them both another beer, leaving Emmy to consider all the revelations from over the past few days.

"Why don't you like him?" Foster asked, sitting back down.

"I don't *not* like him," she admitted, then proceeded to give an abridged version of their attempts at office sharing, at the ways that their collective work together had been frustrating.

Foster leaned back in his chair, kicked one leg over the other. "Em, to be honest, it seems like you're just waiting for Ryan to fuck up so you can add it to your list of grievances. Festivus isn't for a while, my dear."

"I'm not —"

He held up a hand. "Let me finish, you Amazon. You're assuming the worst. That's impacting your work and, I'll be honest, your ability to know a really great guy."

"But my anxiety—"

"Not done yet, Emmy. I know, and I know that's how your brain works. But what are the things that your anxiety has prevented you from doing?"

Emmy sat silent for a few minutes, letting Foster's words soak in. She hadn't applied to big colleges out of state because she was so worried about being rejected. She hadn't submitted her research to national journals because there was the possibility that they would hate her work. She still hadn't even applied to present at the national conference because what if she embarrassed herself in front of the entire country?

"I just wanted to beat some undergrads at trivia," Emmy mumbled into her beer.

"I think what you meant is 'Oh, Foster, thank you for the great advice. I *will* reconsider things and apologize to Ryan, and then I will introduce you to all of my single female friends.'"

Emmy laughed. "Yeah, that's it." She smirked. "Why can't I just date you?"

He shrugged. "The world is a mystery."

"Phoebe?"

"Please, you do know I work in the bar industry in this town." He laughed. "I'm pretty sure I'd be hearing about it from a certain tattooed bartender in about seven seconds."

Emmy scrunched her face. "I'll find someone for you. Just after I figure out my own shit."

Foster barked another laugh as he saw Emmy out of the brewery and walked her to the bus stop. "Em, if that's the case, I'll be a shriveled corpse before I find love." Emmy said goodbye by flashing him a middle finger as she stepped onto the bus.

20

Ryan

Ryan had awoken the day after trivia with a headache and a text from Satya that said, “Good job, doofus,” so he assumed he had one too many beers and said something stupid around Emmy. Saying dumb things around Emmy had become his default state at this point. He slogged through his morning swim, and as he approached The House, he looked up at the window where their office was and noticed that the light was already on. Preparing himself to apologize, he climbed the stairs and opened the door.

Emmy wasn’t there, but it was obvious she was already at work. Her bag was open and her notebook was on her desk, which meant she wasn’t far from the office. He’d dropped his bag next to his desk and had sat down before he noticed a cup of coffee at his desk with a piece of notebook paper folded on top with his name on it. He moved the paper to the side, took a sip of the coffee, and smiled. A vanilla latte. Turning on his computer, he opened the note:

Doc -

I've been an ass. Let's talk about exhibit stuff today.

Em

Only Emmy could write an apology that felt honest and heartfelt that didn't involve the words "I'm sorry." He folded the note back up and was tucking it into his wallet when Emmy came back in the room.

"Oh," she said. "Morning."

"Hi, Em. Thanks for the coffee."

"It's nothing," she said, though he noticed her cheeks pinked slightly. "Do you have time to chat about exhibit ideas today?"

"Why not now?" Ryan said, not needing to look at his calendar to know the morning was free.

"Great, sure, perfect," Emmy replied, walking over to her desk. She slipped off her shoes and sat cross-legged in her chair, turning to face him. There was an awkward silence between the two, and Ryan didn't know how to start this process, remembering that every other overture had been shot down.

"I'm going to set a two-minute timer," Emmy said, breaking into his thoughts. "You can talk for that entire time, and I'm not allowed to interrupt you."

Ryan laughed. She *did* know herself. "Where did you get this idea?"

"My therapist does it at the midpoint and end of every session," she said. "Apparently, I have a tendency to interrupt and jump to conclusions when people are speaking."

"You don't say." He chuckled and was rewarded with a half smile from Emmy.

"Okay, I am setting the timer." Pulling out her phone, she set her app for two minutes, showed Ryan to prove she wasn't lying, then sat back and listened.

"Uh, well." *Great start, Ryan.* "Okay, well, uh." *Even better*. If this was a swim meet, he would already have been rescued by the lifeguard. Emmy pressed her lips together, staying silent. *The one time she's quiet.* He shrugged his shoulders, took a breath. "Okay, well, something that I think is really important that, I guess, I've been batting around in my head is this idea of pulling back the curtain on science."

He waited for Emmy's comment, but she raised her eyebrows and looked at her phone. He still had one minute and forty-five seconds. *Shit.*

"Okay, well, so there's this thing called the Draw-a-Scientist test. Have you heard of it?" Emmy mimed zipping her lips shut and tossing a key over her shoulder. "Fine, I'll explain it to you. In this study, they ask kids to draw a scientist. And that's it. No other instructions. And most kids draw this cra— this wild version of Albert Einstein. A guy by himself with all this hair and test tubes and explosions. Obviously, he's wearing a white coat." He took a breath and looked at Emmy, who was smiling at him. She nodded, moved her hands in small circles to communicate for him to keep going. "Okay, and well — that's not science. No one does science by themselves. We're all linked as teams and, you know, standing on the shoulders of giants. Plus, a lot of it doesn't happen in a lab. And it's messy, you know? Like, science isn't this monolith that has all the answers.

It's constantly changing, and we're always learning new things and adjusting our hypotheses and ideas. I mean, shit, we saw that over the past few years as everyone tried to figure out COVID and —" He was interrupted by the buzzing of Emmy's phone.

Two minutes had gone by quicker than he expected once he got going. He took his glasses off, polished them on his sweater, then looked back at Emmy.

"Damn, Doc," she said, smiling.

"Is that a good *damn* or a bad *damn*?" he asked.

"Really good. Like, wow." Emmy was grinning.

"What are your thoughts?"

"First off, I knew about the Draw-a-Scientist test, but I loved hearing your interpretation." Ryan blushed at the compliment, should have figured out that she would have known. "You're also forgetting that kids always draw the scientist as a white man, too." She tapped a pencil against her lips, then sketched a few ideas in her notebook. "I love the idea of pulling back the curtain — it's the same with history. There aren't answers to everything in collections, because the people who ran museums didn't think that everything was important to collect and —" She paused and laughed at herself. "I'm getting ahead of myself."

"I think there's a lot of overlap between the two," Ryan said, thinking aloud. "I wonder how we could connect it to the research that's going on at the university now." He turned around to his computer and quickly navigated to the biology department's website.

"You know," Emmy scribbled another note in her notebook, "we've got a lot of the journals from the early professors at VU, and I think we've got their lab reports — is that the right word?" She looked at Ryan for confirmation.

"Scientific notebook is usually what we say, but it'll depend on each scientist and on how they approach their work."

"Cool. Well, we have those, and there could be something really interesting if we tied what's going on now to what happened at the beginning." She chewed her lip and flipped through her notebook. "I wrote a paper a few years ago on how Sara funded some of the early labs, so we could reuse that research." Ryan's mind caught on that word. *We*. Emmy continued unabated, her mind whirring at a million kilometers an hour. "I could head to the archives and find some of those, uh, scientific notebooks and...well, I know you have your specialty, but you know enough that you could help me translate the research, right? Connect it to any important discoveries?" She laughed. "I mean, I'll have to read them to you, because they're still in cursive. But you, like, know science better than me, right?"

You could help me. Ryan searched his brain and couldn't remember Emmy asking for help — not to reach a book on the top shelf, not to fix the air conditioner when it randomly kicked on one day in October, not for anything.

"Yeah, Em," he said and flicked his eyes back to his computer monitor so he didn't stare at her. *This* was the woman he had seen in those videos. She was positively magnetic when she was like this.

"And this is interdisciplinary." Emmy was still talking. "This could make a big splash. I mean, I know we're in the *Brady Bunch* of museums still, but isn't this the purpose of the new mission?"

"Now you're not so skeptical?"

"Hush, Doc. I'm still skeptical and don't trust Carter as far as I can throw him – which would be far – but..." She paused a moment. He watched her close her eyes and take a deep breath. *It's weird to stare at her chest while she's breathing.* She opened her eyes, and they were sparkling, like a polished sword. Her voice was a whisper, her cheeks flushed. "This could be really important. This could make a name for the museum. On a national scale."

"Want to go to the archives today?" Ryan pushed down the thought of what had almost happened the last time he was in that tiny room with her.

"I thought you'd never ask," she joked, tossing her hair. *You have no idea.* "However," she held up her paper planner, "we have a massive meeting this afternoon to plan for the gala." Ryan groaned and slid off his chair, sprawled on the floor. "Quit your dramatics, Doc," she said, laughing, nudging him with her bare foot, which did things to Ryan's insides that he was not proud of.

21

Emmy

When the gala rolled around in early December, Emmy had taken a half day of work, giving her a chance to get a workout in to calm her nerves before she was planning to meet Phoebe to get ready. It was being held at the old science museum because it still had old exhibits in place, so Emmy had spent her morning dragging over small pop-up exhibitions so there was some representation from history. Phoebe had unpacked all the education loan kits so there would be more artifacts and hands-on opportunities for donors to see that their collections mattered, too.

Emmy had refused to step foot in the CST since the merger, but she and Phoebe had figured it was easier to get ready there than try to walk across campus in heels. It also made things easier, considering the fact that free alcohol was a perk of working these events. For Emmy, it helped curb her natural tendency to make smart-ass comments to potential donors and it gave Phoebe the courage to talk to strangers when she would usually avoid that.

Emmy pushed open the heavy wrought-iron doors, which squeaked when she walked through them, then made her way up the old stone stairs to the bathrooms. She had been here a few times, had begrudgingly loved the central staircase and how it opened up into ornate doors, with the exhibit hall behind the staircase.

"Phoebes?" Emmy said, walking into the bathroom.

"Here!" she called from one of the stalls.

"Which dress did you decide to go with?"

"Neither. I went back and found a jumpsuit that walks the line between professional and sexy to get donors to throw money at our education programs," Phoebe responded. Emmy laughed as she unpacked her bag and plugged in her curling iron, audibly groaning. Her hair was straight and struggled to hold most hairstyles, which was why she defaulted to down or up in a bun.

"Phoebes?"

"Yes, I can curl your hair."

"Love you," Emmy said, thankful for a best friend who could read her mind.

"What do you think Ryan is going to wear tonight?" Emmy was suddenly no longer as grateful for Phoebe's powers of observations. When she had gone shopping with June and Phoebe, she had, through her hangover, thought about how Ryan would look at her in this dress, donors be damned.

"Probably a suit," Emmy said, trying to keep her voice calm. She hastily applied makeup, adding a bit more eyeshadow and eyeliner than she would normally, dusting a bit of highlighter on her cheeks. She slipped into the stall and slid the dress on. It was a deep blue 1950s-style vintage dress that highlighted her collarbones, shoulders, and hips — her favorite parts of her body. Emmy put her feet into her patent-leather pumps, completing the outfit, then walked out.

"Oh shit," Phoebe said, wolf whistling. "Turn around, turn around." Phoebe motioned her finger in a circle, and Emmy gave in to her sillier instincts and did a small twirl. "Are you *totally* sure you're straight?" Phoebe asked. "I mean, if you're ever inclined to explore any bisexual tendencies..."

"Yes, you goon," Emmy said, laughing.

"Damn shame," Phoebe said, picking up the curling iron. "Grab that chair over there and sit down so I can do your hair. You're too tall."

"You're too short," she replied but complied so Phoebe could get to work on Emmy's hair. The two made small talk about the event — what terrible snacks they anticipated, how long it would be until Jeremy broke his one-glass-of-wine rule, which board member would say something inappropriate first.

"Remember that one board meeting on Zoom where the secretary fell asleep?" Phoebe laughed.

"They're all idiots with too much money and no clue how a museum actually works," Emmy said. She looked at herself in the mirror, studied the soft curls Phoebe was arranging around her shoulders. "Should I wear lipstick?"

"Men love staring at a woman's lips," she replied, like it was a biblical truth that everyone should now.

“Fine.” Emmy applied a deep plum color that contrasted with her light skin and dark hair. “Am I giving off vintage witchy vibes tonight?” Phoebe nodded. “Good. Do you want to get drinks after?”

“I told Dec we were planning on being there,” Phoebe said, fixing her own hair quickly. “Plus, June and Colin are down, so we can invite them, too.”

“Do you ever look at them and get jealous?” Emmy asked, cocking her head, continuing to look at her own reflection in the mirror. “Like, it’s so clear that they’ve each found their person, and it was so easy for them.”

Phoebe snorted. “It’s not always easy, and it wasn’t for them. Colin didn’t have the backbone to ask June to stay, and June ran back to Vanberg. Plus, they’re still figuring out how to live together.”

“That’s not exactly answering my question.”

“Of course I’m jealous.” Phoebe sighed, her voice a bit quieter. “But I’m so happy for them. Colin’s my favorite person in the world, and June makes him happy and challenges him. That’s all any of us could ask for in a partner, I think.”

Challenges him. An image from last week appeared in Emmy’s mind. Ryan, his glasses slipping down his nose, looking closely at a scientific journal in the archives, almost touching the paper, doing his damndest to try to read the document. He had resorted to making up words, reading them with a stoic sincerity that had Emmy laughing so hard her stomach hurt, until they were shushed by another researcher in a different study corral. A few times, Emmy had even brought up the idea of submitting their work to the MAA Conference. If she was being honest, she never *directly* suggested it, but she talked about it in vague terms. Still, it was a step.

They had slipped into a tentative working relationship over the past month, only interrupted when Ryan left for a four-day trip to Minnesota. He claimed that his mother would have his head if he didn't fly home for Thanksgiving but had spent the week before raving about all the dishes that each sibling was responsible for making. He was in charge of the cheesy potatoes.

Emmy spent Thanksgiving Eve at Jeremy's house, an annual tradition for the two of them, then went over to Phoebe and Colin's mother's house to watch the parades the next morning. June had provided commentary on the different float designs, while Emmy had corrected misconceptions about Thanksgiving the announcers spewed. Jeremy baked pies with Colin while sneaking mimosas, and the five had napped the afternoon away in their basement.

With the fall break over, the museum had shifted from any work on research or exhibit design to an all-hands-on-deck approach to the gala planning. It mostly consisted of doing personal outreach to various businesses and wealthy families of Vanberg, and Emmy had let Ryan take the lead on most of the schmoozing via Zoom or phone call. Tonight, however, she had to do it herself. Had to talk to these donors *and* ignore Ryan at the same time. Multitasking was never her strong suit.

"Ready, Em?" Phoebe asked, tidying up both hers and Emmy's belongings and shoving them into their bags.

Emmy swore in response, which Phoebe took as an affirmative.

22

Ryan

"I feel like a penguin," Ryan said to his reflection in the men's bathroom at the CST.

"At least you'll fit in a natural history museum," came a wry voice from the hallway. Ryan's eyes widened in surprise as he took in Jeremy, who looked like he was born to wear his dark purple suit, complete with matching velvet dress shoes. "I'm Jeremy? We work together?"

"I know who you are," Ryan replied, rolling his eyes. He fixed his tie one more time, then adjusted one more curl on his head. Why was he so nervous? He worked with Emmy every single day of the week, much to her chagrin. So what had changed?

There had been a noticeable thaw in their relationship since the day the gala was announced, since Ryan had touched her warm skin with his cool hand and apologized on the pool deck. That, coupled with her apology and their tentative steps toward an exhibition, had Ryan getting his hopes up that one day, he could gather up the courage to let Emmy know that he was interested in her as more than coworkers. Hell, this week, they had even begun to work on a few grant applications for a combined database for all the collections. If she trusted him with a grant proposal, what would be next?

"Stop fussing," Jeremy said, gently swatting at Ryan's hands. "You look great." Ryan forced a laugh and tried to stop his face from blushing as his thoughts once again went to what Emmy would be wearing tonight, how gorgeous she would be, how he could maybe press his damn luck with her one more time.

"She's going to notice," Jeremy said again, quieter this time. Ryan looked at him, pretended he didn't know who the "she" in question was. "She's a tough nut to crack, but it's worth it when she lets you in. She would die for her friends. Though I spent a solid six months working with her thinking she hated me. Turns out we had a lot to bond over."

"Thanks," Ryan said without adding any more explanation.

"And stop fucking with your hair," Jeremy added before walking out. Ryan reached up to fix a curl again before stopping himself. He took in his reflection in the full-length mirror and realized it was as good as it was going to get. He wished he had a chance to have a shot of bourbon before the gala, mentally kicking himself for not slipping his flask into his jacket pocket. He was cataloging the options in the bar downstairs when he walked out of the bathroom and saw Emmy standing at the top of the stairs. His jaw dropped.

She was looking down, seeming to be deciding whether she could head into the gala yet, and she hadn't noticed him. Her hair was soft and flowing in a way that he had never seen before, falling gently over one shoulder. Those shoulders were bare, and Ryan could see the curve of muscle that he had been fantasizing about for weeks. The neckline of the dress plunged and showed off Emmy's breasts in a way he had only imagined, and the dark blue fabric hugged her trim waist before flowing out over the curve of her ass. Looking lower, Ryan swallowed, his mouth gone dry. She was wearing these shiny black heels that made her calf muscles pop and broke his brain. Though she could have walked out in a sweatshirt and boxers, and he would have found her attractive.

He'd keep the heels, though.

"Emmy." He nearly breathed out her name. She turned, her hair shifting, and Ryan caught a tiny drift of her tangy scent mingling with the stale air of the museum. She caught his eye and gave that trademark half grin.

"Hey, Doc." She gave an exaggerated look up and down his body, and Ryan had to suppress an audible groan at her perusal. "You clean up nicely."

You're fucking drop-dead gorgeous.

"Not so bad yourself, Ms. Bonaire." Emmy gave him a warm smile — a genuine smile. He had started to learn the difference between her wry smiles and her warm smiles. And what was more disconcerting was how he craved them.

“I don’t want to go down there yet,” she admitted. “I hate schmoozing. I’m too blunt, too honest, and people don’t like that.”

“Your honesty is endearing,” Ryan said, stepping closer to her. “And, hey, I like you.”

“You like everyone.”

“Not true.”

Emmy snorted. “Who don’t you like?”

Ryan screwed up his face and thought hard for a second. “Uh…my high school swim coach. My sisters’ exes. My homophobic uncle.” Emmy rolled her eyes. And then Ryan was too honest. “I like you, Emmy. For real.”

“For real?” She sounded skeptical.

“For real, for real.” He held out his arm, bent it at the elbow. “Ms. Emmeline Bonaire, curator extraordinaire, would you like to accompany me down to the gala?” Emmy gave another genuine grin and slipped her arm through his.

“Why the hell not, Dr. Ryan Andersson, studier of dino poop?” And with that, they walked down the stairs to face the horde of donors.

23

Emmy

The first place Emmy went after breaking away from Ryan's arm was the table with the wine. The second place she went was to find Phoebe.

"Phoebes," she hissed, sipping her horrible wine and pulling a face.

"What?"

"First off, we are in worse financial shape than I thought with this wine. Good god, I've slapped bags with better wine," Emmy said, draining her glass.

"Yeah, but have you seen Ryan tonight?" Phoebe asked, following Emmy's gaze to where it had landed on Ryan, who had found a bottle of beer and was taking a sip.

"What am I supposed to do?" Emmy whined. Phoebe rolled her eyes.

"Be a human. Do your job. Go talk to some boring old donor about Sara. That will get your mind off Ryan." Phoebe sipped her own wine, then made a similar face. "God, I need a better drink." Emmy huffed and walked away to find one of the board members of the old history museum. She needed a few more letters of support for a grant and had been meaning to ask her. However, on the way to talk to the older woman, she got distracted by trying to eavesdrop on Ryan's conversation with an especially prickly donor that Emmy always tried to avoid.

"It's actually been enlightening," he was saying, his fingers tapping on the neck of his beer bottle. "It has definitely been an adjustment for all of us, but I think we have a lot to learn from other disciplines, and this new museum truly has the potential to create some revolutionary new research, in addition to pioneering innovative exhibitions." Emmy's eyes grew big, and she inadvertently squeaked her reaction, which Ryan noticed. His eyes caught hers and, god*damn* him, he gave her the smallest wink, which caused her stomach to do an uncomfortable flip.

She'd blame this boxed wine. Which she needed more of. Ryan's conversation had slid to educating the donor about the "dimorphism of triceratopses" — whatever the hell that meant — and Emmy turned on her heel to head back to the bar, where Phoebe and Jeremy were watching her with matching smirks on their faces.

"What?" she said, picking up another plastic glass and resisting the urge to down the entire thing in one gulp.

"You know what," Jeremy said, his wine glass close to his lips.

"I plead the fifth," Emmy responded.

"I mean, we all know you have an intelligence kink," Jeremy continued. "Remember when you stopped flirting with that visiting researcher because he admitted that he didn't know how to use interlibrary loan?"

"And remember how you only dated that climber because you watched him climb one day and he knew about the geology of the area?" Phoebe added.

"And not only is that man gorgeous," Jeremy kept on, nodding toward Ryan, "but he's a damn expert in his field, and — oh how sweet! — he's talking through that exhibition with Mrs. Winston." Jeremy nodded over toward the small display of dinosaur specimens anchored by a large triceratops skull.

Ryan once again caught Emmy's eye — she should really be more inconspicuous — and he waved her over with his beer bottle.

"Go," Phoebe muttered, and Jeremy gave her a gentle shove on the small of her back. Emmy walked over, regretting that she'd worn these heels that made her over six feet tall, feeling like she was the most obvious and awkward human in the room. A neon sign hanging over her head that said *She Has a Crush*!

"Ms. Bonaire!" Mrs. Winston said, grabbing Emmy's arm with her tiny, surprisingly strong hands. Mrs. Winston had been a member of the advisory board of the museum since Emmy had been in graduate school and had never missed an event. She was never high on the list of donors that Marshall wanted to reach out to, but Emmy had always appreciated the way the woman pretended to be interested in whatever obscure topic a visiting professor was giving a speech on, always telling Emmy her exhibitions were amazing. "This young man," she used her other arm to grab on to Ryan's bicep and — oh great, now Emmy was jealous of an octogenarian —

continued on, "this young man was just telling me about what you've been working on. You know, back when I taught the fourth-grade history class, we would always take a field trip to her house so we could see what a woman of her time lived like." Emmy had heard this story a million times but still smiled and nodded.

"Actually, Mrs. Winston," Ryan interjected, taking his glasses off and cleaning them, then sliding them back on his face, the way she imagined he did with his undergraduate students. "Sara Jonesboro wasn't just a woman of her time. I believe she was, what did you call her, Emmy? Yes, a 'thought leader among the progressive Vanberg community of the time.'"

"Fascinating!" the older woman said while fireworks went off in Emmy's stomach and her face heated. Since when had Ryan been paying attention to presentations about her research in meetings? She racked her brain to think of what she knew about Ryan's research and came up with the unfortunate phrase of "dinosaur shit." She needed to do a better job of listening.

Mrs. Winston had seemingly forgotten about Emmy and had turned her body to fully face Ryan. "And what do you study, Doctor?"

"I study biopaleontology and provide insights into the flora of prehistoric ecosystems," he said succinctly.

Dinosaur shit, Emmy mouthed behind Mrs. Winston's head. Ryan rolled his eyes at her, and Mrs. Winston kept moving closer to him.

"Actually, Mrs. Winston," Emmy said, steering the woman away before she could mount Ryan. "There are some fascinating causes we could use your support for, including the summer programming Ms. Whitford is putting together." Phoebe was waiting by the raffle table and took over the conversation, giving Emmy a knowing smile. Emmy swung by the bar table and picked up another glass of wine for herself, then grabbed a bottle of beer for Ryan. *Peace offering.*

"Thanks for that," Ryan said. "It's been a while since I've had to fend off the advances of a retired schoolteacher."

"She can be a bit aggressive." Emmy handed Ryan his drink and clinked her plastic glass against the bottle. They stood side by side and looked out over the crowd. The event was, Emmy begrudgingly had to admit, a success.

"That's Phoebe's brother, right? With the sandals?" Ryan asked. Emmy could feel his arm just a centimeter away from hers.

"Yeah, he's a dork, but he donated something to be raffled off. And it makes Phoebe happy to see him down here." She sipped her wine, internally warring with herself. "Also, uh," Emmy didn't know how to begin this conversation, "thanks." Ryan looked at her, raised his eyebrows. "I appreciate what you said to Mrs. Winston. About my research. It's really kind of you to pretend to take an interest."

"Your work is interesting." He shrugged, then took a sip of his beer. "You're interesting."

24

Ryan

THE REST OF THE evening flew by in a whirlwind of conversations with donors, and even Ryan, who loved small talk and had been raised on goodbyes that took forty-five minutes, was sick of talking about the museum. He wanted to go home, take his dress shoes off, pour a bourbon, and space out to old concert videos of his favorite bands. Ryan was winding a scarf around his neck — it had begun to snow while the gala was going on — and was heading out to the parking lot when he felt a tap on his arm.

He turned around to see Emmy, Phoebe, and Jeremy, their arms slung around each other. Jeremy's eyes were glazed and Phoebe was smiling too much, but Emmy seemed to be relatively sober, though there was a certain spark behind her eyes that intrigued him more than he wanted to let on.

"*Ryan*," Phoebe grinned, "we're heading for a drink. Well, me 'n' Emmy are. Jeremy gets water and a plate of garlic knots because he broke his rule."

"Rule?" Ryan asked, smiling, looking to Emmy for confirmation.

"One glass," Jeremy slurred.

"Jeremy, for being even taller than you, has the alcohol tolerance of a fifteen-year-old," Emmy explained, biting the side of her mouth to hold in a laugh. "We'll prop him up in a booth and feed him carbs and water until he can realistically not ralph in an Uber."

The three friends made an unsteady path toward the door, and then Emmy turned, looked over her shoulder and asked him, "You comin', Doc?" And suddenly, all of those plans about his couch fell by the wayside as he followed the group out into the parking lot, then across the street.

"So, uh," Ryan said, throwing his jacket on, "where are we going?"

"Next Door!" Phoebe cheered. "Best bar in Vanberg." She stopped in her tracks and whirled around, grabbed Ryan by his coat collar, and pulled his face down to hers. "Listen," she said, deadly serious, "if you tell an undergrad about this bar, I will personally ensure that you are never allowed to step foot in it ever again."

Ryan looked at Emmy again, only slightly terrified. "She's right, you know." Her face was stern, a serious version of Emmy.

"She knows the owner," Jeremy added, stumbling. "He'd do anything for Phoebes."

Ryan held his hands up in surrender. "Fine, fine, I promise. Scout's honor."

"You would have been a boy scout," Emmy said, shivering slightly. Without thinking, Ryan took his scarf off his neck and wrapped it around her arms. "Th-thanks. I left my jacket at The House. Forgot about drinks."

"Don't worry about it." The foursome walked through the light dusting of snow on the sidewalk, then turned into an alleyway, where Phoebe opened a door that had no sign, no indication that it was a bar. Ryan walked in and was surprised to find a gorgeous, old-fashioned bar full of people in their late twenties and thirties.

"This is heaven," Emmy said, throwing her arm out and showing off the bar. Jeremy fell into a booth, and Phoebe walked over to the bartender to get a glass of water for him.

"What do you drink?" Emmy asked him, following Phoebe to the bar.

"Bourbon," Ryan said, grimacing. "Or beer. I know it's what every white guy in his thirties drinks, but I like what I like."

"Boy scout, Minnesota, bourbon. Such an all-American boy," she teased, and Ryan felt back on steady ground with her making fun of him.

Ryan decided he could give it right back tonight. "And your drink? Something prickly, I bet. Something that's an acquired taste." He made a dramatic show of thinking, tapping his finger to his chin. "Tequila?"

"She's a gin and tonic drinker," said the bartender, who placed a clear drink with a lime in it in front of Emmy.

"Declan, you remembered?" Emmy sounded surprised. The bartender, who still hadn't smiled at the two of them, nodded toward Phoebe.

"She ordered for you." The tattooed man turned blue eyes on Ryan. "And you?"

"Bourbon. Maker's. Neat?" Ryan ordered. Declan grunted his reply, quickly poured from a wax-topped bottle. With that brief conversation, he tucked a towel into his back pocket and went back to Phoebe, who grabbed his arm and pointed to specific tattoos, asking him about the stories behind the art.

"She'll be there all night," Emmy explained. "She and Dec have a...thing." Emmy glanced back at Jeremy, who was gulping down water and shoving pretzels into his face. "He'll eat those and then sleep for a bit in the booth. Dec kind of lets any of Phoebe's friends do whatever they want here." She laughed. "Though that bit him in the ass the night I tried to outdrink him."

"What happened?"

"Turns out you shouldn't go against a bartender whose mom is from Ireland and whose dad is from Chicago." Emmy giggled. "I fell asleep on the bar, and Dec just left me there. I woke up at three a.m. to a note on my head that said *better luck next time*. Jokes on him, though, because I puked all over the bathroom after that."

"Em, look at this one!" Phoebe was still holding on to the bartender's arm. "He says it's based on an old forgotten animator." Emmy laughed and walked over to indulge Phoebe. After a few minutes, she took a plate of garlic knots over to Jeremy, who accepted it gratefully, then returned to sleeping. She was still chuckling when she came back to her chair.

"You three are so close," Ryan said.

Emmy nodded and smiled. "It's not an easy city to meet people in, but once you have people in your corner, it becomes home. And then you meet their people, and all of a sudden you have a family here." Ryan wondered if he was slowly inching his way into that family. Maybe as a distant second cousin or something.

"What made you study history?" he asked, running his finger round the lip of the bourbon glass. Emmy laughed to herself, then took a long sip of her drink. "What's so funny?"

"You're not going to believe this," she said.

"Try me."

"I started college as a chemistry major. Wanted to do research in a lab or be a doctor or something that mattered. I loved science in high school, loved picking apart the world and seeing how it worked. I thought it would be the same in college." She took another sip, then continued on. "It was fine freshman year, and then sophomore year rolled around and, with it, organic chemistry."

"Fuck o-chem," Ryan said. Emmy clinked her glass against his.

"You can say that again. Anyway, it all of a sudden became about memorization and curved exams and — fuck — I was in the professor's office every. Single. Week. I went to extra study sessions. I tried so hard. Was in the library until two a.m. at times studying. But those structures didn't make sense in my head." She took another sip and paused, gathering up her thoughts. Ryan gave her time and space, felt like she was on the verge of saying something important. "The turning point was a day after a midterm. I went to office hours for my professor. He was a younger professor, a real hotshot in the department. And I remember asking him what I could do, almost crying. And he looked at me and said 'well, that's just what science is. It's hard and it's not for everybody.' And," Emmy sniffed, "he told me that you couldn't be emotional as a scientist, that you had to just push through and do it."

"What did you say?"

"Nothing. I was flabbergasted. I walked out of the office, into my apartment, got under blankets, and didn't get out of bed for a week. Barely ate. My brain just kind of shut off. Everything I had been working toward, thought I was interested in, was just shit on by one cocky scientist."

"Asshole," Ryan spat.

"Yeah. Looking back now – with the help of time, distance, therapy, and medication – I realize that he was a symptom of that bullshit masculine culture of science. But it definitely still bothers me at times." She finished her drink, her eyes finding Ryan's. "That's probably a big reason I was such a jerk to you when we met."

"If it makes you feel any better, I failed o-chem, too."

She gasped. "There's something about you that isn't perfect?"

"You think I'm perfect?" he flirted, and Emmy's face turned red.

"So what about you, Doc?" she said, rattling her ice in her glass. "What made you study dinosaurs?" Ryan told his standard story about *Jurassic Park* and old VHS tapes about prehistoric animals, but then decided to share more.

"I didn't think I *could* do this," he said, looking at his drink and not at Emmy. "We didn't grow up well off and, well, I was the third to go to college. I went on a swimming scholarship. I wanted to do something that would make money, so I started off as an engineering student, tried to minor in business." He sighed. "Mom and Dad came during parents' weekend and were furious when I had switched from geology. My mom might be shorter than Phoebe, but she is a force of nature when she wants to be."

Emmy chuckled into her drink. "She sounds like someone who loves aggressively."

"Yeah, she's the best." Ryan smiled. "There's something about my life that keeps me surrounded by these powerful women who bend the world to their will." He looked up at Emmy, watched her pulse flutter in her throat. "I'm not mad about it."

Emmy swallowed hard and opened her mouth to say something to Ryan but was interrupted by Declan walking over to ask if they wanted another drink. Emmy nodded her head vigorously, and Ryan made the decision to leave his car on campus for the evening.

25

Emmy

"How long until your ride's here?" Ryan asked Emmy as she walked out of the bar after him, swaying slightly. Maybe she should have eaten another slice of pizza or a few garlic knots to soak up the gala wine and gin. Things had felt easy with Ryan tonight, the way they maneuvered through the gala together, but also how they shared stories about their college years. Emmy usually waited much longer before sharing some of her background. *God damn Dec and his heavy hand.*

Emmy flicked her eyes down to her phone and checked her rideshare app. "Five minutes or so, but who knows with the weather." A few inches of snow had settled on everything while they were in the bar, and Emmy knew that it could make the main streets in Vanberg slicker than expected. She leaned against the brick wall behind her, feeling the ridges and pokes of the brick on her back. Ryan turned and faced her, chewing on his lip as he studied her. She was still wearing his scarf. Ryan's hair was mussed, his peacoat shrugged over his shoulders in a way that was a bit messy. He was not the put-together Ryan she was used to seeing in the office, and certainly not the debonair, charming curator she had seen on display at the gala this evening. Emmy took a deep breath and let it out slowly, feeling the cool air rush out of her lungs. She blinked her eyes open and took in Ryan, who was closer than expected.

"I had fun tonight," she admitted, her eyes scanning his face, jumping between the green of his eyes and his lower lip caught between his teeth. "Turns out, I actually like spending time with you." She laughed, a bit buzzed and uncomfortable with her admission. He continued to chew on his lip, his teeth gently rocking back and forth.

I'd like my lip to be caught between his teeth. The thought drifted lazily through Emmy's head, but she didn't feel the panic and fear that usually accompanied her acknowledgment of her attraction to Ryan. Not after tonight. It felt like a seismic shift had occurred. A current zinged between them right now, crackling in the cold evening air.

Ryan didn't say anything but inched closer to Emmy, continuing to worry his lip between his teeth. The tip of his tongue slipped between his lips and slicked over the slight teeth marks, causing Emmy's insides to clench.

"I like spending time with you, too," Ryan finally said, and Emmy's heart leapt. "Actually," he brushed a hand through his hair and took his glasses off, cleaning the lenses and shoving them into his jacket pocket, "actually, you frustrate the living hell out of me sometimes, which is annoying, because I do genuinely like being around you." He grumbled. "Sometimes I like it too much."

"What the hell?" Emmy said, both frustrated and intrigued. She turned to walk away, not wanting to get into an argument when the rest of the night had gone so damn well, but Ryan caught her by the shoulder and held her there, squeezing a bit.

"Em," he said, his voice softer. "It's nice to be challenged. You've made me a better curator. I'm used to only thinking about the collection, research, and revenue, but you've made me think about the visitor. About the whole experience. And that's really cool."

Emmy knew she loved what she did. She loved museums — always had, even art museums. She loved creating exhibitions. But she didn't know it was possible for her panties to get slick hearing someone talk about exhibition theory.

It was great to learn something new every day.

Emmy let out an uncomfortable giggle and met Ryan's eyes, then suddenly silenced herself. The air grew heavy and warm between them, even as snow continued to gently fall.

Ryan's eyes made that telltale flicker down to her mouth, and Emmy wasn't sure who eventually ended up making the first move, but it happened. Just a brush of lips at first, Emmy's eyes fluttering closed as Ryan steadied himself with a hand on her hip. He pulled back, and when she opened her eyes, she was greeted with his green ones boring into her.

"Okay?" she asked.

"Fuck yes," he replied, capturing her lips again. His mouth opened and moved over hers, and Emmy gasped and opened her own, the kiss turning wet and hot within seconds. Ryan and Emmy kissed like they worked — somehow aggressive and tentative, their tongues battling and retreating as they figured out how they functioned, what the other liked. Ryan angled his head slightly, deepening the kiss, and Emmy's hands slipped up into his hair, finally getting the chance to play with his curls like she had fantasized about a million times. His hair was rough, and Emmy scraped her fingers through it. Ryan's hands settled down on her hipbones, pressing and gripping through the fabric of her dress.

"Move this," he gritted out, unfurling his scarf that had been wrapped around Emmy's neck so he could swing her hair over her shoulder to reveal more of her skin to him.

If she wasn't careful, she'd reveal all of her skin to him outside of a bar on a snowy night.

Ryan's tongue swirled patterns along Emmy's neck, and she let her head fall back against the brick. The cool wall contrasted with the warmth of Ryan's hands on her hips and his mouth on her neck. Emmy gasped as Ryan pulled back and blew a cool stream of air over the wet spots on her neck, causing goose bumps to rise along her arms that had nothing to do with the cold. Her nipples hardened, her thighs clenched, and Ryan gently laughed to himself as he took note of the effect it had on her body.

"You're horrible." She laughed against his mouth.

"The worst," he replied, his lips finding hers again. Emmy's hands had just begun their own exploration under Ryan's coat, and she had just begun to consider lifting his dress shirt up from his waistband, when they were interrupted by a pair of headlights and a honk.

"Uber for Emmy?" the driver called, rolling down the window. Ryan waved the driver over, then turned back to Emmy.

"I'll see you tomorrow. Text me when you get home," he said, running his hand along her hair, cupping her jaw briefly.

"Yours isn't here yet," she stammered, not quite ready to leave this evening.

"I can wait here," he replied with a smirk, leaning down once more and giving Emmy a gentle kiss but slyly running his tongue over her bottom lip. "I'm a big boy." Emmy had felt evidence to support that statement during their make-out session, but she doubted he meant *that*.

"Okay," she said, taking a deep breath. "I'll — I'll see you. Tomorrow. At work. At the museum." Sentences had become difficult to form, and it wasn't because of the gin. He winked at her as she slid into the back seat of the car, immediately pulling out her phone to text Phoebe.

Emmy: SO

Emmy: UHM

Phoebe: Yes?

Emmy: RYAN AND I

Emmy: JUST MADE OUT

Phoebe: Fuck, finally.

Emmy: WHAT DO I DO?

Phoebe: Was it good?

Emmy: OMGGGG

Emmy: YES

Emmy: FUCK

Emmy: WORK

Phoebe: Do you want to do it again?

Emmy: I MEAN

Emmy: YES

Emmy: HAVE YOU SEEN HIM?

Phoebe: Not my type, but yes, I can see his aesthetic appeal.

Emmy briefly considered sending a voice memo that rambled about how Ryan wasn't Phoebe's type because he wasn't tattooed and didn't make her favorite drink, but even she knew that would be pushing it.

Phoebe: Also, please take off your caps lock and stop yelling at me.

Emmy: Sorry.

Emmy: Just feeling a lot of things.

Emmy: Freaking out.

Phoebe: Not surprising. Okay, so do you want to know what to tell him?

Emmy: TELL ME

Emmy: O WISE ONE

Phoebe: You're an ass.

Emmy: I'm just a bit drunk.

Emmy: Also horny.

Phoebe: This is standard procedure for you.

Emmy: Fuck you.

Emmy: I love you.

Emmy: Help me.

Emmy: We have a meeting in two days.

Emmy: About the exhibition.

Emmy: With the directors.

Emmy: PHOEBES

Emmy: We talked about exhibits.

Emmy: And it was so sexy.

Phoebe: Ha ha, all right. So here's the plan…

Phoebe: Text him right now and make plans for coffee before you're in the office.

Emmy: So smart.

Emmy: You're brilliant.

Emmy: And beautiful.

Phoebe: Text Ryan now, and then drink a glass of electrolytes when you get home.

Phoebe: Take an Advil, fill up your water bottle.

Emmy: See?

Emmy: This is why Dec is in love with you.

Phoebe: Good night, you loon.

Emmy: I'M TELLING YOU.

Phoebe: Stop yelling your conspiracy theories and text Ryan.

Emmy thought about sending another voice memo and then stopped. She took a moment and breathed, let her forehead rest against the coldness of the window, watched the streetlights pass under the snow.

One more breath. In for four, out for six.

And just one more, for good measure.

She opened her phone.

Emmy: Hi.

Fucking brilliant, she thought to herself. *The man has a PhD, and the best you can muster is "hi."* She took another breath and continued to type.

26

Ryan

Ryan had just unlocked his front door and was walking in, tossing his coat sloppily over the banister that began right in his entryway, when the phone in his pocket buzzed. He fumbled it out as he slipped off his boots, tramping to the kitchen in search of a bag of chips to take the edge off his inevitable hangover tomorrow morning. Figuring it was Uber confirming that he was dropped off, he felt heat build in his stomach when he saw Emmy's name pop up.

Emmy: Hi.
Emmy: So.
Emmy: That happened.

Ryan laughed, still not used to Emmy's brief and sporadic style of texting.

Ryan: Yeah, it did.
Ryan: I'm not mad about it.
Emmy: Why the fuck
Emmy: Would you be mad about it?

Emmy: I AM A GOOD KISSER

Ryan laughed as he tossed the chip bag into the trash. He grabbed a glass of water and headed upstairs, walking carefully so he didn't end up on his ass at the bottom of the stairs.

Only Emmy would argue and defend her own skills via text after this many drinks and a fucking phenomenal kiss outside a bar. He kept chuckling to himself as he tossed his phone on the bed and slipped out of his dress pants and took his shirt off. *Let her sweat a little.* Ryan had found that he loved toying with Emmy, realizing that she communicated affection in the form of teasing. He flipped on the light next to his bed and told his smart speaker to turn off the overhead light. When he unlocked his phone again, he saw a few more text messages from Emmy.

Emmy: Doc.

Emmy: Ryan.

Emmy: RYAN

Emmy: DR. ANDERSSON

Emmy: RYAN ANDERSSON, PHD

Emmy: I AM A GOOD KISSER

Ryan: You are, you are.

Emmy: Good.

Emmy: We've established that.

Ryan: Do I get any credit?

Emmy: You're passable

Ryan: Well, thank you.

Emmy: So

Emmy: We should get coffee

Emmy: And talk

Emmy: About this

Ryan went to type a sarcastic response, wanted to bring up the first time he had offered to bring Emmy coffee and how poor of a start their relationship had gotten off to. But he remembered that she had brought him coffee, that she had asked if he was okay with their kiss first. He pulled back from that smart-ass impulse, wanting to push her somewhere else.

Ryan: We should get dinner.

Emmy: Sure.

Emmy: But.

Emmy: We need to talk

Emmy: Before work

Ryan: Ok. 7 a.m.? Too early?

Emmy: That's fine.

Ryan: The usual spot by The House? Jumping Goat?

Emmy sent a thumbs up reaction, and Ryan lay back on his pillows, looking up at his ceiling. He could, of course, leave it there, but that didn't feel right tonight. Wasn't how he wanted to play things with Emmy anymore. He was sick of pretending that he wasn't attracted to her, sick of pretending that her grimaces and smirks didn't make him hard in meetings. He stilled his thumbs over the glass of his phone, debating on what to say. *Fuck it.*

Ryan: I wanted what happened tonight to happen for a long time.

Three dots appeared, then disappeared. *Fuck.* Then they appeared again, followed by a text.

Emmy: I think I did, too.

Emmy: Good night.

Ryan: Night, Emmy.

Ryan clicked his phone off and plugged it into the charger, then flopped back into his pillows, shifting to try to get comfortable. Everything was too much – his room was both too hot and too cool, the blanket the wrong texture for his skin.

Fuck, all he wanted was Emmy's skin. He allowed his mind to wander to how she had felt under his hands, the strength of her body evident in the way he could feel her muscles as she moved. Fuck, what would her thighs feel like around his head? Ryan audibly groaned alone in his room and looked down at his dick. Of course he was hard tonight; he had been half hard since the moment he saw Emmy appear at the top of the stairs wearing that dress and those knockout heels that showed off her calf muscles.

Giving into a temptation he had not indulged in since their team-building retreat, Ryan shoved his boxer briefs down just enough to free his cock and wrapped his right hand around it, the pressure providing a small measure of relief. Gritting his teeth, he kept tugging and pulling, not even needing to pull up porn. Just thinking of the way that Emmy had scratched her fingernails along his scalp, the way she had responded to his teasing, the way she had met his enthusiasm with her own. Ryan wasn't stupid; he knew people found him attractive, how that changed the way they treated him. Emmy didn't try to flatter him with her kiss, but had battled with him, tussled with her tongue and dueled with her hands.

Ryan reached under his bed, squeezed a dollop of lube from the bottle he kept there, and slicked his cock, began to stroke in earnest as he imagined being able to lift up Emmy's dress. He'd crawl underneath it, Ryan on his knees and Emmy above, one heeled foot placed on his shoulder to open her to him. How he'd wipe that skeptical grin off her face with his tongue and fingers, make her gasp and moan and break open all over his face.

With that imagery in his mind, he came all over his stomach, his heart pounding. He quickly cleaned himself up and double-checked his alarm so he'd wake up in time to swim a mile and take the world's coldest shower before he met up with Emmy for coffee.

27

Ryan

Ryan figured he could have swum the entire English Channel before he had coffee with Emmy, and he still wouldn't be able to control his body's reaction to seeing her at the coffee shop that morning. She was already there, which was unsurprising, and she was tucked in at a table, hunched over a book with a highlighter in her hand. She chewed her cheek as she read through a paragraph, then went back and highlighted a specific passage. She hadn't noticed him, absorbed in her work, and Ryan took the chance to study her, to let his gaze rove over her body in the ways he hadn't given himself permission to. In the name of their working relationship, in the name of professionalism. Well, he had blown up that logic last night the moment he pressed Emmy against a cool brick wall and kissed her neck.

Her neck was stretched to one side as her lips worked through muttering a sentence as she was reading. Her hair was swept up in her standard bun, and she occasionally played with her bangs as she read. She was wearing an olive green long-sleeved shirt with a brown

1970s-looking ski vest over it, unzipped to show off the swell of her breasts. Not for the first time this morning, Ryan kicked himself for not allowing his hands to wander more during their make-out. *Next time*. Would there be a next time? Ryan didn't want to get ahead of himself, but there was no missing the way Emmy had responded to him during their kiss.

Emmy looked up and noticed him staring at her and rewarded him with a half smirk and an eye roll. Not the wide grin that most of his partners had greeted him with on a date. Nothing eager about Emmy. Reserved, playful, almost taunting.

He loved it.

Emmy tucked her highlighter into the book to mark her spot, shoved it in her messenger bag, got up, and walked over to him.

"Hey, Doc," she said, bumping into him with her shoulder. Ryan didn't know what was expected here. Could he hug her? Emmy didn't seem like a hugger; he hadn't even seen her hug her friends. A kiss on the cheek seemed reserved for a boyfriend, and he was certainly *not* that. He didn't even know what she thought about the kiss now that they had both sobered up.

"Hey, Curator," he responded, and she gave him a quizzical look. "What? You have a nickname for me, and I feel left out."

"Emmy *is* a nickname," she explained stubbornly as they got in line for coffee.

"Yeah, but everyone calls you that," he replied. "I want something that only I call you. Bonus points if it annoys you."

"Well, 'Curator' is a stupid nickname because it's a syllable longer than the name that most people refer to me as."

"Emmeline?"

"Ugh, god no. My full name makes me sound like a French courtesan."

"That's sexy, though."

"It makes me think of, like, stage three syphilis. Mercury treatments. Losing your nose. Early skin grafts." She shuddered as they moved up a step.

"I think most people think Nicole Kidman in *Moulin Rouge*, but I didn't write a paper on sex work in the American West," he said without thinking.

She eyed him warily. "How do you know about that paper? We barely talk about our own research. We barely talked without arguing until, like, four weeks ago."

Ryan felt his face warm, knew there would be a flush of color high on his cheeks. He couldn't even blame being outside in the cold for this. "I, uh..." he started. "I googled you. When we first started working together."

"You googled me?" Emmy scoffed. "What did you find?"

"Your thesis, a lot of articles. All things that were beyond me or my interests. A few articles from your hometown paper about being valedictorian and your scholarships. The videos from shutdown."

Emmy groaned. “Ugh, those were so stupid. I’m pretty sure no one watched them at all, but it made us feel like we were doing something.”

“I watched them,” he protested.

“What? Why?”

“I watched them,” Ryan repeated softly, his hand grazing hers. “You’re brilliant. And you smile in the videos. Especially when you’re talking about history. It was one of the few ways I could see you smile without interrupting time with your friends.”

28

EMMY

I WATCHED THEM.

It was one of the few ways I could see you smile.

In her time with Ryan, it was unusual for Emmy to be speechless. But here she was, unable to even come up with a sarcastic remark to throw back in his face. This was a snippet of a genuine connection between the two of them, and it felt wrong to cheapen it.

"Oh" was the only brilliant reply she was able to muster, but she was saved from having to say more by it finally being their turn to order coffee. Emmy opened her mouth to order her standard black coffee but couldn't get the barista's attention.

A sour heat flared in her belly as she watched the young — young and thin — *blonde* with perfect California beachy waves make doe eyes at Ryan as she asked him for his order.

Emmy was a feminist. She knew that all women were valuable and beautiful and that her muscular body was its own form of feminine power. She *knew* that. But at the moment, she hated that this ideal of coed beauty was shining all of her attention onto Ryan, while Emmy felt like a lumbering ox next to him. That one guy she had hooked up with years ago echoed into her head: "I don't want a woman who can deadlift me." Followed by her father: "I raised a daughter, not a son." Followed by a joke Phoebe had made early in their friendship when she had referred to Emmy as Miss Trunchbull.

"Em?" Ryan said, breaking her out of her anxiety spiral. "Dirty chai, right?"

"No, just a black coffee," she replied. A dirty chai was like $7.50 at this point. Plus she liked oat milk so she didn't poop all day.

"I'm buying," Ryan said, subtly placing his palm on her lower back, sending waves of sensation cascading all over her body. "You said you drink dirty chais when someone else is buying."

"Yeah, okay. Thanks," Emmy said, dazed that he had remembered a throw-away comment she had made a few months ago. Ryan nodded and ordered himself a vanilla latte, Emmy only jumping in to add her non-dairy milk to the order.

They slid over to the side and waited with the mix of undergrads, graduate students, and professionals who were waiting for their orders. Emmy took a deep breath and looked up at Ryan, surprised to find he was looking down at her already.

"Does that happen to you all the time?" she asked before she could think better of it.

"What?" Ryan asked, raising an eyebrow. *Of course he could raise an eyebrow*, she thought grumpily.

"That." She flapped a hand at the cash register. Ryan still looked at her in confusion. "Getting hit on. Getting ogled. I mean, you own a mirror, right? Somewhere in the geology collection, there's a mirror, right? You know what you look like?"

Ryan flushed again, and Emmy felt a surge of joy. "A-ha!" she said, poking him in the ribs. *Fuck, that was a thick layer of muscle.* "You *do* know you're attractive!"

"Do you think I'm attractive, Bangs?"

"Bangs is even worse than Curator."

"Answer the question, Dirty Chai."

If he only knew. She rolled her eyes and huffed out a breath. "Ugh. Yeah, fine. You're really good-looking. And you know it." He grinned — not the playful grin he usually gave her in the office, but a wide-open, almost boyish grin. Emmy imagined it was the same kind of grin that would appear on his face when he made a particularly interesting discovery in the lab.

"Yes," he hissed, pumping his fist. "The hot historian thinks I'm cute."

Emmy was rolling her eyes so much she thought they were going to fall out of her head. "Please, continue to joke," she deadpanned.

"Emmy, you're stunning," he replied, his smile falling slightly. "I about died when you showed up at the museum in that dress last night. Do you know how many days I couldn't focus on an article I was writing because you decided to wear a skirt to work and I had to look at your legs?"

What? All those weeks, Emmy hadn't been imagining the looks she caught occasionally on Ryan's face, where his eyes would go glassy and he would freeze for a bit. "Well, turnabout is fair play," she responded, not letting it show how much she loved hearing that. "Your sweater collection is positively indecent." She indicated the one he was wearing this morning, thick yarn knotted into an intricate pattern that ran across his broad shoulders. Emmy worked hard to not look down at the pair of jeans he was wearing, knowing his thick thighs would be pushing against the denim in unfair ways. *Could he squat me*? Emmy grew a bit warm at the imagery.

New kink unlocked, apparently.

"Ryan? Emmy?" A barista called out their names with their orders, and Emmy walked up and got them. A heart had been drawn next to Ryan's name, and she resisted the impulse to throw the coffee cup into the trash.

Ryan had settled at a small table in the corner next to the window where students jostled through the slushy streets. She passed the coffee to him, and he took a grateful sip.

"Feeling rough today, Doc?" She sipped her own coffee and was not going to let Ryan know she had to take another dose of Advil this morning. "At your age, you probably need it." *Oh no, that was a tell.*

"Emmy, I'm, like, four years older than you. Not forty."

"Did you google my birthday, too?"

"Maybe." He sipped his latte. "I bet you googled me, too." *Yeah, and found an absolutely absurd collection of your college swim photos that did nothing to help me sleep.*

"How else would I know that you qualified for the Minnesota State Swimming Championships in 2003?" Emmy thought for a second, then a lightbulb went off in her head. "*That's* what you always smell like. It's chlorine!"

"You smell me?"

"Shut up."

"Nah, this is more fun." They sat in silence for a few minutes, and Emmy began to pick at her fingernails, her stomach churning.

"Do you regret it?" she asked suddenly, the words tumbling out of her mouth.

"Regret what? Swimming? No, I told you. It's how I got a scholarship to college —" He caught her eye and paused, understanding flashing across his face. "Oh, that." Emmy remained silent. "Our kiss," he said, raising an eyebrow again.

"Er...yeah. It was kind of more than a kiss, though." Emmy toyed with her bangs.

"Our make-out session?" Ryan tried. Emmy buried her face in her hands, groaning. Ryan continued, "I'm pretty sure we would have gotten to at least second base if our rides had been late."

"I hate baseball."

"Emmy, if you're not okay with this, we can go back to how it was."

"You mean sassing each other and not getting anything done?" Emmy took a breath. "We did get a lot of brainstorming done last night, and we've felt in sync since we decided to start planning the gala events." She took another breath and groaned. "Plus, as I've stated, you're really attractive."

"Emmy, I like you."

"And again, as I've stated, you like everyone."

"No." He caught her hand across the table. "I *like* you. I like your brain and your body and your sexy and frustrating personality."

"Oh."

"Let's go on a date and see what happens." He was so damn sincere, desire and kindness glowing from his face. Emmy felt her defenses crumbling and finally nodded, permitted herself a small smile.

"Fine. Can we not tell anyone at work?"

"Whatever works for you," Ryan said, stretching his leg out and nudging his foot against hers.

"Okay, well, I did text Phoebe last night, so she knows," Emmy admitted. "Which means Jeremy will have to know. And since Phoebe knows that we made out, I'm sure Dec already knows, too."

"Who?"

"Bartender last night." Emmy thought for a second, trying to ignore the way Ryan's boot toe was rubbing up and down her ankle. "Though, we made out at his bar, so it's only fair that he knows."

"Focus," Ryan said, tapping her foot.

"Hard to do with someone playing footsie with me at 7:15 in the morning," she shot back. He gave her a cheeky grin.

"Can I take you out on Friday? Away from work, away from museums, just you and me. Dinner. Drinks. Other things."

"What do you mean other things? I've told you. I don't like surprises."

"Nah, I'll keep that a secret." Emmy's stomach clenched, and she knew she needed to be honest with Ryan.

"Doc, here's the thing," she said, reaching over and placing her hand over his. "This isn't a *ha ha, what a cute quirk* thing. It's an anxiety thing. If you don't tell me where we're going or what you have planned, I won't sleep. I'll run through a million different possibilities and imagine the worst outcome. I'll google every restaurant in the city and look at their health ratings and decide we're going to the one that someone got Listeria at four years ago." She took a breath. "I figure you should know all this before you get in too deep. It's...a lot. And it's not easy. Also, speaking of anxiety, you should also know that I take these meds and —"

"Emmy, okay, okay. I get it." Ryan ran a hand through his hair, took his glasses off, and then put them back on. *Well, that puts off having that awkward conversation for a future date.* "The place I had in mind is called Otter & Stone. There's a band I really like that plays one Friday a month. I thought you would like them. There's good food, and they have a full bar so you can get a gin and tonic."

"All right," Emmy said, wrapping her hands around her nearly empty mug to steady them and to keep from biting her fingernails like a middle schooler in front of Ryan right now. "I also, uh, I don't have a car, so can you pick me up?"

"You don't have a car?" he asked, shocked.

"I thought we talked about this. I take the bus because it's way cheaper, and if I'm headed out to the mountains, I can borrow Phoebe's." She shrugged. "Plus, she tends to go skiing and hiking with me, so it's been easier and cheaper for both of us. We all don't have that fancy science money." Ryan opened his mouth to reply and looked stricken. Emmy took pity on him. "Doc, I'm kidding. Sometimes I'm actually not a bitch."

"You're not a...you know."

"It's fine." Emmy shrugged again. "I know how I come off."

"Intense. Passionate. Driven. Fierce." Ryan ran his thumb over his lower lip. "Not a bitch."

"Oh."

"I don't know how I'm going to do this in the office today," he muttered, reaching over and tugging one of her hands off the mug, then lacing his fingers with hers. Emmy overruled her instinct to pull her hand back or to counter Ryan's comment with a sniping remark of her own.

She cleared her throat and asked, "Do what?"

"Be able to look at you the way I want to," he said, his voice dropping. The room constricted, and Emmy's grip—along with other parts—tightened. "Put my hand on yours when you start fidgeting with your nails." He lowered his voice even more, and Emmy had to lean across the table to hear him. "Kiss you." She melted, even though the coffee shop door was open and wind was blowing in the room.

"Well, not at work," she replied, finally pulling her hand away.

"Duh," he replied, rolling his eyes. "Anyway, I have to be in the collection this morning, anyway. Satya has something to let me know about the database."

"Riveting. Well, then, are we still on for an exhibition planning meeting this afternoon?" She pointed a finger at him and eyed him warily. "No protocols."

"Right, right," Ryan said, getting up and taking his cup and Emmy's and placing them in the bus tub. "I remember how that went." Emmy got up and zipped her vest up, noticing the way Ryan's eyes followed the path of the zipper over her breasts. *Hmm.*

"Let's go to work, you perv," she said, nudging him in the shoulder.

"Like you're not gonna stare at my ass if I walk in front of you?"

"First off, it's your shoulders that I'd stare at," she replied. "And I can be professional," she scoffed.

"Walk you to campus, Vestie?" he asked, offering her his arm.

"Still not working," she said, linking her arm through his. "Can't you just call me Emmy like everyone else?" He shook his head and wrapped his scarf around his neck. She flashed back to when he had peeled it off her neck to suck at the skin there.

They walked and chatted as they headed to the museum, swapping conspiracy theories they had both heard about the Denver Airport. In front of the museum, they split paths, with Emmy noticing the way Ryan's eyes trailed over her face and down to her lips as they parted. She nearly skipped up the stairs to her – *their* – office and put on a background playlist on her phone as her computer booted up. When it finally woke up, she had an email marked "urgent" at the top of her inbox. She let out an audible groan as she looked at the subject.

Exhibition Brainstorm (Calendar Invite – Dr. Ryan Andersson)

She tapped an immediate reply.

Re: Exhibition Brainstorm (Calendar Invite – Dr. Ryan Andersson)

Dr. Andersson -

I am not sure why you felt the need to send this calendar invite, seeing as we just discussed and confirmed this meeting not so much as 15 minutes ago. Also, it is in the office we share.

Best,

Emmy Bonaire, M.S.

She/Her

Re:Re: Exhibition Brainstorm (Calendar Invite – Dr. Ryan Andersson)

Ms. Bonaire -

I wanted to see if you got the attached protocol and agenda I developed for the meeting.

Sincerely,
Dr. Ryan Andersson
He/Him

Re:Re:Re: Exhibition Brainstorm (Calendar Invite – Dr. Ryan Andersson)

Dr. Andersson -

There is nothing attached. Please re-send and also please reconsider.

Best,
Emmy Bonaire, M.S.
She/Her

PS - Since when did you put a dinosaur emoji in your email signature?

Re:Re:Re:Re: Exhibition Brainstorm (Calendar Invite: Dr. Ryan Andersson)

Ms. Bonaire -

Made you look. Just wanted to keep myself on your mind this morning.

Oh, and I've always had the dinosaur emoji. I just deleted it from every email that I sent you because it didn't fit your communication style.

Sincerely,
Dr. Ryan Andersson
He/Him

PS -

Re:Re:Re:Re:Re Exhibition Brainstorm (Calendar Invite: Dr. Ryan Andersson)

You would be someone who likes emojis.

Their brainstorming session went surprisingly well, with Ryan bringing up a Wikipedia page on Sara Jonesboro that he had read. Emmy had been so proud of his excitement (and more than a little turned on) that she waited until he was done sketching out his ideas to let him know she had written that Wikipedia page. What had caught Ryan's attention was the fact that Sara had hosted what she called "gatherings" at her house, at *The House*. Emmy had known about those and had assumed that they were chances for Sara to connect with local scientists to see who needed her financial support most. Ryan, however, compared them to European salons, where scholars would gather and share and collaborate on ideas.

When he had started to explain the way that, historically, salons were one of the places in Europe where women had been most involved with the scientific process (a fact that Emmy knew), she couldn't help but to get up and lock the office door, lean over him, and kiss him.

29

Emmy

Emmy got home as quickly as she could with her main bus delayed – she had bounced between two new routes with the help of Google maps, then alternated between a podcast on a weird historical tradition with a reread of a book on her phone to assuage her nerves about the evening. She unlocked her apartment, tossed her keys on the table next to the door, and took a look around.

What if she and Ryan came back here? Was it nice enough? Was it clean enough? Emmy gave it a once-over and noticed the numerous piles of books that had sprung up all over her house. It wasn't her fault that she didn't have enough bookshelves for all of them. Half of these were for her job, and a bunch were from the library for her research. She had to be honest with herself – her salary did not allow for a larger apartment or even more bookshelves, even if she had room.

Emmy checked the time on her phone. Five thirty. And Ryan had confirmed this afternoon that he was picking her up at seven. Based on what she had seen from him at work, Ryan was a person who tended to get to places on time, which she appreciated. But it also meant that she didn't have that long to get ready.

Shower? Don't shower? Shave? Leave it? Do her hair? Makeup? It had been so long since Emmy had been on an official date — not just a "hope for a hookup after a few beers" evening — she didn't know what to do. Kicking off her shoes and walking to her bedroom, she swiped her phone until she found her most commonly called person.

"Yes?" Phoebe answered.

"Help me, please!" Emmy begged.

"Of course." Emmy could basically hear Phoebe's eye roll, knew that she had stepped away from Declan at the bar to head outside to take Emmy's phone call. "What do you need?"

"Do I shave?"

Phoebe, to her eternal credit, took Emmy's question in stride, as she always did. "What parts?"

"Uh, I dunno? Legs? Pits?" Emmy tucked the phone between her chin and her shoulder and began to slide clothes around her closet, looking at what she wanted to wear for the evening.

"Definitely those, just to be safe. What about below?" Phoebe was always bold and direct in her advice. Emmy took a moment to appreciate that this advice didn't take the form of frantic six a.m. texts for Phoebe to help Emmy figure out a way to not see a one-night stand again.

"Er," Emmy said, holding up a dress to her body in front of a mirror. She shook her head, groaned, and tossed the dress onto her bed. "I doubt he has any interest in that."

Emmy put her face close to the mirror, looking at her pores. Were there any noticeable pimples she needed to pop before she showered?

"Emmy." Phoebe used her teacher voice, which always made Emmy feel like she was being sent to the principal's office. "You are a brilliant historian, but you are a very stupid woman at times."

"What do you mean?" Emmy had given up on her closet and had started making her way to the bathroom. Moving Phoebe to speakerphone, she began to tug her clothes off and turn on the shower.

"Emmy, when he thinks that no one is looking, he looks at you in meetings like he wants to eat you up." Phoebe recounted this like she was letting Emmy know that Highway 36 backed up on the way to Boulder – a fact that anyone would know.

"*What*?"

"Ryan's eyes get all smokey and dark – great call choosing a guy with glasses, by the way. And I swear I think Dec's brain is on another planet, because he told me he didn't pick up on anything. To me and Jer, it was clear as day."

Emmy held her tongue about what might have distracted Dec – Phoebe might still be at the bar, and Declan had supersonic hearing. "Ugh, okay, whatever," she said, ignoring the way Phoebe's noticing caused her stomach to boil and churn with a mix of apprehension and arousal. "I don't like fully shaving, because it gets all prickly. So a trim? A cleanup downstairs?"

"Perfect," Phoebe replied, though Emmy knew she would support any decision Emmy made with her body hair. "Also, if he doesn't like the trimmings, he can get fucked." Emmy laughed out loud and thanked Phoebe for her advice. She pulled up a favorite playlist on her phone, clicked up the volume, and popped into the shower, following Phoebe's advice to a T.

Slipping out of the shower, she wrapped her hair in a towel and applied moisturizer. She padded to the kitchen in her towel and filled a glass of water, took a sip, and tried to calm her nerves. Emmy headed back to her closet, opening the door and muttering about how she hadn't had a wardrobe update in a few years because damn shutdown pay freezes.

"Not good, doesn't fit, makes my arms look big," she said, rifling through the clothes. Cocking her head, Emmy pulled out a brown corduroy skirt and a dark teal sweater that she remembered hugging her curves in a way she liked. After their coffee date, she had taken note of the way that Ryan's eyes often, seemingly unconsciously, slid from her face to her chest when they were in conversation. Completing her outfit with calf-hugging brown leather boots and a headband, she snapped a quick picture and sent it to Phoebe for confirmation that it was a good choice.

Emmy: I think this is good?

Emmy: It's not too

Emmy: I joined a cult?

Phoebe: HOT. Dec agrees.

Emmy: Why did you show him?

Phoebe: He just told me he saw you guys making out the other night on his security cameras.

Emmy groaned and took another sip of her water, heading into the bathroom to work on her makeup. She added a bit of eyeshadow and blush but had to redo her winged eyeliner three times because her hands were shaking and she couldn't get the thickness consistent.

When had she ever been this nervous for a date? She wasn't even this nervous for her thesis defense (and her committee chair had been a huge dick). She routinely gave presentations to the board asking for money, had presented at conferences to nearly full rooms (or rooms that were as full as they would be for esoteric western history topics). Why was dinner with a coworker something that was freaking her out so much?

Finishing her water, she propped herself against the countertop in her kitchen.

What if this dinner went terribly and it made everything weird at work?

What if everyone decided that she had crossed a professional line?

Obviously, Ryan would keep his job — he had a PhD — but Emmy would be asked to step down.

If she had to quit, where could she find a job?

Were any history museums in the area hiring?

Was she going to have to move back home?

A buzz from her phone shook her out of her thought spiral.

Ryan: I'm here! I think?

Shit, shit, shit, Emmy thought. She opened her curtains a bit, saw a newer model Subaru idling on her street. She drained the last bit of water and set her glass next to the sink. On second thought, she rinsed it quickly and turned it upside down in the dish rack. *There*. Now it looked like she did dishes and didn't let them pile up. *That was sexy, right?*

With another audible groan and a litany of swear words, Emmy threw her phone, keys, and wallet into a brown leather purse. She tossed a puffy jacket over her arm, checked her hair one final time in the mirror by the door, took a deep breath, and walked out the door of her apartment.

30

Ryan

Damn, did Ryan love a woman in boots. He savored the view of Emmy walking out of her building, honking the horn slightly to get her attention. Her face lit up a bit when she noticed, and Ryan continued to watch her walk over to his car, the cold air turning just the tip of her nose a delightful pink. She held her jacket over her arms, folded across her body, and Ryan wanted her to move it so he could see the full length of her.

He was excited for tonight, and not just for the chance to be physically close to her. For a chance to get to know her better. To unleash the spark that she had at work into their one-on-one relationship. And, he finally admitted to himself, it wasn't for their working relationship at all. It was for the way that his body reacted around her, yes, but also the way that she battled and sparred with her mind when they interacted.

"How did I know you were going to drive a Subaru?" Emmy laughed, opening the passenger door and sliding into the seat before setting her bag and jacket down on the floor next to her feet. Ryan tried — and failed — to not look at the smooth, creamy skin of her thigh that was revealed when she sat, her skirt moving just a centimeter higher to reveal a slight ripple of muscle.

"I am a walking stereotype," Ryan replied, backing out into the street. For the first time in recent memory, he cursed the convenience of backup cameras, wanted the excuse of putting his arm around Emmy's seat as he would have turned around to see behind him. *Stupid technology.*

They drove in that awkward first-date silence, with Ryan fiddling with the volume on the radio — first too loud, then too quiet, then an awkwardly loud commercial blared through the silence.

"So, this place," Emmy said, clearing her throat, clearly making an attempt to push through some sort of conversation. "You like it?"

"Yeah," Ryan said, mentally thinking, *Of course. That's why I'm taking you there.*

"Great," Emmy said. "I looked at their menu online, and it looks good."

"It is," Ryan replied, not knowing what to say as he turned a corner onto the main drag of town. "It's a bit out of town, but I like getting away."

"Yeah, that's nice."

"Yep." Emmy looked out the window and started picking at her nails, her left knee jiggling so much that Ryan could hear the light clinking of her boot zipper. She dropped her hands in her lap, then began messing with her bangs. Where was the back-and-forth he had gotten used to in the office? Where was that beginning thread of connection they'd had at the bar? And — this was where Ryan got nervous — where was that spark that had him pressing her against a wall that night, had her hands threading through his hair?

"This is weird, right?" Emmy said, shattering the silence and looking at Ryan. *Thank god she said something*, he thought as he let out a nervous laugh.

"So fucking weird," Ryan agreed. "Like, clearly we know how to talk to each other?"

"I mean, usually we're arguing, but at least that isn't silence," Emmy said, grinning.

"We had a great conversation the night of the gala," Ryan pointed out. He slid his gaze over to Emmy and kicked up one side of his mouth in a sly grin. "Among other things." He watched his comment resonate with Emmy and a light pink flush blossom on the apples of her cheeks. *God, she's cute*, he thought, which was interesting. Ryan had considered Emmy a lot of things: intimidating, sexy, badass, brilliant, arousing, frustrating, and gorgeous. But never cute. He liked discovering new sides of her.

"Oh, by the way — Dec saw us making out on his cameras," Emmy said conversationally, causing Ryan to almost swerve off the road.

"Huh?"

"Yeah," Emmy said, tightening her lips and nodding. "So we have to be more careful tonight. Scope out the sightlines and stuff." She peeked at Ryan, bit her lip, and scrunched her nose.

Tonight. More careful. Ryan put the pieces together. That meant she wanted to kiss him again. That boded well for him.

Taking a chance with this newfound information, Ryan reached his right hand over and placed it on Emmy's hand that had remained in her lap. She flipped her palm over and interlaced their fingers. A small jolt of victory ran through him, Ryan loving the feel of her rough palm against his own.

"From lifting?" he said, holding up her palm.

Emmy nodded. "I know I'm supposed to treat the calluses, shave them, but I have this fear that I'm going to slice open my entire hand, and then I get too nervous, so I just wait for them to either grow too big that I have to, or they rip off. Which is actually worse than shaving them."

"I hated lifting in college," Ryan added thoughtfully. "Anything on dry land was my nightmare. Running, lifting, anything considered 'cross-conditioning,' I always tried to get out of."

"Maybe that's why you're a dinosaur poop researcher instead of an Olympian," Emmy said, smiling.

"Yep," Ryan said, playing along, "That's it. I was the Minnesotan Michael Phelps before I skipped the required 10k to begin the season."

"Okay, but running does suck," Emmy said. "I tried so many different types of exercise after my therapist told me it would be a good way to channel my anxiety during undergrad, after my" — she paused momentarily, then regrouped — "after my breakdown. I tried biking, but my ass hurt. Running — actually torture. Swimming — no thank you; I like breathing. Rock climbing — it was Ohio, and heights are the worst. And finally got into a gym to try to lift. Was super nervous at first. Knew nothing about it, could barely move the bar, but fell in love with it."

"Badass," Ryan said, pulling into a small parking lot next to a red brick building. "And we're here." He turned off the car, walked around, and opened the door for her — or rather, stood awkwardly by the door as she opened it, because he wasn't fast enough. He shut it behind her, then looped his arm through hers. "Let's go inside."

31

Emmy

Emmy didn't have a huge knowledge of the restaurants of Vanberg or the surrounding area. She had been working multiple jobs for a lot of her career, which didn't leave her a lot of time to get out. And she liked saving what little money she did make for skiing adventures during the winter or a new book. She hadn't heard about this place before but had spent a solid forty-five minutes reading their dinner menu (she was going to order the lamb with a side of sweet potatoes), drink menu (they had her favorite type of gin, so she could splurge on that tonight), and then reading Yelp reviews (the service was generally ranked as good, but the food took a while to prepare). What she wasn't ready for, though, was walking into a place with Ryan.

She was used to him taking up space in the office, as much as it drove her up a wall, but she wasn't used to the way his energy lit up a room in public. She felt like an overly tall Wednesday Addams next to a 1950s high school quarterback as he walked up to the hostess, stepping slightly in front of her to field the conversation.

"Good evening," he said, flashing a grin at the woman, who Emmy guessed to be just out of undergrad. She looked up from her hostess stand – and up and up, because Emmy had forgotten that Ryan was abnormally tall to most people – and her face flushed a deep red.

"Hi," she said, grinning. "Can I help you?"

"I have a reservation tonight. Should be under Andersson? I asked for a table near the back?" Ryan's Midwestern charm was in full force. The girl stammered and checked the reservation.

"You're here, but the table is up front." She tapped her computer a few times, then said something into a radio. "I moved you to the back, though."

Emmy hated the surge of jealousy that flared through her with the way this woman looked at Ryan. He wasn't *hers*, but still. As if he could read her mind, Ryan placed his large palm on her lower back. The hostess, who was gathering menus, noticed, and her eyes bounced from Ryan to Emmy and back to Ryan, a tiny sliver of disappointment running over her face.

Right, Emmy reminded herself. *He asked* you *here. He picked* you *up. He kissed* you.

Ryan kept his hand on her back as they slowly walked past the tables in the restaurant to a small, semi-private booth in the corner. Emmy slid into one side, setting her jacket and purse down, while Ryan took the other.

"Why did you request a table in the back?" she asked, picking up a menu and pretending to scan it, even though she knew her order.

"I've noticed that you don't love crowds," he said. "You tend to hang on the sides of them, so I figured back here would be easier for us to talk. I remembered it from trivia."

Emmy felt a wave of emotion, of gratitude. So she reacted in the only logical way — she made a sarcastic remark.

"I'm surprised you even remember that night." He laughed, and Emmy continued. "You didn't choose a dark corner to ravish me?" She placed a hand on her forehead and adopted a mock swoon. Ryan's eyes flashed something bright green and dangerous, like a jungle viper, when she said *ravish*.

Oh.

"Later, Em," he said, making a production of spreading his napkin on his lap. "But first, we eat."

"And drink," Emmy added.

"But not too much," Ryan said. Emmy raised her eyebrows. "Well, I'm driving, and I'd like to remember our first date."

Oh shit. That's right. This was a date. A real, proper, made-for-TV date. He had picked her up in his car and everything.

"A date," she said, smiling into her water glass. "Not too shabby, Doc."

"I try," he said, sliding his foot across to hers under the table and tapping the side. "I try."

Dinner was lovely. Emmy did order the lamb and a gin and tonic, which she worked to sip slowly. Usually, her impulse was to down her first drink quickly to counteract her nerves, but Ryan had hinted that he wanted her sober-ish, and she could respect that. Especially if she worked up the courage to invite him upstairs when he dropped her off.

It had also been a slight bit of torture — watching Ryan sip a bourbon on the rocks, the way he pulled his lips in to savor each taste, the way he thoughtfully chewed each bite of food. The waiter came around with a check after someone had taken their plates, but Ryan gently asked if he could have a cup of coffee and asked if Emmy wanted another gin and tonic.

"I'd love that," Emmy said, excited that he didn't want their evening to end. "You're good?"

"Yeah, plus, the band is going on soon," he said, pointing to a stage in the opposite corner. "I'll have this cup of coffee, and then another drink when the band starts."

"Mmm," Emmy said as her drink was delivered, taking a delicate sip. "Sounds lovely. What kind of music is it?" Emmy knew, though. She had searched the event calendar, found the band scheduled for Friday nights, then found their Instagram. Then she'd found their recent EP on Spotify.

"Bluegrass," he replied.

"Ahh," Emmy said, trying to sound authentically surprised. "I like bluegrass. One of very few parts of my Appalachian upbringing that I actually enjoy."

Ryan studied her for a second. "You knew about the band, didn't you?"

"Maybe," Emmy hedged.

"You researched everything, huh?" Ryan asked. Emmy felt her face flush, thanked the heavens that the corner was dark.

"Yeah, I am really good at researching," she admitted, rocking her head from side to side. Ryan grinned, a grin that was silly and goofy and told her he had something he wasn't telling her. Unlike most times, her anxiety didn't spike, didn't immediately jump to the worst possible outcome. Maybe it was the gin, or his smile, or the whole evening, but Emmy was intrigued, not worried. "What is it you're not telling me?"

"Oh, my strong and brilliant Emmy," he said, and Emmy pulled a face. "There's something they don't put on the website."

"Which is?"

"Dancing is strongly encouraged." Ryan gently took the glass out of her hand and set it on the coaster. "And I love dancing."

"Oh god. Of course you do," Emmy groaned, slipping down into the booth, trying to fit her five-eleven body into the tiny space.

"Come on, Em," he said, standing up and offering his hand to her. "Let's give it a whirl."

32

Ryan

He had planned all this, he admitted to himself. Had swung into Next Door the day after their kiss and asked Declan what Emmy drank ("always a gin & tonic because a bartender can't fuck it up" was his deadpanned response), and then he had asked Phoebe if she had a favorite kind of gin. Made sure that it was on the menu at the restaurant. Made sure that the band he liked was playing (they could flake sometimes), and he had called ahead to ensure that the dance floor would be open. Not so much a ploy to touch Emmy, but a reason to hold her close and have a whispered conversation. Something that wouldn't have a table or a notebook or a drink in the way, where it could just be the two of them talking.

Emmy rolled her eyes as she took his hand. He pulled her up to him and led her onto the dance floor but still stayed in the back corner.

"My therapist is always telling me that I need to try new things," she explained. "To get out of my comfort zone so I see that the things that I'm afraid of happening very rarely do. Though, I'm sure, one day, something will happen that will confirm all of it, and it will be a setback in all this progress I've made —"

Ryan stopped her by placing his finger on her lips. "Are you worried about your therapy going wrong? You're worrying about the thing that's supposed to stop you from worrying?"

Emmy grimaced, then nodded. "I guess so," she said.

"Does your brain ever stop?" Ryan asked the question before he could think twice, to realize that it could have come off as judgmental or not understanding. "I didn't mean it as a bad thing," he rushed to explain. "But it seems tiring."

"Not really," Emmy said. "It's why I stay busy — at work, picking up extra stuff for the museum, lifting, hanging out with people. The minute I'm alone, my brain takes over. I even have to fall asleep to a podcast or white noise machine so I'm not alone with my thoughts."

Ryan filed that information away for later but tried to not let his brain get ahead of itself. "Okay, let me take over here." Emmy glowered. "Seriously, I'll lead. I can actually dance. I promise." He took one of her hands in his, then guided her other to his waist. Then he placed his hand on her shoulder, squeezing slightly, enjoying the way he could already feel her muscles under her shirt.

"This feels so formal," Emmy said. "Like I'm a southern debutante or some shit."

"You'll relax, I promise," Ryan said, interlacing their fingers together. "It's just simple swaying to the rhythm of the music, with the occasional turn. I'll lead."

Emmy opened her mouth to say something, then shut it and thought again. “Fine.”

“Em? What is it?”

“Nothing. Let’s do this.”

“Emmy, you don’t have to lie to make me feel good. If you’re really against this, we can sit back down and just listen to the music. It’s fine.” He would be disappointed, sure, but he could sacrifice his plan to make sure that the evening didn’t entirely go off the rails.

“It’s just…” Emmy’s grip tightened, and her body stiffened in Ryan’s arms. “It’s just that phrasing. You *leading*. The idea of giving up control is really terrifying to me.”

“It’s just a few songs,” Ryan said quietly. “I’m here for you.”

“I know, I know,” she squeezed her eyes shut. “I can do this. I promise.” Her eyes were still closed, and that tiny line between her eyebrows had appeared again. Figuring that he could do what he’d wanted to do a thousand times in meetings, he pressed his lips to that space. Emmy’s eyes popped open in surprise, then she softened slightly. Sparks danced behind her eyes, and Ryan saw her smile slightly, which meant he knew a sarcastic comment was coming. Which meant Emmy was relaxed, or at least progressing toward it. “How the hell do you know how to dance anyway?”

“Every elementary school gym class in Minnesota taught us square dancing,” he explained. “Plus,” and here, he felt his face warm slightly, “my older sisters insisted that I practice with them before I went to high school so I wouldn't totally embarrass them at homecoming and prom." Emmy snorted a laugh at that last fact and leaned into him just a bit.

Ryan began to sway her slightly, loving the way she fit against his body. He was tall. Everyone in his family but his mom was. His dad was six-five to this day, his sisters all above five-ten. But Emmy was tall, too. And broad. She took up space everywhere she went, unapologetically. Even tonight, she had worn boots with a heel, so she was *almost* eye level with his nose. They shuffled around the dance floor, enjoying the pluck of the mandolin, the pull of the fiddle.

They danced for a few songs, making quiet conversation, Ryan sharing more about his childhood, Emmy poking fun at stories he shared. Occasionally, he was able to pull a tiny fact about her upbringing out of her. She had no siblings, her parents were still alive and still lived in her hometown, and he thought they were still married. Getting Emmy to reveal pieces of her background was a challenge, something that reminded Ryan of the digs he had been on, looking for delicate pieces of the prehistoric past. He needed a fine brush and a dental pick to remove the layers of soil from around Emmy's protective shell, but if there was one thing his academic training had prepared him for, it was patience.

A slower song came on, and Ryan made to head off the dance floor, but Emmy grunted a tiny protest. Without talking, she pulled him slightly closer to her, resting her cheek on his chest. Something flared in his chest, a desire to wrap his arms around this woman and scurry away with her, but he settled for sliding both of his hands down low on her waist and pressing a kiss to her forehead before resting his chin on the top of her head.

They stayed slow dancing through the rest of the song, and Ryan felt a contented hum vibrate from Emmy's chest, which passed through the thick wool of his sweater directly into his own chest — though part of that sensation definitely took a detour a bit farther south. The song ended, and Emmy went to pull away, but Ryan held her tighter for just a second longer than she anticipated, not ready to leave their cocoon.

"Doc." She giggled — *giggled* — and he squeezed her tight, past the point of comfort. "Oof," came the sound from her lips. "You're a fool."

"Yep," he agreed, finally letting her go and heading back to the table. "Do you want to take a break? Finish your drink?" Emmy nodded, looking only slightly relieved to be off the dance floor.

"Question," she said, plopping down into the booth and taking a large sip of her gin and tonic, though the ice had melted down while they were dancing. Ryan nodded, indicating she could go ahead. Emmy squinted her eyes and stared Ryan down. "Does your mom have photographs of you practicing dancing with your sisters?"

Ryan barked a laugh and then silenced himself with the imagery of Emmy meeting his mom and his sisters. Still much too soon to be getting any ideas like *that*. Ryan hadn't brought a girl home since undergrad, and that was only because she happened to be from a town just outside of St. Cloud. His parents had never met his girlfriend in California, though his sisters had and immediately pronounced her "suspicious." They were right. What would they think of Emmy?

Kristin would love her strength, her take-no-shit attitude. Jennifer would get her to warm up quickly and probably be able to find out all of the mysteries of her background that Ryan couldn't. Amanda would keep to herself for a bit but spend the whole time analyzing Emmy's subtle movements.

His mom would love her. His dad would say he finally had a fifth daughter (the fourth was Jenn's wife).

He had gotten so distracted by thoughts of his family and the image of Emmy in front of their Christmas tree in St. Cloud, opening up a stocking his aunt would have cross-stitched, that he didn't hear what she said.

"What?" he said, grateful that Emmy, while talented, couldn't read minds.

"Do you want to dance again?" She had drained her drink and was already standing by the table, hip cocked and expectant.

"I'd love to," he said, smiling as he took her hand. Without warning, he spun her wildly on the floor, capturing her tight to his chest as he pulled her back.

"More skills, Doc!"

"You don't know the half of it," he said, and he held her close, leaned down, and pressed his lips to hers the way he had wanted to since he saw her walk out of her apartment in those fucking boots. He captured her top lip with his, and Emmy responded in kind, keeping the kiss wet and hot but still appropriate for a dance floor that was predominantly populated by people who were their parents' ages.

Emmy pulled back a touch, pressed a kiss to Ryan's neck, and stretched up on her tiptoes to whisper in his ear, "Thanks for teaching me how to dance, Doc."

Ryan had never had a better date.

33

Ryan

Ryan turned onto Emmy's street and maneuvered his car to the side where he had picked her up. He had to let go of the hand of hers he was holding on his thigh to put the car into park. Then he switched off the car but clicked the overhead light on. He liked looking at Emmy, liked watching her lips twitch and smirk as she thought about what she was going to say. He liked talking to Emmy, figuring out the way her mind untangled problems and attacked ideas. And, god knows, he liked kissing and touching Emmy, the way she gave as much as him and took as much as she wanted to as well. Ryan hadn't in recent memory met his match in bed, someone who liked being a bit dominant but also liked when people battled for their own control.

All of these thoughts buzzed through Ryan's head as the engine settled, a last clatter the only sound between them, save the quiet music Ryan hadn't quite turned off.

Emmy looked out the window, slightly bouncing her head back and forth in the way that Ryan knew meant she was thinking about what to do next, taking her time to pick her words and ignore her usual impulsive speech.

Ryan opened his mouth to say good night — he didn't want to push her in any way, didn't want to ruin the good vibe they had going on, the way he had danced with her and kissed her — but Emmy turned around, her hair moving and showering him with her grapefruit scent.

"Do you want to come up?" she asked, picking at a nail with her thumb. She rolled her shoulders down and lifted her head up just a millimeter. Ryan was so busy studying her, processing that *she* invited *him* up, that he forgot to answer. So Emmy continued, filling the silence. "I mean, you don't have to — no pressure. It's probably stupid to ask, and I don't even know if I have any beer or bourbon up there. I drink clear alcohol, and I don't smoke weed."

"Em?" Ryan said, reaching out to wrap his arm around her shoulders. He pulled her close and tapped his forehead against hers. "I'd love that," he whispered, then took her lips in a quick kiss. Because he was touching her, he felt her body relax, slacken just an iota with his affirmative.

"Great," she said, her half smile appearing, her eyes twinkling almost white under the car's dim light. She reached down, grabbed her bag, and was out of the car in five seconds. Ryan opened his own door and waited a second, then walked around the back of the car, where Emmy was meeting him. He would have opened the door for her, ran to wrap his arm around her, but he figured that adjusting himself took precedent. He didn't want it to be so evident how excited he was to be going upstairs.

Emmy slid in front of him and dug around in her purse for her keys, unlocking the large wooden front door to reveal a wide-open entryway with mailboxes and a bulletin board. "Upstairs," she said, a bit awkwardly, nodding her head up the stairs. She walked up the stairs in front of him, and Ryan adjusted himself again as he watched her ass sway from side to side. *I can't wait to get my hands under that skirt.*

Emmy turned left to a simple wooden door that had a pine wreath hung over the apartment number, surprising Ryan. She opened the door, and a warm scent of cinnamon floated out. Emmy walked in and hung her keys up on a holder near the door, below a whiteboard with her weekly schedule laid out, along with a list of "Goals for the Week."

Emmy bent down and unzipped her boots, kicking them off in a neat and organized way by the doorway. Ryan followed suit, toeing off his dress sneakers. He liked the look of their shoes next to each other. He followed Emmy into a small apartment, a galley kitchen to his left, then a main area with a couch, coffee table, bookshelves, and a small TV. To the right of the couch was a darkened hallway — her bedroom?

"Do you want something to drink?" Emmy walked past him and back into the kitchen, socked feet roaming across worn carpet. "I might have a beer from when Colin came down last time, but I've got stuff for a gin and tonic if you want that." She had opened up the fridge and bent over, heading out of Ryan's sight line, but she popped back up, holding a brown bottle.

"Anything is fine, really," he said, standing around, unsure of where to sit.

"You can sit on the couch," she said, the sounds of a drink being made emanating from the kitchen. Ryan walked around to the bookshelves, where there were various candles, incense holders, and photographs. Most of the pictures featured Phoebe and Jeremy doing a variety of things – going to concerts, skiing, hiking, drinking at that bar by campus. A few photos of Foster and Flo with Emmy at the brewery. A photograph of Emmy in her master's cap and gown, smiling in front of the historical center. Tucked away behind a few books was a map of Ohio with a penguin with a red scarf. Ryan had just begun to study what kinds of books she had when she appeared next to him, handing him a beer.

"Like my exhibit, Doc?" she asked, taking a sip of her own drink.

"Just trying to learn more about you," he said honestly. "It looks like most of your pictures are from Colorado. No family photos?"

Emmy snorted. "I'm an only child of very disinterested parents from a dying city. What's here is important to me."

"So you like books?" he asked as Emmy led him to the couch where he sat near the center. She sat at the edge, tucking her feet underneath her in the same way she did in the office.

"Yeah. Awkward child who was really interested in school and had no problem speaking her mind? Books were the only consistent friend I had in elementary school." She studied Ryan. "I bet you were super popular in high school, huh? Like prom king and shit?"

"I was over six feet tall by seventh grade but didn't add any muscle until my college coach made me eat more calories than I knew I could. I was into science and swimming and didn't know how to talk to girls at all." Ryan shuddered, remembering. "My mom has spent her entire life trying to follow fad diets and raised my sisters with the same philosophy. She didn't know how to feed me, but it's not her fault." Emmy raised her eyebrows, skeptical as usual. "You know," he said, tapping her nose, "patriarchy and everything." Emmy rolled her eyes but grinned at him. Something in his stomach flipped.

"Anyway, I was a big nerd and then grew into myself freshman year of college. Lost my virginity, all that shit, and then realized girls liked me." Ryan took another sip of his beer, trying to decide how much to press Emmy tonight. "What were you like?"

"Nerdy, anxious, abrasive, ambitious — kind of like how I am now." Ryan scoffed, and Emmy shrugged. "I know how people perceive me. But that got me to where I am today, and I'm proud of that."

"I like that woman," Ryan said, stretching his arms out, almost able to touch her.

Emmy turned more to face him. "What's your family like?" she asked. Ryan grinned. He loved his sisters, loved his parents. "I've got three sisters — two older, one younger. Jenn and Kristin are both married. Jenn's wife had twins a few years ago. Kristin's pregnant right now, and her husband is beside himself." He took another swig of beer. "Amanda does something with computers in Seattle, but the other two are in Minnesota, just like Mom and Dad."

"That must be so nice," Emmy said. Ryan didn't detect any bitterness but thought she genuinely liked the idea of his family. He tried to not let his imagination run away, how he would love to see his nephews terrorize her and his sisters embrace her.

"I'm pretty lucky," Ryan admitted. He finished his beer, then got up and set it on a table, making sure to use a coaster after Emmy cleared her throat. Heading back to the couch, he took a chance and sat closer to Emmy. He pressed his thigh into her knees and reached his arm out, his large palm spanning the back of her neck. He pressed his fingers into muscle, massaging slightly. Ryan was rewarded with a groan that emanated out of Emmy, and her hand slid across her legs to rest on his thigh. That movement caused her body to lean forward toward him, her lips close to his.

"I think I'm lucky now," she said, her breath whispering against his mouth a second before she kissed him, sliding her tongue across the seam of his lips. In a second, his mouth was open, and he was sliding his hand up her neck and into her hair. He tightened his grip slightly on her hair, tugging a bit, and Emmy moaned. She caught his lip between her teeth, biting just enough for Ryan to gasp in pleasure. Emmy's hands roved all over his body as she took control, pressing him backward on the couch, her body half lying over him. She kept pressure on his chest as she moved her lips from his mouth to his neck, kissing down until she got to his sweater.

"This damn sweater is in my way," she grunted. Smirking, she pulled back. "What I meant was aren't you too warm, Doctor Andersson?"

Ryan had never been with a woman who mentioned his PhD in bed, had been perfectly fine getting by with being known as "Ryan." But as he struggled out of his sweater with Emmy still on top of him – *difficult woman* – he realized that having Emmy call him Dr. Andersson made him immediately hard.

Work was going to be much more difficult.

Tossing his sweater and undershirt off to the side of the couch, he lay back down, and Emmy resumed her position hovering over him, her hands tracing the nips and tucks of his muscles along his shoulders and arms. "Damn, Doc," she muttered. "Why the hell have you been hiding all of this under those sheepherder sweaters?" Ryan laughed and pulled her down to him, kissing her again. Her hands pressed into his pecs, her nimble little fingers finding their way to his nipples and twisting slightly, causing a groan to come out of Ryan's mouth.

"Ha!" she said, excited about her new discovery. Her fingers kept working, twisting and turning, as she kissed down his neck and over to his shoulder, her tongue tracing a bit of muscle definition. For a moment, Ryan had gone entirely still underneath her, temporarily overwhelmed by the sensation of her taking control and holding him down. However, as Emmy began to run her fingers down lower, her nails scratching lightly over his abdomen, Ryan remembered that two could play at this game.

"Not yet," he said, pulling her up his body and gathering her hair in his fist, pulling just enough to remove her mouth from his. He kissed *her* neck this time, scraping his teeth just enough to let her know that he liked this, this balance of pleasure and pain and dominance they were playing with.

"Oh," Emmy gasped, and Ryan continued to kiss and nip his way down her neck to her collarbone.

"Now your sweater is in the way," he said, reaching down and pulling off the teal top with ease. Emmy was still straddled over his lap, and Ryan reached both of his arms around her, bending her backward slightly as he took control. It was his turn to admire her muscles, to sink his teeth into that damn pop of a tricep that had haunted him during their high ropes course all those months ago. He maneuvered her off his lap and sat her on the couch, panting and waiting, her hair an unfamiliar mess from his fingers. Her lips were bright red and swollen, and Ryan was sure his matched, as neither of them were shy about using their teeth to elevate their kiss.

Just to tease her, to frustrate, to remind Emmy that there was a bit of him that would be in charge for now, he toyed with her bra strap, snapping it against her skin, but left the garment in place, then slipped off the couch. With the way her fingers had zeroed in on his nipples, he imagined it meant hers were sensitive as well. He kissed down her stomach, ran his tongue along the top edge of her skirt that sat over her abdomen. Just before he would have typically pulled it down or slid his fingers under her skirt, he pulled back, sitting on his heels for a moment.

"Dammit, Doc!" Emmy said in frustration, wiping her bangs from her forehead. Ryan gave her a coy smile and removed his glasses, taking an absolutely absurd amount of time to fold them delicately and place them on the table next to his beer. Turning back around to Emmy, he continued to take his time sauntering back to her on the couch, loving the way she couldn't help but move, her fingers flexing and gripping the couch cushions, her toes curling with anticipation.

Ryan couldn't blame her. It felt like months of buildup were coming to fruition on this couch, the damn Yellowstone Caldera about to erupt after 640,000 years.

Easy Andersson. Stop thinking about geology when you're about to go down on Emmy for the first time. Not sexy, just weird.

"I'm just deciding my plan of attack," he said, kneeling on the floor again. Emmy took him in and impulsively tossed a pillow down at him, which bounced off his bare chest. "What the hell was that for?" he asked, confused and unsure if he was supposed to be offended or stop.

Emmy blushed slightly. "Your knees," she explained, raising her eyebrows.

Ryan grinned and settled in, adjusting himself to make his knees and painfully hard cock more comfortable. He began at Emmy's ankle, running his fingers over the thin skin there, then tracking the line of her calf muscle with his forefinger. "These damn legs," he muttered. Dropping her left leg, he picked up her right leg and performed the same gesture, letting his finger travel just a bit higher to circle her knee. Ryan set both of her legs down, wider than they had previously been, and ran his palms up the sides of her thighs, feeling the muscle flex and tense under his palms in the way he had been fantasizing about. Her skirt pushed up as he continued the upward path of his hands, giving Ryan a tantalizing peek at something light blue and lacy.

What he was about to do amounted to one of his favorite things in the world – taking a woman apart piece by piece, cataloging and archiving her reactions to him, and watching her shatter and come back together. The taste, the heat, the sounds – all of it combined for an experience that turned Ryan on almost as much as he thought it turned on his partners.

"You good?" he asked, looking up at Emmy. Where he expected her to be as turned on as he was – her gray eyes shining with sex, her cheeks flushed – he found her shy, nervous, and slightly fearful. Quickly removing his hands from her body and clasping them in his lap, he sat back.

"Emmy?"

"Huh?"

"You're not good."

"I'm fine," she said, sounding like she was trying to convince herself.

"I don't believe you," he said honestly. "It doesn't feel like you're into this or ready. That's *fine*. But I'm not going any further until I understand what's going on."

Emmy clenched her legs together, crossed her ankles, and slumped back on the couch. “I’m so sorry,” she said, pressing her palms into her eyes.

Ryan sat on the couch next to her – adjusting himself *again* – and gently pulled one of her hands from her face. “You’ve got nothing to be sorry about.” He turned her hand, kissed her palm. “What’s going on?”

34

Emmy

She hadn't planned on having this mental meltdown. The entire evening with Ryan had been wonderful, light years better than she had expected. And damn, she loved kissing and touching him. He hadn't seemed to be turned off or intimidated by her when she got a bit aggressive, as previous partners had been. He had even made his intent *very* clear that he wanted to go down on her, so point to him.

But Emmy was always a bit nervous about sex for a host of reasons, and something that Ryan had said earlier kept sticking in her brain, playing on repeat.

You don't have to lie to make me feel good.

"Uh," Emmy began, tucking her feet underneath her and pulling the pillow off the floor and holding it across her stomach. "So, I've got pretty gnarly anxiety."

Ryan nodded, still holding on to her hand. "Yeah, I know that."

"Okay, well, I also take some pretty gnarly brain medicines to balance it all out and, like, allow myself to function."

"Okay?" Ryan said, the familiar look of confusion glittering across his face. "I mean, that's fine. My sister-in-law started taking meds after she had the twins, for postpartum stuff."

"Have you ever talked to her about the meds?" He shook his head. "About any side effects?" Another head shake. Emmy took a deep breath and prepared herself to reveal one of the most embarrassing facts about herself.

"Okay, well, I love the meds, and they're necessary for me to, like, function, but one of the major side effects is the fact that it makes, well...finishing...difficult." The words spilled out quickly, like Emmy needed them out of her mouth as soon as possible. Rip the Band-Aid off about the truth, give Ryan an out, and then she could go on with her night with an item in her bedside drawer. "Like, I can't come. A lot. Most of the time," she finished with a bang. *Or not.*

"Hmm," Ryan said, dropping her hand and running a hand through his hair. Emmy had seen this gesture before, when they were in meetings and he was tossing around ideas with his fellow scientists. "Can I ask a few follow-up questions?"

Emmy was a bit stunned. "You're not leaving?"

"Why the fuck would I leave?" he said, pulling a face. "It's not like you said a pterodactyl is a dinosaur or something horrible." Emmy tried to follow his train of thought but got lost. He grimaced and continued. "Does it still feel good?"

"What?"

"Like if I were to go down on you, and you didn't come, would it feel good?"

Emmy had never appreciated a scientific mind as much as she did right now. "I mean, yeah. I like the connection with someone else. It can be frustrating as hell when you build and build and build and never go anywhere, but I can always take care of it on my own later." Ryan frowned, and Emmy put a mental pin in the conversation about introducing her favorite silicone devices for now.

"Em," he said, leaning over to her and pressing a kiss against the hollow at the base of her throat. "You do know what I have a PhD in, right?"

She scoffed. This, now? "Yes, Doc. Some boring old dinosaur shit. Literally." Any other smart-ass remarks were swept away when Ryan sucked hard below her collarbone.

"I'm a geologist by training, my lovely historian. My research takes place over thousands of years." He tugged the pillow away, set in on the floor next to him. "Ages." He kneeled back down to where he had been previously. "Eons. Geologic time." Emmy relaxed back on the couch again and tentatively uncrossed her ankles. "I'm a patient man, Em. I can take my time. Plus," he shrugged in a faux casual way, then smirked at her, "I can't fucking wait to go down on you."

Emmy gasped, and he palmed her knees, opening them up again. *Just one more thing I have to say*. "And please promise me that you'll stop if you get bored or hate it." AnxietyBrain, that fucking bitch, had a way of always popping in at the most inconvenient times.

Ryan, who was already occupied with pushing her skirt up over her hips, bunching the corduroy around her waist, grunted his acknowledgment. Emmy breathed out shakily as Ryan hooked his fingers around the waistband of her panties — she had picked out a pair of her favorites today in case the date went well — and pulled them down around her ankles, then off her feet, taking an extra moment to caress the top of her foot, sending a new shiver up her leg and right to her clit.

Oh.

Ryan placed one of his hands on her, spreading his fingers wide in the space underneath her belly button. His other hand gripped her thigh, spread her wider to him, before he leaned in and pressed his face to her. He took a moment, breathed her in, then licked her in long, slow strokes. Eventually, he slid his fingers down and was able to spread her wider. Lips. Tongue. Teeth.

Emmy's anxiety had started to dissipate, replaced by a low boil of arousal that thrummed through her blood. "Fuck, Ry," she hissed as he found an especially sensitive spot.

He pulled back enough to grab a gulp of air and to ask *soft or hard*, barely even waiting a second for her to respond.

"Hard," Emmy moaned, reaching down and running her fingers through his hair, gripping tight and pulling herself closer to him, beginning to twist her hips.

Someone somewhere needed to be thanked for telling Ryan what to do between a woman's legs. Instead of bouncing between various positions and techniques,

Ryan seemed to pay attention to what worked for *Emmy*. He found the side of her clit that was most sensitive and stayed there, flicking his tongue up and down in a perfect rhythm. He only varied his pressure and tempo to occasionally scrape his teeth against her clit.

It took a while – Emmy wasn't going to lie about that – and she eventually added her own hands to her nipples to heighten the sensation that was building low in her belly. Finally, she held her breath and felt her insides pull into a vacuum, hold, then explode throughout her body, sizzling all over her skin.

Ryan pulled back, running one hand down her calf in a soothing gesture, wiping his mouth on the back of his other hand. "Yeah?" he asked, that boyish grin blossoming on his face again as Emmy nodded her head frantically, breathing heavily. Emmy got the sense that if he was alone, he would have pumped his fist in the air, just like he had done after winning a race in the pool.

"Yeah," she whispered, shoving off her bra that she had pushed down as she approached her orgasm. "Yeah, really fucking great, Doc." She was so damn grateful that Ryan had not freaked out a million times this evening – not when she got rough, not when she told him about her meds, not when she had ground her hips into his face, his nose nudging her clit.

She wanted to do the same for him. Needed to. Her blood still burned hot, and she needed to make this heat, this energy, go somewhere.

Emmy stood up, unzipping her skirt that was bunched over her hips and stepping out of it, totally naked in front of Ryan. She watched his reactions as his eyes scanned her body, followed the small curve of her breasts, bounced between her arms and her hips, finally landing between her legs, which she knew still glistened with her pleasure. She straddled his hips on the floor, her knees hugging his waist, his erection pressing up.

"Dr. Andersson," she said, having seen the way his eyes sparked when she used his formal title before. "You look like you're in need of some attention yourself." She leaned over him, wrapped her hands around his wrists and guided his hands above his head, pinning him down. Obviously, Ryan probably had a good seventy-five pounds on her and could have flipped her without breaking a sweat, but she also got the sense that he liked occasionally giving up control – but only if Emmy worked for it. They had more in common than she had thought before, she realized, smiling to herself.

Ryan's obliques stretched and rippled as he kept his arms above his head, eyes almost a radioactive green as he watched Emmy hover above him. Keeping one hand spread across his wrists, she leaned down and ran her tongue along his neck. The slightly salty taste mixed with the faint chemical tang of chlorine that seemed to always linger on his skin. She felt the groan rumble through his throat as she pressed her mouth to it, then moved herself down lower, having to reluctantly let go of his hands. He had already undone his belt and zipper, so Emmy took his pants and boxer briefs off as she continued to slide herself down.

Reaching his hip bones, she ran her teeth along the V of muscle that had haunted her since she saw him at the pool, saw how it shot right to his dick. Laughing to herself, she peered up at Ryan, who had crossed his hands under his head and was looking down at her.

"Expecting something, Professor?" she teased. He raised his eyebrows, affected that fake shrug another time.

"Oh, nothing," he replied, his pulse thrumming in his throat betraying his casual attitude toward Emmy's proximity to his dick.

Tit for tat, Doc. Mostly tit.

"Okay," she replied nonchalantly. She sat back and stretched her arms behind her, popping her triceps and pressing her breasts out. Then she rolled back down and began to trace light patterns over his abs with the edge of her fingernail, loving the way the muscles contracted and flexed beneath her touch. She watched his chest start to rise and fall more quickly, though he kept his face stoic. It had been so long since she had a partner to play with like this.

Emmy wrapped her palm around the base of his cock, pressing it up, then began to lightly kiss the shaft, occasionally slipping her tongue out to give it a little lick. Tiny kisses, just a tease, up and down, her hand occasionally squeezing to apply pressure. Covering all the skin, though Emmy avoided the sensitive head, just to drive him wild.

"Em," he gritted out. She looked up from underneath her lashes, trying to look innocent even though her lips were pressed to an especially prominent vein.

"Yes?"

"What are you doing?" Ryan's jaw pulsed, his throat muscles tight as he swallowed, his breathing shallow.

"Oh, nothing," she said, mimicking what he had said earlier. Another light kiss, a flutter of her lashes as she held his gaze.

"Fuck, woman," he panted. "You're killing me."

"Oh?"

"*Please.*" It was that word that unlocked something in Emmy. This man was so polished, so organized, with his sweaters and iPad and scientific papers, his degrees and his protocols. But here he was, naked on her floor and begging after he had taken her apart with scientific precision.

"Fine." She sighed dramatically, then got to work, sucking and pulling and using her tongue in all the delicious ways that Phoebe had told her about from articles and blogs she read. Wet, slick, sliding, her lips pulling, she heard Ryan whisper "*fuck*" and she looked up to find him lifted up on his elbows, watching her with those emerald eyes again.

"Close," he warned, his voice warbling. Emmy moaned her affirmation around him, then he jerked and swore and came into her mouth. Emmy breathed through her nose, continuing to suck him through the aftershocks, then closed her lips and swallowed. She slid up to the couch and took a sip of her gin and tonic to chase away the aftertaste.

Emmy tucked her feet under her on the couch and watched Ryan on the floor. He was taking deep breaths, sweat shimmering deliciously along the ridges of his torso. "You good, Doc?" she called, taking another sip.

"Nope," he replied, rolling onto his stomach on her carpet. Ass *like a Greek statue*. "I'm done for." He lifted his head and looked up at her with that playful grin that she had only recently begun to cherish. "Will you make a diorama out of my body?"

"I'm going to put you into the back of a collection where no one will find you and you'll get dusty. I'm not even going to put you into the database," Emmy said. Ryan reached over and found the pillow that he had kneeled on, then threw it up at Emmy.

"Oh, hush," he said, his Minnesota accent coming through. For a moment, they locked eyes and just looked at each other, and Emmy knew that her own small smile mirrored the one that was on Ryan's face, his eyes now a calmer, deeper forest green.

"Are you staying?" she asked on a whisper, holding the pillow close.

"I want to, but I can't," he replied, his chin on his hands. "I have an early family Zoom call with my sisters and my parents." A slight blush stained his cheeks, but Emmy felt her own heart give an extra *thump* as Ryan smiled, thinking about his family.

"Okay, that's so cute I feel ill, so you can leave now." He looked up at her, and she gave him a small wink. "See you soon?"

He gathered his clothes, put his beer bottle in the recycling, put his glasses back on. Emmy had grabbed a blanket from the arm of the couch and wrapped it around herself, unwilling to put clothes back on just yet. When Ryan had all his belongings, he walked over to her on the couch, kissed her lightly on the lips, and whispered. "See you as soon as I can."

35

Ryan

"Come on, you damn slide. Focus so I can see what you are," Ryan said to his microscope the following Monday. He twiddled with a knob on the side. Looked again. Adjusted. Looked. Repeated ad nauseam. "You son of a bitch piece of shit
—"

"Talking to yourself, Doc?" he slid his chair back quickly and put his glasses back on his nose. Turning around, he saw Emmy, a half smirk on her lips, leaning against the doorframe. She was dressed in a deep red sweater, paired with loose plaid pants and chunky black shoes, a bit of holly on a headband. Surprisingly festive, this woman.

"It's a habit I picked up from this historian I'm around all the time," he said, grinning at her. She had never come down to the collections before, had never seen his lab. This had to be a good sign, right?

"Ah," she said, pushing off the doorframe and sauntering over. "She sounds horrible." She placed her hands on the back of his chair, hovering over him.

"Literally the worst," he said, leaning back and looking up at her. She was still smirking, leaning down and keeping her lips just a centimeter away from his.

She pulled away suddenly, just as Ryan was about to stretch his neck to press his lips to hers. "What do you do down here, anyway?" Emmy made a show of walking around his lab, poking around through papers and specimens.

"Science," he replied, willing his definitely not-workplace-appropriate boner to go down. *Think about your research. That's not sexy.* A few deep breaths, and he had lost Emmy. He quickly searched for her and found her leaning over one of the lab tables to look at specimens, her ass on display.

Well, so much for *that* specimen going away.

"Do you want to see something cool?" he said, wincing at how much he sounded like a little boy who wanted to show his crush a thing he found on the playground. Emmy turned around and let her eyes dance over his body, and he flushed as she saw the state of his pants.

"There's a joke there about bones and rock-hard things, but I'm too lazy to make it," she said, grinning.

"Stop your sass," he replied, walking into another room that held their cabinets. Most of their collection were small specimens held in drawers that were pulled out to show the artifacts, and Ryan walked down a darkened aisle until he found the one he had looked up a few weeks ago in a forgotten attempt to impress Emmy. He pulled out a drawer that he had marked with a blue Post-it and held up a tiny impression fossil.

"What's this?" Emmy said, leaning over to peer at the fossil. Her question held none of the sarcasm, none of her usual inclination to make a joke at his expense. She was interested.

"It's a crinoid. An impression of an ancient marine animal," Ryan explained.

"Can I touch it?" she said, lifting her hand up, keeping it a few centimeters away from the fossil.

Ryan chuckled. "It's thousands of years old. It's not going to break." Emmy murmured some smart-ass comment about rocks that he couldn't quite catch but reached out one finger. Her nail was painted a deep green and wasn't chipped for a change. He suppressed another groan as she delicately ran the tip of her finger over the impression, chewing on her lip as she took in the dips and grooves of the stone.

"Want to know something else about it?"

Her eyes glimmered. "I want to know everything." *I know. That's what I adore about you.*

"This fossil isn't just any fossil."

"How so?"

"It was collected by a very special paleontologist."

"Who was he?" Ryan loved teasing Emmy, watching the anticipation and excitement radiate out of her body.

"*Tsk, tsk, tsk,*" he said, pulling the fossil away from her wandering hand, causing her to frown.

"What did I do?"

"Assumed, and you know what that means —"

"Do not go all folksy on me now, Ryan."

"It wasn't a *he* paleontologist. It was a *she* paleontologist." He grinned at her, the cheesiest smile he could muster, and he could feel her resisting the urge to roll her eyes again. Without talking, she took the small fossil from his hand and placed it in her own palm, looking at it carefully.

"Tell me about her." Her voice was softer now.

"Her name was Winifred Goldring, and she was the first woman to be named a state paleontologist in the US." Ryan loved teaching about science and missed the classes he had assisted with during graduate school. "She did most of her work in New York, but we somehow have a few of the items she collected here." He grew bashful, suddenly embarrassed at his eagerness. Quieting his voice, he added, "I thought you'd like it."

Emmy was silent for a few beats, continuing to trace her finger over the impression in the stone. "This is what I love about collections, about museums. If you didn't tell me that, I'd know that this was old, but adding the context – *the history* – adds that other level. To know that a woman was making her own way in science, making discoveries at a time when she was barely allowed to know herself. Holding this is unlike anything else. That's why exhibitions are so special. We have the ability to provide this insight to anyone who comes to the museum." She looked up at him, finally meeting his eyes, hers glittering with excitement.

"You said *we*," Ryan said.

"I guess I did." A smile. Ryan and Emmy chatted about the specimen, about the history of women in science, about the fact that "She Sells Seashells (by the Sea Shore)" was based on a real woman. After a few minutes, Ryan took the fossil back from a reluctant Emmy and put it away.

"Remember when you followed me to the archives that one day?" Emmy asked, leaning back against the shelving unit. Ryan hummed his acknowledgment as he slid the drawer closed, then turned around to look at her. Her hair was still down – rare for Emmy this late in the day – and her eyes sparkled almost silver in the dim light of the collection. "I thought you were going to kiss me."

"I wanted to," he said, honestly. "Though I can't imagine that you would have taken it well."

Emmy's eyes grew sharp, her lips twisting. "Wanna try again?"

Did he want to try again? Ryan wanted to try everything with Emmy, wanted to ask her what she wanted to try and have her make *those sounds* again and then have her pull the same sounds out of him. Before he could scramble those thoughts into a coherent sentence, Emmy asked another question, pressing her hips forward a touch. "Does anyone come down here?"

"Just me, usually. And our grad students and Satya. But she's off today, and no one is scheduled to work today and –"

"Great," Emmy said, staying exactly in her same position. His collection, his control?

"Oh, like now?" he said, smirking.

Emmy crossed her arms. "Yeah, Doc. Like now." Ryan crowded her against the collections shelves, placed his hands over her head, and leaned down, kissed her neck.

"Oh." Another kiss. "Okay." A bite. "I think I can make that work."

"Let me get my planner," she said, slipping her hands through his hair and scratching his scalp in a way he *really* loved. She held his head in place as he worked the space just below her neckline with his lips and tongue, making a delightful set of tiny moans.

"Shh," Ryan said, lifting his head up and silencing her with a nip to her mouth.

"There are a lot of fossils here I can use as weapons," she said against his lips, but Ryan could feel that smirk.

"You are always threatening me," he said, wrapping his hands around her wrists and holding them above her head. "One of these days, I'm going to do something about that."

"I'm hoping," she said, and then the conversation ended for a while as they battled through their kiss, their hands tangled above her head. Ryan let go of Emmy's hands to slide them down the sides of her body, to lift the hem of her sweater up and run his hands over her smooth stomach to the lower edge of her bra, noticing the way that she wrapped her own arms around his and pulled him closer to her.

Ryan was hard, and his length rubbed against Emmy's center. He mentally cringed at first, but when he realized Emmy noticed, when he felt her take a sharp intake of breath, he took a chance and pressed himself even more firmly against her. As usual, she one-upped him by lifting her leg up slightly and wrapping it around his hip.

"God, Em," he whispered, reaching a hand down and hauling her thigh closer to his body. She had begun to writhe beneath him, moving her hips in a rhythmic thrust against him. He took the shell of her ear between his teeth, bit gently, then asked, "You like that?" She pursed her lips, gave a smug smile that let him know she wouldn't admit it easily. He pressed into her again, grinding his hardness into her. "Yeah, you do." Another smirk. "Are you wet, Em?"

"Why don't you find out?" she hissed as they found a quicker tempo.

"God *damn*," he muttered, kissing her again, sliding his hand that was on her ribs up over her bra and pulling the cup down, pinching her nipple. "Fine, you vixen." He dropped her leg and cupped her outside her pants, gripping.

"In my pants, Doc," she panted. Ryan had just undone the top button, ready to slip his fingers down, when they both froze at the sound of a door opening. Footsteps.

"Shush," he whispered.

"You shush," she hissed back.

"You are not shushing!"

"Well, neither are you." They waited, bickering back and forth in hushed tones until the footsteps receded and the lab door shut again. Ryan slid his hand over Emmy's smooth stomach, grabbed her hip. He pressed his forehead against hers and looked down at her. Her eyes were clenched shut, and she was shaking with suppressed laughter, so infectious that Ryan couldn't help but join her.

"What are we, seventeen?" he asked her.

"What were you doing in high school?" she asked through her laughs.

"Not this," he replied, pressing his hips back into her. "You?"

"I would have somehow spent even more time in the library if this was a possibility." Emmy took a deep breath, reaching under her shirt to adjust her bra back into position. "I guess that's a sign from the Museum Powers That Be that we should go back to work, huh?"

Ryan put on an exaggerated thinking face.

"What?"

"I'm trying to think of some famous curator from history who would be okay with continuing this, but I'm coming up with a blank." He kissed her forehead. "Though I'm sure *Jurassic Park* was full of people sneaking off to canoodle in dark corners."

Emmy peeked down the aisle of the cabinets, then turned around. "Did you just say *canoodle*?"

"It's a perfectly valid word," he said, taking her by the arm and leading her out into the halogen-lit lab. He couldn't stop touching her, especially when they were here and alone and he was still so worked up. "What are you doing tonight?"

"I've got plans," Emmy said, grimacing. "Jeremy and I have a standing monthly date at the teahouse." She chewed her lips for a second, thinking. "I'm supposed to go hiking with Phoebe this weekend, so you could join us?"

"How about we go to trivia this Wednesday?" Ryan suggested, not wanting to wait until the weekend to spend time with her outside of work.

"Fine," she said, then her eyes sparkled. *Wicked woman.* "I propose that we each play individually, though. Head-to-head." She wiggled her body, her eyebrows disappearing into her bangs.

"Fine, Ms. Bonaire. I'm gonna start studying tonight," he replied. "Brush up on my presidents and the cabinet secretaries."

"Snore," she replied, rolling her eyes. "Everyone knows the key to bar trivia is obscure historical facts and eighties music." She adjusted her top one more time, then grinned at him. "See you in the office tomorrow, Doc." And with that, she was gone.

36

Emmy

Ryan had offered to pick her up for trivia, but Emmy still wasn't ready for that step. If she took the bus, she'd have an out at the end of the night. Yeah, of course she could always call an Uber, but she felt like she was on this precipice with Ryan, and one wrong — or right — move could have her falling faster than she anticipated.

Better to make sure there was some kind of cushion at the bottom for when she inevitably tripped.

Walking into the brewery, she found Flo behind the bar and chatted about her upcoming brews and the fact that the brewery was doing extremely well. So well, in fact, that she was thinking of hiring an assistant brewer for the first time. Emmy mentioned that she could connect Flo with the brewery certificate program on campus, but Flo shook her head and laughed.

"I don't trust people with too much education," she said.

"I can see that," Emmy said. Flo shot her a look.

"I hear that you've been spending time with someone with quite a lot of education."

Emmy felt her face flush. "Now, where would you get an idea like that?"

"I knew you'd beat me here!" Ryan had perfect timing. He came up behind her at the bar and slipped his arm around her hips.

"It's not the only thing I'm going to beat you at," she said, turning in her stool to face him. He leaned down and pressed a sweet kiss to her lips.

"You wish, Em. You wish."

"Hello, Ryan," Flo said, pointedly.

"Hey, Flo!" He smiled at her, to which she rolled her eyes. Emmy knew she liked Flo for a reason. "Can I have the IPA you just put on tap?" He turned to Emmy. "You drink a stout here, right?" She nodded, once again impressed by the way Ryan picked up on tiny preferences she had. They got their beers, then found a table on the side of the brewery and both pulled out their phones to log on to the trivia website.

Emmy entered in her usual solo team name, logged on, then looked at the list of team names. She looked up at Ryan, a skeptical purse to her lips. "Really?"

Ryan grinned at her. "I don't know what you're talking about."

"Doctor DinoSwimmer? That's so corny."

"It's also my username on all my social media," he reached over and tapped her phone. "So now you can follow me." Emmy had already found Ryan's Instagram, of course, but now she clicked to the app and followed him.

He got a notification on his phone, then let out that laugh — the one she was pretty sure began in his toes and resonated through his big body. "ThatHistoryBitch?" Emmy grinned back at him while he shook his head, took another sip of beer. "You're too much."

"Nah, I'm just enough."

"Happy trivia night!" Foster's voice rang out throughout the brewery, and Emmy pulled her phone away from Ryan.

"No cheating," she said, fixing him with a steely gaze.

"Wouldn't dream of it," he said, then leaned across the table, his lips close to hers. "I don't need to."

"If I win, you have to go on a historic tour of the mine outside of town with me."

Ryan made a pained face. "If I win, you have to teach me how to ski," he replied.

"As if."

"It's on, Stout."

"Actually the worst nickname you've come up with so far."

They were evenly matched through the first six rounds, with Ryan having a significant advantage in the sports round, and Emmy pulling ahead after a round on the Brontë sisters. Round seven took place off phones, with every team trying to complete a word puzzle on a piece of paper the fastest and run it to Foster. Emmy finished a few seconds before Ryan and was jogging to Foster when Ryan came behind her, grabbed her by the waist with both arms, spun her around, and submitted his paper first.

"Foul!" she called. "Red flag! Penalty! Error! Sports Terms!"

"Emmy, if you can tell me what sport they use a red flag in, I'll forfeit this round." He smirked at her, his chest heaving slightly from the effort he put into getting his answers in first.

"Uh," she sputtered. "Soccer?"

Foster made a buzzer sound. "Incorrect, Em! This round goes to Ryan." He pumped his fist, to which Emmy rolled her eyes and flipped him off, but she couldn't help the grin that spread across her face as they walked back to the table. Right before she sat down, Ryan smacked her ass lightly.

"Doc!"

He stuck his tongue out at her in reply.

Emmy took round eight, which was on classic rom-com movies, though Ryan complained that he should know these because he had to watch so many with his sisters. Round nine was on geology, and Emmy was shouting at Foster that this was rigged and unfair. She was silent, though, when he announced round ten as Colorado history.

"Did you tell him we were coming?" Emmy asked after they had submitted their final answers.

"I may have mentioned something," he said, finishing his beer and licking his lips. Emmy tilted her head, took in this tall scientist with his blond curls and wide smile, and felt a wave of comfort fall over her. Getting up, she walked across the table, threaded her fingers through his hair, and kissed him.

"What was that for?" Ryan asked after she had pulled away and returned to her seat.

"Nothing." She shrugged. "Just wanted to."

"Em, I wanted to ask —" But he was interrupted by Foster.

"Final results!" he called, looking over at Ryan and Emmy's table.

"Get ready to learn about silver mining, Doc," Emmy whispered.

"Get ready to turn me into Picabo Street," he replied.

"It's a tie!" Foster said. "I need the two teams of," and then Foster guffawed, "the Fresh Princess of Bonaire and Doctor DinoSwimmer to come up to the front for a tiebreaker."

They made their way to the front of the brewery, where Foster was grinning at them both. He pulled the microphone away from his mouth. "When did you start dating?"

Were they dating? Were they exclusive? Should they talk about that? Emmy's mind started to spiral, and Ryan picked up on it, because he shot Foster a look and said, "Let's worry about the tiebreaker."

Coughing his skepticism, Foster read the tiebreaker question:

"What was the name of the first cloned animal?"

Emmy drew a blank, but she saw Ryan's eyes flash emerald.

"Dolly!" he yelled.

37

Ryan

"Dolly!" he cried. "The sheep was named Dolly because they used DNA from a mammary gland!" He looked over at Emmy, who seemed to be equal parts frustrated and impressed.

"You only knew that because it involved boobs," she muttered, a smirk on her face.

Ryan shrugged. "Doesn't matter how I know it. I still win." He gave a pointed look at Emmy's chest, to which she scoffed and crossed her arms. Joke was on her, because that position only served to emphasize her breasts even more. *God, she's so beautiful.*

"Congrats to Doctor DinoSwimmer!" Foster said, interrupting their stare off. Emmy gave a half-hearted golf clap as Ryan took a dramatic bow, though no one in the brewery was paying attention to them at all. He followed her back to their table to finish their beers.

"So when are we going skiing?" he asked, putting his chin in his hands and batting his lashes at Emmy. "I'm thinking of buying one of those obnoxious eighties-style snowsuits for the occasion."

She looked at him over the top of her beer glass as she took a sip. "Please," Emmy said. "If you get off the bunny hill, I'll be impressed."

"Mmm, *get off*," he teased.

"Who's getting off?" Foster said, walking to their table. "Is it me? Have you finally found me a girlfriend?"

"That's impossible," Ryan quipped. "We'll have solar powered cars before that happens." Emmy rolled her eyes and whispered *nerd.*

"It seems you've found yourself one," Foster said, his eyes flicking between Ryan and Emmy. *Shut the fuck up, Foster.* Ryan wished he could telepathically let his friend know to not say this, not to push, not when he wasn't sure where this was going and had begun to tentatively let himself hope.

As Emmy excused herself to the bathroom, Foster eyed Ryan with a skeptical glare that bordered on threatening. "Having a hard time getting your new coworker to like you, are we?"

Ryan blushed, then mumbled, "Okay, well, she does seem to like me a little."

"Yeah, *that* much was obvious," Foster gave a dry laugh. "I'm surprised you didn't follow her into the bathroom."

"Gross," Ryan said. *What if that's what she wanted? What if I'm taking it too slow? Wait, I already ate her out. That's not slow. Did I move too fast?* Foster started a sentence, then stopped. Started again, then stopped. Ryan pushed his glasses into his hair. "Spit it out, dude. It's clear you want to say something, so go ahead. You don't need to tell me she's out of my league, because I'm well aware of that scientific fact."

Foster gave another wry chuckle, then grew serious. "All I'm gonna say is that she seems really into you, and you're obviously into her and — well, I know Emmy, and she loves Vanberg. So, what I'm asking is, does she know?"

Fuck.

"Know what?" Emmy said, returning to the table, drying her hands on her pants, her face still a bit flushed.

"Know that Ryan here held the record for losing three tiebreakers three weeks in a row," Foster said, easily deflecting from what he had been about to discuss with Ryan.

Emmy pursed her lips, tilted her head to the side. "Let me guess. The topics were about the Brontë sisters? Or Austen?"

"I read *Wuthering Heights*!" he argued, though Emmy continued to pin him with her steel gaze. "Well, I read the SparkNotes." She stared, unconvinced. "Okay, I had my sister read the SparkNotes."

"I knew it." She sighed in a faux-dramatic way. "How can I ever bond with you over what a sad piece of shit Heathcliff was?"

"I've read it," Foster said unhelpfully. Ryan almost growled at the man, who gave a wide grin and said good night.

38

Emmy

"You do know it was a special kind of torture to follow your ass the entire way up the mountain, right?" Ryan said from behind her on the steps that Saturday evening. The sun had just begun to set on their drive back from the hike outside of Boulder, and Ryan and Emmy had dipped out of Phoebe's invite to dinner. Emmy snorted a laugh as she unlocked her door and kicked off her shoes in the
doorway.

"You know it's a special kind of torture to share a car with you after you've been hiking?" Emmy shot back, grabbing a glass of water and gulping it down quickly.

"You're sweaty, too," he said, stealing the glass of water out of her hand and taking a gulp. Emmy felt fire sizzle through her veins and locked eyes with Ryan.

"Hey, Doc?"

"Yeah?"

"Wanna get clean?"

"I mean, I can head home, and we could meet up later and —" Ryan looked down at her and saw the way she pulled her lip into her mouth, the way her eyes suggestively flipped down to his waist. “Oh.”

“Yeah. *Oh*,” she replied sarcastically.

It took just over two seconds, it seemed, for Ryan’s body to catch up with his brain, but when it did, he surged forward and wrapped his arms around Emmy, slanting his mouth over hers and plunging his tongue into her mouth.

“Oh,” she breathed against his neck, “you understand now.” She couldn’t help but to prod him and rile him up.

“Yeah” was all Ryan could grit out as she snuck her hand down between them and palmed the bulge in his shorts.

“Get your fucking clothes off,” she said, tearing her own shirt off and struggling to get her sweaty sports bra off at the same time. Ryan’s big palms came under hers and helped to urge off the garment, the clothes landing on the floor with a *plop*. “Not mine,” she said, sliding her hands under his shirt. “Yours.” They grappled with each other as Emmy led him toward the bathroom, leaving a trail of socks, shorts, leggings, and underwear behind them.

Emmy reached in and flipped the shower on, then opened the curtain and stepped in, letting the hot water sear her skin, a moan escaping her mouth. She opened her eyes to find Ryan watching her from outside the shower, his hand absentmindedly stroking his cock. She indicated it with her chin and said, “Hey, that’s my job.”

“You should see yourself,” he hissed.

“Get in here with me,” she demanded.

“I’m too big.”

"I think I'll be the judge of that," she said, pursing her lips. Ryan laughed, then stepped over the edge of the tub, crowding her in the shower.

"Let's try," she said, shuffling around to the back, angling Ryan under the water at the same time he said, "What if I?" Ryan was now under the water, but that meant Emmy only got the occasional splash of water that bounced off him, her blood turning to ice.

"I'm cold!" she whined.

"Okay, you go under the water," Ryan said, attempting to slide past her but letting out a shrill shriek when his ass touched the shower curtain. Emmy sighed in relief when she was under the water but laughed as Ryan's nipples hardened with him out of the water.

Okay. So Emmy was tall, and her apartment shower wasn't meant for two tall people. Maybe Ryan was right that this thing wouldn't work. Shower sex was always better on video than in reality.

"So," she said awkwardly as she soaped her hair with shampoo, "I'm gonna attempt to take the world's fastest shower, then you'll shower, and then we'll meet in my room."

"Thank god," Ryan said, his teeth almost chattering. "I've done polar plunges that are warmer than this bathroom."

"Oh, do you have a sauna?" Emmy asked, rinsing out her shampoo and running conditioner through her hair. "I forgot I was in the presence of royalty."

"You can find out when we go to my house next time," he said, reaching out to squeeze her ass cheek when Emmy bent over to grab her soap.

"Easy, Doc," she said, swiping a washcloth over her breasts, loving the way Ryan's eyes followed the soapy trail over her body.

"Hurry," he whined. "My balls are inverting."

"Super sexy," Emmy said, her eyes flicking down to check him out. *Everything looks fine*, she thought, Ryan's cock still pointing straight up at attention. One final rinse, then she stepped out of the shower, letting Ryan know that she left an extra towel out for him.

Emmy wrapped her hair in a towel, then her body in another, and sprinted to her bedroom, almost sliding across the tile floor. She tossed off her towel and slipped under her blanket, wrapping it around her body, trying to build heat.

It felt like a million years that Ryan was in the shower, Emmy trying to warm up her legs by rubbing them together. Her arousal had dimmed slightly with the logistics of failed shower sex, but the anticipation was currently killing her. Finally — *finally* — Ryan appeared in her doorway, the towel slung low on his hips.

"It's unfair, you know," she said conversationally, her eyes tracking all over his damp body.

"What's unfair?" he asked, walking around the bed to the empty side. Emmy slithered over, under the covers still, and slipped a hand out of the blankets to indicate Ryan's torso.

"This swimmer business," she said, inching her fingers to the edge of his towel. She grabbed and tugged and was rewarded when the towel fell to the ground.

"You like it," Ryan said, shrugging as he pulled back the covers all at once.

"Nah."

"Yeah," he whispered, covering Emmy's body with his and kissing her deeply. She loved being this close to him, loved the way the little bit of water on their skin allowed their bodies to slide against one another, building heat and wetness between her legs. Ryan's hand tugged her towel off her head, and he tossed it aside, then ran that same hand down to her breasts, rolling her nipple between his fingers.

"Harder," she hissed, and Ryan's fingers squeezed, followed quickly by his mouth, teeth grazing the sensitive bud. "Fuck yes," she cried as he moved to the other breast with his lips, his hand sliding lower and lower to press into Emmy's heat.

"God, you're fucking wet," he muttered in her ear, sending shivers cascading down her spine. "It's gonna feel so good when I'm in you." Ryan pressed a finger inside her, deep and solid.

"Aren't you in me now?" she teased, clenching around him.

"Semantics," he replied, adding a second finger. Emmy pulled his face back up to hers and kissed him, this time taking over control and thrusting her hips against his hand. Something was building, but it was far away, and she gave a frustrated grunt into Ryan's mouth. "Yeah, Em?"

"Fuck me," she said, somewhere between a demand and a plea.

"No argument," he replied, pulling his hand away from her, leaving her temporarily empty and clenching. Fire burned through her as he slid his fingers into his mouth, sucking, then pressed one to Emmy's lips. She nipped at the pad of his forefinger in reply. Ryan groaned, closing his eyes for a moment like he was in pain. "Do you have a condom? If not, I've got some in the car." Emmy was crawling over him before he finished the sentence, draping her body across Ryan's as she dug in the drawer under her bed for the foil packets she had tossed in there. Grabbing a handful, she threw them over her shoulder at Ryan.

"You think I'm gonna need all of these?" he said, rubbing her ass that was pressed up in the air.

"I won't complain," she said, squirming. Ryan spread his palm over one cheek, and she moved more, getting Ryan to gently smack her ass. *Exactly*, she thought, doing it again.

"You want that?" Ryan said, disbelief sliding into his voice.

"I don't mind it," she said, and Ryan responded by slapping her ass a bit harder. "C'mon Doc, show me what you can do," Ryan hit harder, and Emmy moaned. "There it is." Ryan flipped her over quickly, then slid the condom on. He caged her with his arms and big body, dropping his hips between her legs. She was wet, he was ready, and it took an instant for him to slide inside, matching groans leaving their mouths.

"God damn, Em," he said, pressing his hips forward. Emmy pressed back, but something in the back of her mind started to twitch. It felt good, yeah. She loved the feeling of Ryan in her, stretching her, the way he panted and whispered above her. He even slid a hand between them and pressed his fingers to her clit, finding the rhythm that matched the press of his body that he clearly remembered from before. He kept thrusting but would occasionally pull back, waiting for Emmy to catch up.

Fuck.

Fuck. She wasn't going to come.

The first time Ryan fucking Andersson had his dick in her — the thing she had been craving for months — and her stupid fucking mind wouldn't let her enjoy this. Emmy tried to push the thought out of her head, tried to push her focus to the way their bodies moved, the clench of Ryan's muscles, the grunts that were pushed out of his mouth. However, Ryan — damn him, the observant scientist that he was — started to notice.

Still inside her, he slowed down, brushed her wet hair out of her face. "Em?"

"Yeah?" she said, pressing her hips up.

"Em, stop," he said, cupping her jaw in his hand. She stilled her hips, and he slipped out of her, rolled to the side. "What's going on? What can I do differently? Doggy style? You on top?"

Emmy's eyes stung and she blinked quickly. "It's – it's not you. I just know I'm not going to come, and it's fine. Get back on me, and we'll go."

"Em," Ryan said, his eyes glittering a spring green. "I am not going to use your body that way."

"I'm consenting!"

"Nope," he said, running a hand down her side. "What have you done in the past?"

"Faked it," she spat back. "I'm a great actor."

"You better not fake it with me," he said, squeezing her hip.

"Make me come," she retorted, then regretted it. "Except you can't because I'm broken!"

"Not broken." Ryan slid the condom off, tossed it in a wastebasket.

"You're not even hard right now!" she said, looking down.

"A minor detail, Em," he said, a soft smile on his face. He kissed her neck. "How do you get off alone?"

"Vibrator," she replied immediately.

"Not your hands?"

"Nah, it doesn't provide enough stimulation," Emmy said, pulling a pillow over her face. "Like it feels good, but like, I'm never going to get off from just fingers."

Ryan looked puzzled. "But, uh...but last time..."

"Yeah, you've got a killer mouth," she said, "but even that's not gonna do it all the time." She groaned again. Here was where the other shoe dropped, here was where Ryan left and got frustrated at how her brain and body didn't communicate with each other.

Ryan took a moment and sat back on his heels, and Emmy looked him over. He was so fucking sexy. Long lines and just enough muscle, lean torso and quads she wanted to wrap her arms around. She felt embarrassed and exhausted, and she'd never been less sexy in her entire life.

"I'm sorry. You can go. It's fine," Emmy said, willing her eyes to keep the tears away until he left. The last thing she needed on top of all of this was for Ryan to see her *cry*. She rolled over to the side and hugged that pillow to her chest. *Breathe.*

"Em, why would I leave?"

"Because we're not having sex?"

"Okay?" She felt him slide under the blankets and curl his body around hers. "We can just, I dunno, *be*."

"Just be?"

"Yeah." One of his big arms wrapped around her, and he began to run his fingers up and down her arm, following the dips of her arm muscles. "We can just be."

"I can try that," she whispered into the sheets, and Emmy felt Ryan let out a small chuckle behind her.

"Tell me about something," he said.

"Why?"

"Because I know your brain is going, and I want to distract you." He was always so honest, never really played his cards close to the chest. He probably let his nephews win at every single game they played. She let out a big sigh, feeling her body decompress just a bit. "There we go," Ryan said into her hair. "Tell me about your thesis."

"You mean the dusty thing on my shelf that exactly five people have read? And I don't count Phoebe, because I'm pretty sure she skimmed it to make me feel better." At that, Ryan let out a full belly laugh behind her, so much that her body jostled with his joy. She cracked a smile but buried it in the pillow so he wouldn't see. *This man.*

"Yes, you remarkable scholar. *That* thesis."

Emmy sighed again and began to unravel the research she had done almost a decade ago, spinning tales about odd, wealthy women who benefited from the Colorado silver boom and who used that money to support scientific research throughout the Rockies. She even tossed in a few stories about the Unsinkable Molly Brown just to make it interesting, to make a few jokes about being old enough to remember *Titanic* on two VHS tapes. Ryan held her the entire time, and eventually, she rolled over and draped herself across his chest as she continued to talk.

In those moments, Emmy didn't feel sexy or desired, but that wasn't what she needed. She felt safe. And that was new.

39

Ryan

THE REST OF THE night had passed with Emmy and Ryan wrapped around each other, gentle passes of hands and slight presses of kisses to shoulders and wrists, but nothing more. They had left the bed, dragging all the blankets to the couch, to order Thai food and watch a documentary before heading back to bed to sleep.

Ryan woke up at four to pee and grab a glass of water. At the sink, he reached and grabbed a second ornately decorated glass to leave by Emmy's side of the bed in case she got thirsty, too. He walked back into Emmy's bedroom balancing the glasses. He set one down next to her, then took a gulp of water from his own before setting it down. Turning to head back and flip the lights off, he caught a glimpse of Emmy in her sleep.

She was sprawled across the bed on her stomach, her right hand hanging off the edge of the bed. Emmy had fallen asleep with her hair in a bun, but that mass of hair had tilted to one side. Her body was devoid of the tension and strength he usually loved to play with, and her breath caused her body to move in a slight, gentle manner. The blanket had pulled down low on her hips, exposing the slope of her back, the light from the hallway casting shadows that danced over the ridges of her shoulders and spine.

His eyes following down the length of her body, he noticed that her toes were peeking out from the edge of the blanket. God, every single part of her was beautiful. Ryan tilted his head to snag a better look and grinned to himself when he found that her toenails were painted a neon pink.

His Emmy, who dressed like a witchy librarian, had pink toenails.

His Emmy, who kept her ideas in a leather notebook, had pink toenails.

His Emmy, who cared about the legacy of a widow from one hundred years ago that she had no reason to, had pink toenails.

His Emmy.

He liked the sound of that.

Ryan quickly went to the kitchen to turn the lights off, then headed back to the bedroom, walking carefully across the floor. He slid back into bed, and Emmy, in her sleep, grumbled, "Dammit, Doc," even as she flipped her body over and moved closer to him.

"My Emmy," he whispered into her hair. He was going to figure this out.

Like most of Ryan's best ideas, this one came in the middle of swimming laps. After a quick shared coffee with

Emmy, he had gone home to grab his swim bag and made it to the pool in record time. He pushed through the final five hundred yards, then took the quickest shower he could manage, tugging on a wool beanie as he left so his hair didn't frost at the edges. He slipped a pair of AirPods in his ears and flicked his thumb across the screen. His sister answered on the first ring.

"Oh, hello there, mountain man," she said, her smile coming through her voice.

"Hi, Jenn," he said. "How're the kids?"

"Exhausting." She laughed. "Don't have them, ever."

"Not planning on it," he replied, though he suddenly wondered if Emmy wanted kids. He once overheard her asking Phoebe why the hell she chose to work with tiny humans who made no sense. "Uh, anyway, I have kind of a weird question."

"You're a weird guy. It makes sense. You brought a dictionary to show and tell in kindergarten."

"They said to bring my favorite gift, and it had a really cool illustration of the solar system and – no. I'm not getting into this with you. I—" He groaned. "I need your help with something."

"Shoot."

"Are the kids around?"

"No, Marisa has them right now. What's up?"

Ryan didn't know where to start. He felt like it was high school again, and he was asking his sister how he was supposed to understand anything about girls. She had replied that she didn't know either, which was doubly frustrating as she was a girl and also wanted to kiss them. "So I've been seeing this new woman —"

"It's the historian, isn't it?"

"How did you know?"

"Sisterly sense. Also, you sent me a picture of you two at that museum fundraiser. She's stunning."

"Okay, we agree on that." Ryan tugged at his hat, suddenly unable to find words. "She's great — well, actually, she's frustrating and sexy and annoying and everything else. But we've been, uh." Ryan cleared his throat.

"Baby brother, you're killing me. Just say it."

"She takes brain meds, and she — ugh, this is so weird to talk to you about — she can't, you know."

"Come?"

Ryan blushed, seven states away. "Yeah. That."

"I know what you mean. Ris has the same issue with her meds. It's totally normal."

"What do you do?" Ryan scratched the back of his neck. "Emmy said she likes to use a vibrator. But, like, then, what is my purpose in the whole situation?"

"Why, 'cause you can't use your dick?"

"Kind of?"

"Does it make the sex that I have less valid because there's not a dick involved?"

"No!"

"You could always do some mutual masturbation stuff," she suggested.

"Jenn!"

"Dude, I shared a bathroom with you in high school. I know you jerked it every time your shower ran long." Ryan was wishing this conversation would end sooner rather than later. "Give me a second. I'm gonna call Ris into this conversation. She's got a way better perspective."

Ryan unlocked his front door and flopped onto his couch, confused about why something that had always been easy for him – sex – was suddenly so complicated.

Emmy *was* complicated, but damn if that didn't make him like her more. Her body was a dream, strong and steady. And all Ryan wanted to do was drive her wild, just like she did to him. He wanted her to come on his face, on his cock, anywhere she wanted. Wanted to infuse every muscle fiber with pleasure and make her beg to have it released.

He had started to get hard at the idea of all the things he wanted to do for Emmy, but that was quickly solved when his sister got back on the phone, joined by her wife.

"Putting you on speakerphone," Jenn said, and Ryan heard the click and press of buttons.

"Hey, Ross Geller," Jenn's wife, Marisa, said, using the nickname she had decided on the first time she met him and had refused to deviate from.

"Hi, Ris," he said, groaning. "Thank you for coming to the most awkward conversation of my life." He had lain back on the couch and closed his eyes, pinching the bridge of his nose.

"Okay, let's get down to business here. I'm gonna just be blunt, and you're gonna have to deal." Ryan had always liked Jenn's wife because she took no one's shit. And he didn't expect this to change now. Ris and Emmy would definitely get along.

"Great."

"I'm assuming, because you're smart, that you understand the need for foreplay." Ryan grunted a yes. "Okay, double down on the foreplay, and not just on her pussy. Play with her tits, kiss her neck, bite her ears. And ask her what she likes — she knows her body better than you do, so ask her what feels good."

"How?"

"How do you usually talk to her? Think of it as, like, extending your foreplay."

"This feels like homework."

"You went to school for seventeen thousand years, so you can deal with asking about your girlfriend's orgasms."

"She's not my —"

"Whatever," Ris continued on, blowing through Ryan's protest. He got up and walked over to his desk, where he grabbed a pad of Post-its and a pen and began scribbling reminders to himself.

Ask her.

Whole body.

"Okay, then the next thing you're gonna want to do is either get a vibrator to keep at your house or figure out her favorites."

"Do I just walk into a sex store?" Ryan suddenly had an image of going into Pumpy's, the sex store off campus, and seeing one of his graduate student assistants, or worse, an undergrad he knew. "Is it weird for a dude to buy these?"

“Get over your puritanical bullshit,” Jenn chimed in.

Ryan gritted his teeth. Sisters were something else. “I literally called you so my girlf — so Emmy could come. That’s not puritanical.”

“You’re at least old school. No one shops in person anymore. Go online. You’re gonna wanna check out this website I’ll text you. They’ve got great porn, too. Figure out how they’re used so you’re prepared. If her meds are anything like mine, she’s gonna have trouble getting wet, so get some lube. You should have some anyway —”

“I. Have. Lube,” he muttered through a clenched jaw. “I’m not twenty-two anymore.”

“Great. I’d suggest a vibrator that, like, sucks on the clit, because those are the most successful for us and our friends.”

Ryan wrote down:

Belisa (sp?)

Clit sucking

Get one for my house

“How many batteries do they take?” Ryan said, getting up to look through his junk drawer. His question was greeted by two identical groans. “What?”

“Everything is USB rechargeable now, you dork,” Jenn said. Ryan added that to his list, along with tips about what type of lube to buy and how to wash the toys (which was something he had never even considered).

“Is that it? I’d like to go swim another two miles today to recover from this conversation,” he said, getting up and tossing his glasses on the kitchen counter.

“I think?”

Ryan let out a big sigh and decided to be honest. “I just want it to be really great. Like, amazing. Seeing her come is so fucking sexy. I want her to feel confident, and I want to help make her feel good.”

“Oh, you have it *so* bad,” Jenn teased.

“Okay, goodby—”

Ris cut him off. “One more thing, and this is major.” Ris had adopted her serious tone, the one she used with the kids when she was talking about important things. “Do not rush her. She’s got enough on her mind already, and the last thing she needs is you telling her to come right now or some dominant shit. You can do that or whatever gets your freak on in a way that doesn’t make her feel like there’s a schedule to stick to.”

Ryan nodded, then realized they couldn’t see him. “Gotcha,” he added quietly.

“Tell your historian love that your big sister says hi and I hope she knows how to play Hearts so we can kick her ass next Christmas.”

“Goodbye, Jennifer Louise Andersson,” Ryan said firmly, hanging up and thinking. He opened his phone’s browser, started to google the website his sister had mentioned, then ended up clicking into incognito mode.

Scanning the site — and ignoring the video clips that he really wanted to explore — he navigated to the store and was immediately overwhelmed. Looking back at his notes, he clicked on *Vibrators*, but made a mental note to check out a few other tabs. Most notably *Couples*, *For Him*, and *Anal*. Scrolling through the options that seemed to focus on the clit (*good god, his tongue could never do half of these things*), he took the approach that he did when ordering wine in a restaurant – avoid the most expensive and the cheapest. Choose something in the middle. He paid extra for overnight shipping, then sat back on the couch, feeling accomplished.

And then he walked up to his bedroom, threw off his clothes, and opened the video portion of the website and searched *Toys*.

To research.

For science.

40

Emmy

Emmy was up early on Saturday, scrolling through her phone in her bed, trying to ignore the way her brain insisted on replaying the events of Thursday night over and over again. Her sleep had been shit since Ryan had left Friday morning — had been shit that night, if she was honest. Her brain was doing that wonderful thing where, as soon as her mind stilled for a second, it replayed every awkward situation she had ever experienced. Highlights included: the time she cried in English class in high school, interviews she had fucked up, and, of course, the way Ryan looked at her in bed on Thursday. Confused, a bit fearful, like she was a street
cat.

Ryan: Morning, Em! What are you up to today?

Speak of the devil.

Emmy: I was going to go to the gym.

Emmy: And then I have no plans.

Emmy: So I need to find something.

Days off were the worst. When Emmy didn't fill her days with activities and events, her brain would end up getting the best of her and running wild. She made a mental note to text Phoebe and see what she was up to. Maybe there was a hike they could do in the afternoon. Then they could see what Jer was up to and maybe hit up Mountain Friend for some beer. Maybe Foster was working –

A buzz from the phone in her hand distracted her.

Ryan: I would like to request that your afternoon be spent with me.

Emmy: Okay. After lunch?

Ryan: I'll be eating, but not food.

A jolt of heat spiked between Emmy's legs. Was…was this what she thought it was? She pressed his message, responded with a question mark.

Ryan: You're brilliant. You know exactly what I'm referring to.

Ryan: Speaking of, I have a homework assignment for you.

Ryan: Think about what you like.

Emmy: ????

Ryan: In bed. And text me. I want to be prepared this time.

Emmy started sweating, even though it was a chilly morning and her apartment's heat wasn't the best.

Ryan: Come over around 3? And bring your stuff.

Emmy: You think I'll be there long enough to need a bag?

Ryan: I plan on you not being able to walk to get home.

How the fuck was Emmy supposed to safely lift weights when these types of text messages were coming through her phone? She changed into her workout clothes, threw her lifting notebook and a water bottle in her drawstring bag, and went to the gym close to her apartment instead of the on-campus gym. She couldn't think about running into Ryan, didn't want to be distracted while she moved a few hundred pounds of metal off the floor and put it back down again.

Tossing her things into the locker, Emmy grabbed her phone, then put it back. Too distracting.

As she moved through her warm-up and then her lifts (deadlift day was always her favorite), her mind wandered to Ryan's texts and how she would respond. He was...different. If a partner had an issue with the way she liked to play with control, then she would just not see them again, but Ryan liked to wrestle, too. Usually, Emmy didn't make such a big deal about not coming, but Ryan was too observant. There was something different here. Ryan had seen her at her most vulnerable on Thursday and had stayed. Had reached out again. Still wanted her.

She was nervous for the first time since undergrad, when she had resorted to shots of tequila one night to finally ask one of her friends to fuck her so she could get the whole virginity thing over with. It ended about as poorly as she should have expected.

But not this time. There was a glimmer of unfamiliar hope, coupled with typical nerves, in Emmy's brain.

Finishing up her workout, Emmy gulped down water and went back to the locker room, not bothering to shower, just to grab her bag and walk home. She clicked open her phone to find – good god – fifteen text messages from Ryan.

Ryan: This is research, background info, Em.

Ryan: Because I know you get off on research, too.

Ryan: I'm just going to send you a list of things and you can thumbs up or thumbs down react to let me know what you're into.

Emmy scanned the series of text messages, her eyes snagging on a few keywords. Never one to really follow directions, she replied individually to each.

Dirty Talk – I think so but not if it gets weird.

Hair Pulling – Always.

Slow – Nope. Except how slow I am at coming.

Sweet – Ha! (That's a no)

Kissing – Yes, please. You should remember I'm good at it.

Spanking – Into it. Remember?

Anal – Maybe? Haven't tried it but not opposed.

Tying Up – Light bondage is cool, but I need to be able to see.

Choking – FUCK NO. I have to breathe.

Foot stuff – Maybe? I hate my feet?

Dominant – I like to do both. Like being in control and also not.

Rough – Yes.

Oral – Obviously you know this.

You on top – Not my favorite. Hard to come.

Missionary – I think people shit on this one too much.

Doggy style – It's fine.

Ryan: I'm not ignoring you. I'm writing all of this down.

Emmy: If you screenshot this thread, I'm going to beat you over the head with a fossil.

Ryan: You and these threats.

Ryan: Oh, and by the way, this is my list.

Emmy got a screenshot of a message:

Dirty Talk – YES especially from you.

Hair Pulling – I like to do it, and I like it to be done to me.

Slow – If you want.

Sweet – We both know this isn't us.

Kissing – Yes.

Spanking – Yes to doing it. No to having it done to me.

Anal – This one is totally up to you but

Tying Up – I'd love you to tie me up.

Choking – Seems scary.

Foot stuff – YES.

Dominant – Yes, and you can be dominant with me, too.

Rough – Yes

Oral – I cannot wait to make you come on my tongue again.

You on top – I get to watch you, so yes.

Missionary – Sex is awesome.

Doggy style – See above.

Emmy's pulse skyrocketed as she read his list, most of which she could have guessed based on their time together. She was slick as she walked into her apartment, chucking her clothes in the hamper and reaching for a vibrator. Holding the slim purple wand, she clicked it on but stopped herself before she pressed it to her body. Did she want to waste this? Or could she build up the tension in her own body all day, carry that momentum into this afternoon?

Her phone buzzed again, and Emmy ran to pick it up, praying it was Ryan. It was. Turning off the vibrator and sitting on her bed naked, she looked at her phone.

Ryan: Re: Dirty Talk. I have a clarifying question.

Emmy: Shoot

Ryan: Would you like it to be, like, compliments and praise? Or like...

Ryan: Not nice things.

Emmy: I like being celebrated for my accomplishments.

Emmy: I like being told I'm doing well.

Emmy: A guy once called me

Emmy: His cum dumpster

Emmy: And I kicked his ass out of bed.

Ryan: That is certainly an...interesting choice of phrase. I'd go with, like, "dirty little slut" or something, but bold choice.

Ryan: Also ditto.

Ryan: Except you can be a bit mean to me.

Ryan:

Emmy: The emojis really sell the sexting.

She had a vision of Ryan telling her filthy things, that slight smile always in his voice growled into her ear. How she could tell him what he looked like as he slid into her. She remembered the way he had loved it when she called him Dr. Andersson.

Before heading into the shower, Emmy looked at the clock on her nightstand. It was only 10 a.m.

Fuck. It was going to be a long day.

41

Ryan

Ryan looked at his bedroom, checking
off the mental list he had made.
"It's for you," he said, clicking it on and holding it in the palm of his hand like he had practiced, hoping the vibrations would hide how his hand had begun to shake slightly with his nerves. "Is it okay?"

Lube? Check.

Sheets? Washed.

Glasses of water by the bedside table? Yes.

Condoms? A brand-new box, already opened.

And the pièce de résistance? Shiny new vibrator, charged and ready. He looked over the pink device, practiced holding it. It looked so tiny in his big hand, but if it helped Emmy, it was worth the shock of opening up a package that had apparently held containers to find the "Pleasure Pearl."

He'd already jerked off twice today in his preparation for the afternoon, and it had barely taken the need out of his system. Jenn and Ris were right – this type of communication was like an extended foreplay, and he hoped it was working for Emmy like it was for him.

Ryan: Thanks again.

Jenn: Stop texting me and go wait for your girlfriend.

Ryan: We haven't had that conversation.

Jenn: Make her come, then ask her.

Ryan laughed and walked downstairs, using his phone to turn on some music in the kitchen, trying to set the mood. He had selected a slower folk and bluegrass band, the singer with a scratchy voice that screamed sex.

"I'm here," came Emmy's voice from the outside. Ryan tossed his phone onto a countertop and opened the door.

"Normal people use a doorbell," he said by way of greeting.

"Normal people actually send a text message," Emmy replied. "I just like to show up." She sighed. "Actually, I'm avoiding my phone in case you send another dirty text message." Emmy set her bag down and cracked her knuckles, looking at Ryan. "Okay, let's do this." She walked over to him and went to kiss him, but Ryan held her back at arm's length.

"Slow down there, Ms. Bonaire," he said, squeezing her shoulder. "We have all afternoon." Emmy bounced from side to side, energy and nerves radiating out of her system. "I plan on taking my time with you." He kissed the side of her neck, then dropped his voice. "You can be patient for me, right? You can be good?" Emmy's eyes widened, and she nodded, licking her lips. "Let's go upstairs," he nodded to where his bedroom was located.

Emmy went to slip off her shoes, heeled ankle boots with an ornate pattern embroidered around the edge.

"No," he said, his mouth going dry. "Leave them on."

Emmy laughed, running her fingers along the top of her shoe. "Right, I forgot. Foot stuff." She straightened and looked at him. "Does that mean, like, a foot job? I don't think I'm that coordinated with my toes, to be honest."

Ryan laughed, easing some of the tension that crackled between them. "No, I just like looking at your feet and legs. Like a lot. I'd like to touch them and kiss them if you're not too ticklish and it doesn't weird you out." He started up the stairs. "I don't know why people are fine with, like, spitting in someone's mouth but not a bit of foot play."

"Don't spit in my mouth," Emmy said from behind him. "But what you suggested is fine." He laughed again and nodded.

"I'll update the file," he said as he reached the top of the stairs. Ryan pushed open the door to his bedroom, relieved to find it in the same condition that it was ten minutes ago, as if some type of gremlin would have come and fucked everything up.

Emmy sat on the bed and crossed her ankles primly. "Does this look like a school picture day pose?" she said, laughing. "Like, I'd have a giant 07 behind me or something. Well, you'd probably have a 1946 behind you because you're old."

"I'm not old," Ryan said, momentarily offended. "Thirty-seven is a perfectly respectable age." He kneeled next to the bed, and Emmy placed one heeled foot on his shoulder. "Good god, woman, you couldn't be any sexier," he breathed, turning his head and pressing a kiss to the skin above her ankle.

Her eyes flashed steel and silver. "I know how I could do it. Be sexier, that is. I could recite, uh..." Ryan looked up at Emmy, who seemed to be struggling to find words. "I could recite types of rocks." She grinned, that feisty smile he adored stretching across her face. "There's the one that's volcanic."

"Igneous," he said, kissing up her calf.

"Yep, that one," she said. "And the one that's compressed sand and shit."

"Sedimentary." A nip to the back of her knee. "Emmy, I know these things. Talk to me about something I didn't spend years studying." He looked up at her from between her legs, right before the hem of her skirt. She raised an eyebrow and pressed her foot into his shoulder, moving him back slightly.

"You mean, like my own research? Museum theory? Exhibit design?" Her eyes flashed again, molten with heat. "Or do you want to hear about how fucking desperate I am?" Ryan somehow got harder. Emmy slid her foot off his shoulder, ran the toe of her boot down his chest, and just barely pressed it into the bulge of his pants. *This woman.*

"Desperate for what?" he said thickly.

"You," she whispered, and Ryan almost collapsed right there. "I've been wet since you texted this morning, but I didn't allow myself to do anything about it." She let out a strained breath. "Dr. Andersson?"

Fuck. There it was — that damn name, the way she said it with sex and snark and play all wrapped up in her voice. “Happy to provide my services,” he said, reaching up and pulling the string at her waistband. “But I need these clothes off first.” Emmy reached for the hem of her shirt, but Ryan gripped her hand and set it aside. “Nope, my job.”

“But —”

“Do. Not. Rush. Me,” he said, deadly serious. He stood up slightly, hovered his body over her. “I checked your Google calendar, and I’ll head downstairs to double-check the damn paper planner you insist on using that I know is in your bag. Your schedule is empty today, and I plan on filling it.” Ryan wrapped her ponytail around his fist, tugged slightly. “And I plan on filling you.”

Emmy moaned at the hair pull, and Ryan got to work, pulling her shirt off and unclipping her bra quickly. “You won’t need these the rest of the night.” He tossed the clothing across the room, where they were shortly joined by her skirt and panties. Ryan trailed his fingertips over her chest, then hopped off the bed and took his own clothes off.

“Lie down for me, Em,” he said. “Spread your legs and let me look.” Emmy obeyed. And fuck, Ryan was overjoyed that she had kept those boots on. He removed his glasses and set them on his table, then allowed himself to look at her, strong, muscular, and already trembling slightly.

“Don’t you need those?”

“Only for faraway things.” He ran his tongue over his bottom lip. “And I plan on being very close today.” He continued to look at Emmy, watch the way she buzzed with anticipation. Her left hand slid over her hip and was inching toward the gorgeous, wet space between her legs. Ryan couldn't have that.

"No," he said, leaning over and grabbing her wrist. "I said lie there, not to touch."

"You need to be clearer with your instructions," she said, eyes sparkling.

Ryan straddled her hips and took both wrists above her head, holding them in his hands. "And you need to listen." With her hands held above her head, Ryan leaned down and kissed her, realizing that he hadn't done that since she'd arrived. She opened for him eagerly, licking into his mouth. He took a break from her mouth to whisper against her ear, "Don't move your hands."

"Or?"

"Don't test me, Em." Ryan nipped at her earlobe, sucked the flesh into his mouth. Emmy moaned.

"Fuck, Doc," she breathed. "Are you gonna go down on me?"

"I'll get there," he said, and true to his word, he slid up and down her body, taking his time kissing, touching, pinching, whispering. For minutes, he spent his time reacquainting himself with Emmy's body. He nipped her hipbone, sucked below her breast. "You're doing so good," he said into her ribs. "So patient."

He slid himself down the length of her, gently pulled off her boots. Finally, he had arrived at her toes, painted a light silver.

"This is a secret part of you," he whispered, massaging the arch of her foot.

"What do you mean?" she gasped.

"You paint your toenails." He lifted her foot, ran his tongue from her heel along her instep, was pleased to hear the way she gasped at the new sensation.

"Lots of people do," she said, the end of the sentence cut off with a loud moan as he sucked her pinky toe. "Good god, Ry!"

"Hmm?" he asked, pulling away, switching his hands to her other foot.

"It feels" — he sucked again — "sur-*fuck*-prisingly good."

"There are over seven thousand nerve endings in your foot," he said, tongue snaking out.

"Usually it's ticklish, but, oh—" Emmy's voice wavered.

"Studies say," he whispered against her ankle, nipped at the thin skin there, "it's one of the more popular fetishes."

"So mainstream," Emmy said, the bite of the sarcastic phrase weakened by the way she started to pant when Ryan kissed the ball of her foot. He continued to experiment with Emmy, running his tongue along the top and bottom of her foot, varying the pressuring, scraping his teeth.

"I'm dying," she said. "Touch me, *please*." Ryan laughed and ran his hands up her legs, loving the way his fingers ran through her short pubic hair. Emmy, apparently, was done being patient. She thrust her fingers into his hair and gripped tight, that edge of pain that Ryan loved with his pleasure. He looked up at her, and she was breathing heavily, her eyes glassy and hooded. "Please, Ry."

"Okay," he said simply, and she kept her fingers in his hair as he made his way down, spreading her wide and pressing his mouth to her.

"Oh!" she keened, and Ryan smiled against her and continued to work. He pressed a finger into her, feeling how she was warm and tight and so fucking wet. He could feel her building toward an orgasm, remembered the way she had started to grind her hips into him when she was close. He pulled his mouth away but kept a finger running through her lips.

"What the fuck?" she panted, her eyes wild. "Don't you dare edge me."

"You're being so fucking perfect," he said, climbing off the bed. "Your body is perfect, your pussy is perfect, your mind is perfect, your fucking mouth is perfect." He opened the drawer and pulled out his newest purchase.

"What is that?"

"I..." And here was the part where he had to be vulnerable, had to admit that he was trying something new. "I thought it could help...you. Me. Us. Because you deserve all the pleasure."

"What is it doing here?"

"It's for you," he said, clicking it on and holding it in the palm of his hand like he had practiced, hoping the vibrations would hide how his hand had begun to shake slightly with his nerves. "Is it okay?"

42

EMMY

"IS IT OKAY?" RYAN'S question had shocked her more than the first time they had kissed.

"Where did you —"

"Internet."

"How did it get here so —"

"Overnight shipping."

"Why did—"

"For you."

"How can —" Her brain was full of questions she couldn't manage to get out fast enough.

"Emmy, I adore your inquisitive nature, but I'm dying here." Now it was Ryan's turn to look desperate, his eyes twin flames of desire, his breathing quick. "I want to see you come so fucking badly, and I want to see it so many times."

Her brain sputtered, paused, then roared to life. "Yes," she said, opening her knees wider.

"Thank god," he said. He clicked the toy on, then pressed it to her inner thigh, allowing her to get adjusted to the speed and patterns. “Talk to me, tell me what to do.”

“I’ve never had a problem doing that,” she said sarcastically, but any further smart-ass comment was gone from her brain when he moved the toy to her clit.

“Good?”

“Great,” she said, breathing heavily. “Perfect.” Emmy was on her back, legs spread, and Ryan was next to her, his left hand running over her throat and down to her nipples, pinching and tweaking slightly. “A little to the left,” she said, and he watched her, adjusted. Then he hit that glorious spot, and she lost the ability to make complete sentences. Instead reverting to just swearing and groaning. Ryan was talking enough for both of them.

“You should see yourself,” he was saying. “I’m going to film you one day and then fuck you while we watch it. God, your fucking muscles and power and your flawless tits and pussy.” Emmy loved his words, loved the desire in them. He leaned down and wrapped his mouth around a nipple and used his teeth to apply a little pressure.

“More,” she gasped, tugging on his hair again, and he responded with his mouth and by adjusting the vibrator up a setting. She felt the tension in the base of her spine build to the point that it was almost unbearable. If she didn’t come tonight, she was going to implode, end up as a pile of dust to be swept away. More tension, and now she could sense that release was soon, felt herself begin to open and clench and, god damn, she wanted Ryan in her next time. “I’m so close, I’m so close, I’m so —”

"Holy fuck," Ryan muttered as she brought her knees together, holding his hand to her as the tension spiked through her body. She reached down and pulled the vibrator away, then wrenched Ryan's lips to hers and kissed the ever-loving shit out of him.

"You," she said against his mouth. "You are so smart." She kissed him again. "So resourceful." Another kiss. "And now I need *you*, Dr. Andersson." She grabbed the vibrator from his hand and moved it to her left side, preparing for later. Ryan, who apparently needed no other hint, was scrambling for a condom, almost dropping the foil packet in his haste.

"You bought more, right?" Emmy said, trying to get a look at what he was digging for on the floor.

Ryan rolled on the condom and shot her a look. "Yes, because, ideally, this is not the only time we do this." She snorted a laugh. "Are you laughing at my dick?"

"Hell no," she said. He hovered over her but slid a hand down her stomach and felt between her legs. He disappeared again for a second but came back with a small light blue bottle that he flipped open and drizzled over her.

"Yeah?" he asked, his tip rubbing over her clit.

"Yeah," she answered on a sigh, then he thrust into her. She was already open and ready, and it felt even better this time, especially because she had already come and could check that off her mental to-do list. Ryan pulled her up against his chest, their bodies moving together, and Emmy scraped her nails down his back.

"Harder?" she asked. Ryan nodded, and Emmy used her muscles to press him down so she was above him and began to roll her hips. Ryan reached for her to flip again, but she held his arms down, gripped his wrists. "My turn to be in charge, Dr. Andersson," she whispered, running her tongue over a nipple. Emmy was grateful for the recent core work she had been doing as she rolled her hips, still holding Ryan down and watching his dominance begin to fracture to a frenzied submission.

"God, Em, you're magnificent," he panted, thrusting up.

"About time you realized." She smirked, then moaned as he hit a particularly sensitive spot.

"Perfection. Can you come like this?" She went to shake her head, then remembered the tiny pink device next to her. She pressed it on, then held it to herself. "I think," she replied. She felt herself begin to pulse and open, and she saw Ryan's eyes squeeze shut, knew that he felt it, too. More heat, more movement. The second orgasm came faster than the first, making her so sensitive that she removed the vibrator quickly. Ryan held her hips steady and thrust up a few more times. Then he followed her with a grunting moan. Emmy leaned over and pressed a gentle kiss to his lips, and Ryan held his hand to her cheek. For a moment, they looked at each other, sharing air and each unwilling to break the silence.

"You're amazing," she said. "That was amazing."

"I can't wait to do it again," Ryan replied, and Emmy felt herself already warming but knew that this was a marathon, not a sprint.

"I need water," she said, rolling off him. "Then I need to pee, and then we need to decide what to eat for dinner, and *then* we can do it again."

43

RYAN

EMMY WAS ALREADY AWAKE when Ryan woke up. He was usually up early during the week to swim before work, but on weekends, he allowed himself to sleep in and be a bit lazy. Emmy was lying on her side, her back to him, scrolling through her phone.

"Morning," he said, rolling behind her. Emmy put her phone down and looked over her shoulder.

"It's about time, you snooze machine," she said, pressing a light kiss to his lips. "I've been up for an hour already."

"Why are you still in bed, then?"

"Your sheets are really comfy," she said, snuggling in. "And then I went down a weird rabbit hole of Wikipedia entries about the history of refrigerators, and well, here I am."

"Coffee?" he asked, stepping out of the blankets and looking around for a pair of shorts. God, they had really wrecked this place throughout the night. Clothes were everywhere, there were three — no, four — condom wrappers around the bed, and most of the pillows had fallen off. They had barely slept, snagging bits of rest between the moments where one of them woke up feral for the other.

"God, please. And an Advil? I feel like I've been hit by a truck," she said, standing with a groan. Ryan was sore himself, but he had to will himself not to press her back down to the bed as Emmy stretched. There were hickies on her hipbones, and Ryan knew his own back bore the marks of her nails. Emmy walked over to her bag and threw on a T-shirt and shorts, and Ryan studied what she was wearing. Even in boxers and an oversized shirt, she took his breath away.

"What's that mean?" he asked, nodding toward her shirt.

"It's a quote from the founder of the Exploratorium in San Fran," she said, pulling out her T-shirt to look it over. *Nobody ever failed a science museum.* "That place is revolutionary. Have you been?"

"Never made it, even though I did my PhD in California. Is it good?"

"Ry, you'd *die*. You have to go."

"We should go," he said. She chuckled and rolled her eyes.

"You should make me coffee," she replied, walking out of the bedroom and into the hallway. Ryan followed her downstairs and into the kitchen, where she perched on one of the high-top stools that were placed around his center island.

"What do you want to do today?" he asked her as he got out the necessary supplies. Emmy shrugged, toying around with her phone. Suddenly, Ryan got an idea — and it wasn't just from staring at her chest, though that is what he had to do to reread the quote on the front.

"Wanna exhibit plan?" Emmy's eyes snapped up to his, and her face split into a grin. "I take it that's a yes?"

"Literally the sexiest thing you've ever said to me," she quipped. Ryan pulled a face, remembering a lot of what they had said to each other the previous night. "Okay, well, top five," she amended. He handed her a cup of coffee and couldn't help but to mess with the bun she had put her hair up in.

"You're cute in the morning," he said honestly.

"You have morning breath," she replied, sipping her coffee.

"So do you, sweetheart. But you're still cute." The endearments for Emmy felt natural. Better than a nickname. "Okay, Em, I'm going to grab a shower, but I'll show you my office and allow you to get settled."

She eyed him warily. "No protocols?"

He laughed. "No protocols. You set up the way your gorgeous mind decides makes sense, and I'll let you drag me along for the ride." She followed him to a small room on the first floor, sparse with a computer, bookshelves, and a whiteboard. Ryan took a quick shower and came down, dressed in a sweatshirt from undergrad, the hood pulled up, and a pair of running shorts. He didn't miss the way Emmy's eyes zeroed in on his legs when he walked into the room, but she was in curator mode, and quickly went back to what she was working on.

"Okay, Em," he said, walking over to where she had commandeered the whiteboard that he had installed but never actually used. "Explain." She had found a marker and had written SARA JONESBORO SALON EXHIBITION on the center, and then she'd started to make a map of all the main ideas that connected to it.

"I like to try to get as many ideas as possible down and then weed them out from there," she said, beginning to scribble a series of words surrounded by bubbles, then connecting them to the center title. "There are unexpected connections between things, and I find that you can only really see them when they're all out in front of you. We can look at all of these things that may seem unrelated, but the topics might connect and create a new way of looking at things for the visitor." She gave him a smirk. "And we have to keep them in mind, right? It's not just about our collections and the science research, but what someone can get out of this exhibition."

"Riiight," Ryan said, walking over and plucking the marker out of Emmy's hand, and drawing an arrow, connecting the bubble labeled *historic science experiments* to his own writing that read *contemporary lab connections*. "And what comes next?"

Emmy chewed her lip, eyes scanning what she had already written on the board. "I usually work with ideas first, then spend some time in the database, looking for what in the collection can supplement the narrative, though sometimes a really amazing artifact can be the reason to tell a story." He nodded for her to continue, so she said, "And then Phoebe and I usually draft label text – she's better at putting things into words the public can understand. And then Jeremy comes down and figures out the way to organize everything so it makes sense in our tiny space."

"That seems like a pretty easy process," Ryan said.

"If we have time and funding, I like to do some prototype testing with visitors, but that's been harder and harder to come by, especially since the last administration and our shit budget." She grinned. "Maybe we can finagle some science money this time."

Ryan cocked his head. "Damn, you're smart. I can't wait to see you as Dr. Emmy one day." Ryan heard a sharp intake of breath from Emmy and looked at her. Emmy's lips had pressed into a hard line, and her face had gone stone-like. *What happened*? Ryan thought to himself and was just about to ask Emmy what had upset her when her face relaxed and her eyes found his.

"Yeah, right." She sighed, shaking her head slightly. "Quit your daydreaming and add your ideas." They worked in silence for just over a half hour, eventually running out of room on the whiteboard, shifting to Post-its that scattered around the board like buckshot. They would occasionally take a marker or a pen and Post-it from the other and put it on the board, moving around each other in a little bubble of ideas and flow.

When the creation of new Post-its had begun to slow, like the end of a bag of popcorn popping in a microwave,

Emmy gently laid a hand on Ryan's arm and encouraged him to step back from the board a few feet.

"Now we take it all in," she said softly, and Ryan's eyes widened at everything they had created in that small amount of time. Yes, it was a bit hectic, and yes, there wasn't anything organized yet, but it was dense with ideas. Ryan and Emmy had taken this tiny concept of Sara Jonesboro's salons and support of the original university science departments and begun to connect it to the research that professors were doing. Emmy had written a few notes that emphasized that the original research at the university was much more interdisciplinary than what was done currently, and perhaps this exhibition could be what she called a "meta-commentary" on the merger of the museums. He assumed that was a good thing.

"This is really cool," Emmy said, scattering papers around herself, snapping a picture of the board. "I think we should submit this to a conference." Her eyes flashed. "MAA?"

Ryan couldn't help himself anymore. He came up behind her and kissed the back of her neck as she looked over the plans. "You're so sexy when you're in historian mode."

Emmy giggled but tried to pull away from Ryan to get her notebook. "Doc, I need to write down an idea."

"It can wait," he said, pulling her down to the floor of his office, scattering her papers even further.

"My notes!"

"This is why you need to go digital," he quipped and took her lips, running his hands up and down her body to let her know exactly what new ideas this planning session had sparked in him. After a frenetic couple of minutes and many fewer clothes (and a frantic naked sprint to get a condom), Emmy was lying on Ryan, pressing tiny kisses into his chest.

"Anyway, want to spend Monday morning putting this into a report and then present it to the board at the meeting on Thursday evening?" she asked. Another kiss.

Ryan nodded and watched as Emmy crawled across him and found her planner, added a note to the Thursday page.

"Do you want to stay here tonight?" Ryan asked, hopeful.

Emmy gave him a quick shake of her head. "I have to get my shit ready for the week. Meal plan, grocery store, all that kind of good stuff." Ryan wanted to offer to go grocery shopping with her, sit with her while she figured out what to make for lunch during the week. He wanted to take out the trash with her, vacuum the house. Anything, even the most menial tasks, he wanted to do alongside Emmy.

Heat blossomed in his cheeks when he realized what it all meant.

"Okay," he said, though a part of him wanted to beg her to stay. He had to keep *some* appearance of being cool. He couldn't quite help himself from offering to pick Emmy up in the morning on the way to work, promising a dirty chai if she agreed to let him drive her. She said she agreed because she hated waiting in the cold for the bus, but Ryan knew better.

44

Emmy

The week went by quickly for a change, with the tension in Emmy and Ryan's office reduced by a few thousand degrees. They were able to figure each other out, getting a sense of when one of them needed quiet time and when they needed someone to bounce ideas off. And when they needed someone to slip their arms around them while they were working on a computer. And when they needed to double check that the door to the office was closed and locked so they could make out.

Emmy was surprised that Phoebe had only walked in on them once (she had opened the door to find Ryan's hand up Emmy's shirt, only to roll her eyes and mumble something about how every fucking person around her was doing this now), and even Jeremy had taken to texting Emmy a five-minute warning before he headed to her office.

After that first Monday morning, Ryan had started texting her each night before bed to ask what time she wanted him to pick her up. Emmy liked the convenience of starting her day with him, taking their fifteen-minute commute from her apartment to work to continue to get to know each other better. They swapped embarrassing stories from high school, started a shared playlist of songs the other *had* to listen to, and debated the relative merits of different hikes in the area.

On that Thursday, Ryan and Emmy presented their exhibition proposal to the board and received full approval to move ahead. Which was good, because a few weeks after their successful – *ahem* – planning session, they had also submitted a proposal for a session on their cross-disciplinary collaboration and the benefits it would have for their work and the museum profession as a whole. Ryan had brought a tiny bottle of champagne to the office and popped the cork when Emmy was able to finally toss the sun faded blue Post-it in the recycling that read *submit to MAA conference.*

All in all, things were going...well. Which made Emmy suspicious. Any time things had been going well, the other shoe was due to drop. That was how life went. She had been doing well in college until her breakdown. She had finally gotten her feet under her in Vanberg, had become a curator, and then COVID shut the world down. She had come back, and then the museums merged. It all felt too easy.

But it continued to be easy, with Ryan holding Emmy's hand on a ski lift when she became convinced the wires would snap. With Emmy yelling at him to turn his skis into pizzas, not french fries, before he gave up on the entire concept of downhill skiing and went to the lodge. And later that evening, when Emmy had spent the whole day on the mountain, and Ryan had nursed hot toddies all day until she joined him. They had sat in front of the fire in the lodge, Emmy leaning into Ryan's side with his arm around her.

"You're my girlfriend, right?" Ryan had asked.

"I hate that word," Emmy said. "It makes me feel like I'm sixteen."

"Womanfriend?"

"That's the best you can do?"

Ryan took a sip of his bourbon, and Emmy sipped a gin and tonic. "You're my sweetheart."

"Too 1950s."

"Beau?"

"Too 1850s."

Ryan thought again and kissed Emmy's temple. "Whatever you want to call it, you're mine, right?"

"Only if you're mine, too," she had replied, and somehow, that had settled it. They had become Emmy-and-Ryan, or Ryan-and-Emmy, spoken about in one collective noun. As winter thawed into spring, Emmy-and-Ryan worked on the exhibition plan, drafted papers together, hiked mountains, tried new restaurants, and tumbled into bed with each other almost every night.

On a Sunday morning in March, Emmy was up before Ryan, as usual. They had met Phoebe, Jeremy, Colin, June, and June's old coworker Kevin and his husband for a special weekend trivia night at Mountain Friend, where they had then destroyed the rest of the competition. Ryan had insisted they be called the Histori-sauruses, which Colin had loved. They had spent the night at Ryan's, which had become their more common location, and Emmy was doing her standard morning scroll when a new email caught her eye:

SUBJECT: MAA Conference Proposal

Emmy threw her arm out and smacked Ryan's chest while her stomach dropped like she was on a roller coaster. "Ry, wake up," she said, her voice trembling. He groaned and rolled over, his arm snaking over her stomach, his hand searching for her breast. She batted it away. "No, not now."

"*Why*?" he whined, his fingers continuing their half-awake search. Emmy pushed the phone in his face, and Ryan blinked rapidly, then scrambled his hand on his bedside table for his glasses. "It's here already? What does it say?"

"I'm too afraid to read it," Emmy said, letting go of her phone. "You read it and tell me." He pulled her back to his front, settling her in his lap, and rested his chin on her shoulder. He took a deep inhale of her hair, kissed the top of her head, then held up the phone in front of her face to unlock it. He thumbed to her email, opening where she had closed the app.

"We are happy to inform you..." he mumbled in her ear, and she was momentarily distracted by the way that a wave of goose bumps rose on her skin. "...accepted...highlighted session...Saturday."

“Ryan,” she said, turning around in his lap, knocking the phone from his hands. “Ryan, we did it.” She launched herself at him, kissing him wildly, fiercely, taking control and holding him down.

“We did, you minx,” he replied when Emmy made a particular swiveling movement against his growing hard-on. He flailed his hands under the pillow to find an extra condom that had flown across the bed during an especially vigorous session the previous night and moved Emmy’s hips out of the way to sheathe himself. When he’d guided her back on top of him, she allowed him to move her body, building a mild heat between her legs. Her mind was going a million miles an hour thinking about the conference, making plans for more research, for how they would present, that she barely noticed that Ryan was grunting underneath her.

“Sorry,” he said as he came.

“Just what every girl wants to hear.” She laughed, kissing him. “It’s fine.”

“Nope,” he said, rolling her body off him and looking in his bedside table. “I keep this charged for a reason,” he added emphatically, pressing the vibrator to her clit just as he took her nipple in his mouth and rolled it between his teeth.

“Fucking brilliant, Dr. Andersson,” Emmy gasped, and then words became increasingly difficult.

—

Later that morning, Emmy and Ryan had gone for a run and showered (together — his shower was much larger) and were in his kitchen. Ryan was whipping up scrambled eggs, Emmy had made coffee, and the entire situation felt...normal. Domestic. Emmy looked around at Ryan's kitchen and couldn't remember the exact moment she had learned where he kept the spoons and forks and mixing bowls. Knew what type of creamer he kept in his fridge, knew that he had a bag of kale in the back that would get sadder and sadder until he eventually threw it out and began the process again.

"I can't wait to go to Boston," Emmy said. "There are so many amazing historical sites, and they were one of the first cities to take historic preservation seriously, so there are so many things we can see!"

"One of the first American natural history museums is there, at Harvard," Ryan added. "We could go."

"I'd like that."

"It will also be a good chance to make connections, especially with east coast museums or big ones out in LA or San Francisco." Ryan turned back to the stove. Something caught at the back of Emmy's mind, and AnxietyBrain woke from a deep slumber. It wouldn't allow her to let it go.

"Why would I need to make connections?" Emmy said.

"For your next job. Or for grad school," Ryan replied, flipping the eggs. Cue a record scratch in Emmy's mind.

"Wait, what?"

He turned and looked at her, twirling the spatula in his hands. "I mean, VU isn't the endgame for me. I always planned on staying here for a short bit of time, on the way to a bigger museum."

And here was the other shoe. "What the fuck is wrong with VU?" Emmy asked, slamming her coffee mug down. "It's a gorgeous campus."

"Sure, Em, it's been great to live here. But..." He paused, finally seeming to pick up on her anger. "Wait, you're planning on staying here? Like long term?"

"Yeah," she said slowly. "And you're not?"

"Not really," Ryan said simply. He sighed. "Think of what you could do in a bigger city. You could work at the Smithsonian!"

"Do you have any idea how hard it is to get a job in the humanities in a museum? Let alone one like that? I have a full-time one here. With benefits! I'm not going to leave that to start all over at the bottom of a staff ladder, working thirty hours a week without that safety net. I have a massive amount of influence here," Emmy said, her voice rising. "I'm doing work that matters to me and matters to this town. I like my job."

"But think if you went back and got a PhD —" he began.

"With what money, Ryan? I've busted my ass to get here, to be in a position where I'm out of debt and living by myself and can afford a life I like."

"Well, when I was in grad school, I got paid."

"Hey, Ryan, what the fuck did you study?" He was silent. "Yeah, there's money in science. The last time I looked at PhDs in history, the entire year's salary was twenty thousand dollars. Before taxes. In California. If I got funding." He remained quiet. "You don't get to tell me what it means for me to be successful."

They stood there looking at each other, Emmy's coffee cooling, Ryan's eggs burning on the stove. "I've always planned on leaving Vanberg eventually, but you could come with me if you wanted," Ryan said, quieter this time.

"If I wanted. My career would follow yours." Emmy's voice had gotten deadly calm.

"Or not. It's up to you." For some reason, the lack of fight in him, the way he just accepted that there was a place in the future where their paths diverged, infuriated Emmy. And she exploded.

"Well, we should probably have talked about that," Emmy spat. "What was this? Just a quick few fucks on the side while you get ready to move on to bigger and brighter stages?" Her heart was racing and her breathing was picking up. This is why Emmy should always listen to AnxietyBrain. She had gotten lazy, she had gotten content, and she had let her guard down. And now she was getting stomped on.

"Em," Ryan said, turning off the stove and reaching for her. "Can we –"

"No," she said, pulling out of his grasp. "I can't believe you would just assume that I'd leave this life and follow you wherever you went. Like my work doesn't matter."

"That's not what I said," Ryan urged, pushing his glasses into his hair.

"Then enlighten me," she said, her tone turning harsh. "What did you mean?"

"I don't know. I haven't thought it through, and you caught me off guard, and –"

"You don't think things through, do you?" Emmy was having the realization of a lifetime here. "I'm a planner, and I'm always working toward something. But not you. No." She snorted. "Everything just falls in your lap perfectly, huh? It always works out for you. You're going to go to Boston and charm everyone and then just leave this place. Leave me."

"That's not the case, Emmy, and you know that."

"God, I'm such an idiot," she said, slightly dazed as the picture became clearer. "Of *course* you wanted to submit to the conference. You could go and present and make the connections and use my work as a stepping stone. It was never about creating something new, was it? It was only about what was beneficial to you."

Emmy was moving out of the kitchen now, hastily throwing her belongings in a bag, trying to find her shoes, anything to get out of this house, back to her space, where she could call Phoebe and cry and get drunk and just forget that she had been on the verge of giving her heart to someone who was only using her.

"Emmy, no. I believe in the work we're doing," Ryan was saying as he followed her outside.

"Not enough to let me know you wanted to leave," she said. "Not enough to believe that my work is good enough here. I should have known better. This is always what happens when men and women mix relationships with academia."

"What?"

"You're going to take this and move to some fancy-pants full-of-money museum. I'll stay here. That's what always happens. The man gets the credit, gets the success, and the woman is a footnote in history." She turned around, walked up to him, and pushed her pointer finger into his chest. "You listen to me, Doctor Ryan Andersson" – she spat his title, so different from the way she had said it in bed an hour ago – "I will not be a footnote. I'm the whole damn book." With that, she started walking down the sidewalk.

"You don't have a car. I can drive you home," Ryan said from his driveway, but Emmy shook her head, already opening her phone to call Phoebe for a ride.

"No. Don't you follow me." Emmy whirled around and looked at him, standing in the doorway in pajama pants and a T-shirt. "I'll see you at work. We are *only* colleagues now. Until you leave. Then we will have been *former* coworkers. That's it." Phoebe answered on the first ring, and Emmy walked in the direction of her apartment.

It was going to be a long three weeks until the conference.

45

Ryan

Ryan watched Emmy's figure grow smaller and smaller until she turned the corner at the end of the block. What was he supposed to do now? When he had mis-stepped before, she had stayed and talked through it. She'd shared her perspective and how she had interpreted what he said or didn't say.

This time she just...left. And from what he knew about Emmy — and he felt like he knew a whole hell of a lot these days — that meant she had made up her mind.

He wasn't worth the fight.

His toes growing cold on the brick steps outside his house, Ryan went back inside to his kitchen. Her coffee was there, half-drunk, his eggs half-scrambled on the stove. His stomach was full of acid. No energy to even throw the eggs away or put dishes in the sink. He'd deal with all of that later. Ryan grabbed his phone off the table — fuck, why had he made his background a photo of Emmy? A photo of Emmy after a day of skiing, her cheeks red with windburn, a hat with a ridiculous pom-pom on top of her head, that trademark smirk plastered across her face as she made eye contact with the camera.

He'd known that day. Realized it when he was driving her back down the mountain and she had slept, curled up in the front seat. She had been explaining the history of how a WWII division that trained in the Rocky Mountains had been responsible for the development of the Colorado ski industry and had fallen asleep midsentence. One minute she was telling him about cutting ski runs into mountains, the next, he could see her breath fogging up the window. She was literally so passionate about history that she thought about it from the moment she woke up until she couldn't anymore. He loved that about her.

Loved her.

Fuck. He went to walk upstairs, then realized that his sheets would still smell like grapefruit and he would probably find a sock of hers in his bed. Ryan turned, went to the couch, and collapsed on it. He turned on the TV to whatever it had been on last — some replay of a baseball game — and stared into space. He occasionally picked up his phone, but who was he going to call?

He couldn't call Jeremy, because Ryan was sure he was already on the way to Phoebe's.

He couldn't call Phoebe, who he assumed was already raiding the museum's collection for some obscure torture device to use on him.

He couldn't call Foster, because Emmy was friends with him, too.

He couldn't call Satya, because they didn't really discuss personal matters outside of bar trivia.

He'd lived in Vanberg for, what, five years now? And he had no one he could call to work through the worst heartbreak of his life. Whereas he imagined Emmy would be surrounded by people who could step into the space he'd left.

At some point, he'd fallen asleep with announcers talking about a hot young rookie second baseman, but Ryan hadn't paid attention. He woke up to the buzzing of his phone in his hand and audibly groaned when he saw Emmy's face on his lock screen. Again. Blinking his eyes, he grabbed his glasses from where they had fallen onto the floor, put them on, and looked at his phone, which let him know he had a lot of text messages.

Jenn: Logging on!
Kristin: Give me a few. I have to pee.
Kristin: Again.
Amanda: This is why I'm not ready for kids.
Amanda: Ryan, you're so lucky.
Jenn: He doesn't want them anyway.

Then a few minutes later.
Jenn: Ryan, where are you?
Jenn: Ryan, stop having sex and log on.
Amanda: Everything okay?
Kristin: Ry, pick up.
Kristin: We've all tried to call you.
Amanda: LET US KNOW WHEN YOU GET THESE.

He clicked around and found seven missed calls. He didn't have the energy to call them, one-by-one, and tell them what happened. The downside of growing up in a close-knit family was that any change in his voice or mood was analyzed to a microscopic degree. He opened up a group text.

Ryan: Hey, everyone. Shitty morning. Sorry I missed the family call.

Ryan: I'm fine but not in the mood to talk.

He turned off his phone before he could deal with the inevitable wave of attempts to get him to talk. He grabbed his remote, navigated to a shitty action movie that would take exactly zero brain power, then sat back down.

One more thing. He walked over to a shelf, grabbed his bottle of bourbon and a glass, then sat back down on the couch. Who gave a shit if he was hungover at work tomorrow? He was planning on hiding in the collection, anyway.

The first sip of bourbon burned, which was another reason Ryan never drank before two p.m. But the second, third, and fourth went down a bit smoother. He reached for his phone, wanted to call Emmy and beg her to come back so he could explain, finally tell her what he hadn't been able to. Ryan had never had a problem speaking his mind – people liked him, listened to him. Why had he not been able to tell Emmy what she meant to him?

He racked his brain, thinking of every romantic comedy or romance film he had watched with his sisters.

Emmy wouldn't care for flowers, chocolate, some grand declaration of love in front of her friends. She would need space — that was the most painful realization — but she also needed a way to see that he trusted her, loved her mind and body and everything else. Not only loved them but knew and respected them.

Taking another sip of the bourbon — this time straight out of the bottle — Ryan figured he could work on that plan tomorrow.

Tomorrow, when he had to go back to the museum.

Tomorrow, when he had to see Emmy again.

Fuck.

46

Emmy

"Coffee?" Emmy looked at her phone. It was six p.m.

"It's too late for that," she said, sitting up and groaning. How did her head hurt this much? And how had she gotten to her apartment?

"I'll make you tea," Jeremy said, patting her on the thigh. Phoebe was sitting on the arm of the couch, looking down at her.

"What happened?" Emmy said. She remembered fighting with Ryan, walking out, and Phoebe picking her up. Then there was red wine at ten in the morning and crying. And then Jeremy was there, and then she woke up on this couch.

"Ryan was a fucker," Phoebe replied. She took a moment, reconsidered. "Well, I'm pretty sure he was. When I picked you up, you were crying so hard I couldn't understand you. But I'm sure you're right."

Jeremy came back with a warm mug. Emmy sniffed – peppermint. "Thanks, Jer." He sat on the couch next to her.

"So what did —" Phoebe began, but Jeremy shushed her.

"Not now, Phoebes," he said, and he pulled Emmy into his side and gave her a hug. Emmy took a big breath and sank into her friend. "Em, just stay here, drink this tea, and breathe." She leaned her head against Jer's shoulder as he ran his fingers through her hair. "Sip the tea." She followed his instructions, appreciating the way he continued to shut Phoebe down when she wanted answers.

Emmy didn't have answers. Emmy hadn't even processed what happened yet. Could she?

Finishing her tea, she got up from the couch and took her mug to the kitchen. She loved her friends, but right now, she needed them out of her apartment, needed to be by herself.

"I love you both, but—" she began, walking back into the room. Jeremy was already putting his jacket on and hurrying Phoebe to do the same.

"Text us if you need anything," he said.

"I love you," Phoebe said. "I'm happy to stay here if you need someone around."

"Thanks, but," she sighed, "I think I just need some time by myself." Her two friends nodded and then were gone.

It wasn't supposed to happen like this. She wasn't supposed to get the biggest opportunity of her career, on a national stage, the same day that her heart was broken. She wasn't supposed to have trusted someone in a way that allowed her to be hurt like this.

She wasn't supposed to have fallen in love.

Emmy wrapped her comforter around herself in a sadness cocoon and was reminded of her sophomore year of college. Her bed had felt like a sanctuary on that first day she fell into it, a way to protect her from the outside world. But as her breakdown had progressed, as she had gotten further trapped by her own mind, the bed had become a sort of prison.

Not this time. She had more on her side this time. Therapy. Medication. True friends. A home. Purpose in her work, a legacy to look forward to.

Ryan.

No. Not him. Not anymore.

Emmy set five different alarms for the morning. She *would* wake up. She *would* get out of bed. She *would* push through.

The office felt emptier than normal when Emmy had arrived. She tried to not even look at Ryan's desk as she walked in and booted up her computer. She had taken the bus to work this morning, hadn't even realized how much she had gotten accustomed to commuting with Ryan every day.

"Has that fuckface showed his face in this office yet?" Phoebe poked her head around Emmy's doorframe, a stern look on her face.

"He usually works Monday mornings in the collection," Emmy replied with little enthusiasm, hating the way that she knew Ryan's schedules and patterns. *At least that will make it easy to avoid him.*

"Do you want me to work here all day? Provide a buffer?" Emmy sighed. Phoebe would have ripped out her own hair if it would make Emmy feel better. She had once driven all the way from Breckenridge in a snowstorm because Jeremy needed help moving something into his new house. She had rallied the graduate alumni community during June of 2020 in order to run a fundraiser for Declan that allowed him to take over partial ownership of the bar. She was the definition of *giver*, but Emmy couldn't accept today.

"Phoebes, look — I love you, and I know you want to do this for me, but I can't have you fight my battles. I'm a grown-up, and I can do this." Emmy sighed, rested her head against the door behind her. "It'd be easier if the whole office didn't smell like him, though. I'll never be able to walk into a pool again."

"Fine," Phoebe said, pouting slightly. "What's *your* plan for today?"

"Same shit I used to do," Emmy said, kicking off her shoes and pulling her feet up onto her chair. "Suffer through emails, attend meetings, try to fit in a little research."

"Yeah, but..." Phoebe toyed with a piece of her hair.

Emmy slowly slid her eyes to Phoebe. "But what?"

"Isn't most of your research, kind of..." She continued to play with her hair and finally sucked her teeth and finished her sentence. "Your research is all tied up with Ryan's now. You submitted to the conference; you've got papers out for publication. It just all seems *messy*."

"Yeah, don't I know it." Emmy glanced at her email and saw the conference acceptance. "Oh, by the way, we got accepted to the conference."

"What?"

"Yeah, featured session, too. Whoo." Emmy's voice was flat as she shared the news. How was *this* the way she was reacting after getting this professional recognition?

"And you're co-presenting?"

"Yeah."

"How are —"

"I don't know, Phoebes." Emmy squeezed her eyes shut.

Squelch the dreams of a professional and personal collaboration. Squelch the hopes of changing the way departmental collaboration worked. Squelch that pesky damn word that had floated around her mind when she thought about Ryan. *Remember why you started.* This had to be about her research again. *Just* her research. Emmy could still do what she had always planned on doing. She had always planned on doing it by herself, the way she had done everything else in her career.

This would be a bump in the road. She had overcome a breakdown, a move, COVID, and now she would overcome a paleontologist.

Easy.

47

RYAN

RYAN WAS SITTING ON his couch. Again. It had basically become the only place he was, aside from the collection, this week. He hadn't been able to go into the office, had begged Satya to get what he needed from The House. Even the collection held memories for him — his body pressed up against Emmy's down a dark row of cabinets. He called in sick on Friday and stayed home, attempting to watch all the *Fast and Furious* movies in one day.

He had just started *Fast Five* when he heard a knock at the door. He opened his phone. He hadn't remembered ordering delivery but got up and peeked through the peephole. Foster's olive green eye stared back at him. "Open up, asshole!"

"What?" Ryan said, all Midwestern kindness out of his voice as he opened the door.

"I know your mother did *not* raise you like that," Foster replied, pushing past Ryan and walking into the foyer. He was followed, surprisingly, by Jeremy. Jeremy, who Ryan had very rarely seen out of work and never out of business casual. He was wearing athletic leggings underneath shorts paired with a long-sleeved hooded shirt.

"What?" Jeremy parroted, looking him up and down.

"I've never seen you, like..." He waved a hand up and down.

"I do exist outside of the museum," Jeremy replied haughtily. "I do things that aren't design. Occasionally." He gave Ryan another perusal. "Also, really? You can't say anything." Ryan looked down at himself, realized that his old North Stars T-shirt was stained.

"I'm sick?" he tried.

"Bullshit," Foster said. "Also, you smell like bourbon and sadness, so..." Ryan, dazed, followed the two men into his living room.

Jeremy shoved a thermos into his hands. Ryan opened it and took a tentative sniff. "Peppermint?"

"Trust me," he said, sitting down on a chair. "You need the energy boost from the mint."

He looked at Foster, who was holding a brown bag with a grease stain on the bottom. "I brought you a burger and fries," he explained. "I'm assuming you need something in your stomach to soak up all the bourbon."

"Thanks," Ryan grumbled, taking the bag and making his way back to the spot on the couch.

"So," Jeremy began.

"So," Foster added.

"Sick?"

"I'm not sick," Ryan admitted.

Foster hummed a thoughtful noise. "If you're not sick, maybe you're tired."

"Or maybe you really needed a day off to learn about *family*," Jeremy said, pointing to the frozen car chase on his TV screen.

"Maybe you —"

"Are you two stupid?" Ryan said, frustration boiling over. "I love her and I fucked up!"

"About time you realized," Foster said, to which Jeremy sniffed his agreement.

Ryan slumped back on the couch, and Foster placed the fast-food bag on his lap. "Eat and talk to Uncle Foster."

"I don't know. I just assumed that Emmy and I would have similar long-term goals. We've got so much else in common."

To that statement, Jeremy let out a full body laugh that Ryan had never heard. It sounded like a combination of a goose honking and a semitruck horn.

"What was that?" Ryan asked, slightly horrified.

"It's my laugh," Jeremy replied primly. "Deal with it. However, I laughed because what you just said is the most inane statement I've heard in months."

"Yeah, he's not wrong," Foster added, reaching into the bag and stealing a handful of fries. Ryan gave him an offended look, to which Foster replied, "Advice tax."

"Listen, Ryan, you're quite nice. I like you, and I love Emmy," Jeremy began, "but you two are nothing alike."

"Opposites attract," Foster added. "Listen, I'll eat that burger if you don't." Ryan glared and picked up the sandwich, took a bite just to spite him. *Food was a good call.* When was the last time he had eaten?

"As I was saying," Jeremy continued, "you're nothing alike. Yeah, you're both nerds about your own work, but that's where the similarities end. And that's why this worked. You pushed her, and she pushed you. But it's also why it's hard."

"How do you know?" Ryan asked, taking another bite of the sandwich.

"I've seen real love, like, only three times in my life. My parents were one example. My mom was an artist and my dad was an engineer, but they complemented each other perfectly. Phoebe's brother is another one, and god only knows how that happened." He sniffed, grabbed Ryan's tea, and took a sip for himself. "I have a sneaking suspicion you and Emmy are the same way, but you're going to have to find a way to let her know."

"Something that speaks to *her*," Foster added around a mouthful of fries.

"You're a smart guy," Jeremy said, slapping his thighs and getting up. "Let me know if you need access to our collection or something to help."

"I'm here for moral support," Foster said, popping another fry into his mouth. He checked his watch. "All right, this bro support train is leaving the station."

"Don't you want to stay and watch Ludacris go on a heist?" Ryan laughed.

"As lovely as that sounds, I will gladly pass," Jeremy said. Foster looked interested, but Jeremy tapped him on the shoulder. "You promised you'd try this spin class with me." Foster groaned, and both men gave Ryan a sympathetic pat on the shoulder, then were gone.

Ryan sat on the couch, movie still paused, a half-eaten burger in his hand. He'd never had this. He'd never had people who weren't his family show up for him. That had to mean something, right? Had to mean something about these people, this museum, this town tucked into the foothills of the Rockies?

He shoved the rest of the burger into his mouth, pressed play, and started thinking.

48

RYAN

THREE WEEKS LATER

As Ryan was getting dropped off by his Uber at the Denver Airport, his phone buzzed in his pocket. A number he didn't recognize popped up, and he flicked his thumb over the screen.

3035554102: You'll want to check the art deco bar in terminal 3.

Ryan: Who is this? And why?

3035554102: It's Jeremy. That's her spot where she always drinks before a flight. Make sure she doesn't have more than three gin & tonics, or she'll get sick during takeoff.

Ryan didn't need to ask who "she" was.

Jeremy (Suggested Name): Happened to me when we went to a conference in Miami. She's a horrible sick person.

Ryan: Why are you telling me this?

Jeremy: She hates flying.

Jeremy: And I know you'll take care of her.

If Ryan had been able to focus on anything over the past three weeks except how much he had fucked up, he'd have anticipated how Emmy would hate flying. He had spent most of his time sitting on the couch – alone – and drinking bourbon. He hadn't even told his sisters about this, couldn't face them and tell him what he had done. He had spent his mental energy developing a thousand different apology plans and throwing most of them away.

Of course Emmy hated flying. It involved giving up control and heights, two of her least favorite things. Though he figured right now, he probably counted among her least favorite things, too.

He had half-assed his portion of the presentation preparation, hiding near his microscope for the vast majority of working hours. He still caught glimpses of her in the museum, still caught the faint trace of grapefruit in the office when he popped in from time to time. They still had to communicate, but that happened exclusively via email or during group meetings, with them sitting as far away from each other as possible.

Jeremy had offered an olive branch at work early on, sitting next to Ryan, sharing his design ideas for the exhibition, and, one time, a cup of lemongrass tea that did wonders for a sore throat. This, combined with the dressing down he'd gotten from him with Foster, had opened up a new appreciation for the exhibit designer. Phoebe, however, did not offer any type of goodwill and, instead, spent most of the meetings shooting daggers from her eyes across the table, her body close and fiercely protective of Emmy. Ryan had taken to avoiding Next Door, too, in case Phoebe had convinced Declan to slip arsenic in his drink or something.

The hardest part was watching Emmy in meetings. How she bounced between days where she came in all fire and fury and fought for her ideas in the exhibition and got even the most antisocial or skeptical or boring lab directors to contribute their research to the exhibition. The worst days, though, were the ones where she came in without her spark, the color of her face and hair dimmed slightly, like on an old television. On those days, she tended to sit in the corner of the dining room, letting other people speak over her, making notes and sketches in her notebook that Ryan was dying to see.

He let his thoughts drift as he waited in line for security, pushed down the usual impulse he now had to randomly Wikipedia everything around him to find out the history of it — seriously, what was up with that creepy blue horse? Flicking through his phone to find his boarding pass, he noticed that his flight was in terminal 3. It wouldn't hurt to check on her, would it? He wouldn't want any coworker to get sick on a plane.

He found her at the corner of the bar, her nose stuck in a book, hair piled on her head, and a tiny straw from her drink stuck between her teeth. He didn't have to look at the glass to know what it would contain.

"Hey, Emmy," he said, sidling up next to her and setting his bags down. He approached her tentatively, ready to pick up his bags and head to the gate if she told him to fuck off.

"Hullo," she said glumly, pulling the straw between her front teeth.

"Do you mind if I sit here?" He pulled out the barstool, waited for her answer. She shrugged and took a sip of her drink. If Ryan hadn't spent so much time looking at her – in the office, over dinner, underneath him – he wouldn't have noticed it. But he knew her reactions and how she hid her emotions from the world. Today, her body held a slight stiffness and rigidity, and her left leg jiggled almost imperceptibly. This was Emmy at her most anxious.

Ryan waved the bartender over and ignored the way she flashed him an extra grin and a wink when he ordered a bloody Mary. He tipped his head toward Emmy and indicated that he'd get her next round, too.

"You good?" he asked, the first time he had allowed himself to talk to her about something that wasn't related to the exhibition in three weeks.

"I hate – *hate* – flying," she said through gritted teeth. Her eyes followed his hand as he took his drink from the bartender, flicked up and down his body. "You don't like to drink before noon, I thought."

"I don't like seeing people drinking alone," he said, tapping the edge of his glass to Emmy's and hoping that a stray piece of celery or an olive didn't fall into her drink. "Plus, airports and flying are boring. A drink makes it fun."

"You think this is *fun*?"

Ryan nodded, taking a sip of his drink. He didn't actually like bloody Marys but thought ordering a straight bourbon at nine thirty would be a bit weird. Plus, bourbon made him too honest recently.

"The people watching is interesting, and being here means you're going somewhere, and that's fun." Ryan didn't get to travel a lot growing up and had spent most of his breaks from school trying to find a cheap flight to somewhere new.

Emmy picked at the corner of her napkin, then rolled her eyes. Something heated in Ryan's lower belly, a reminder of the way they used to prod and poke at each other. If this was a month ago, he would have made a game out of people watching to get Emmy's mind off the flight, then suggested that they find a dark corner of the airport to get even more distracted.

"How long have you been here?" he asked, trying to make conversation.

"Long enough to have only one drink," she said. "I'm sure Jeremy texted you. I know my limits on flights now." Her gray eyes shot to him, cold and metallic. "You don't need to watch over me."

"I'm just being friendly," he said, a bit defensively. Looking for a change in topic, he looked at Emmy's phone, where she had been absentmindedly scrolling through unfamiliar looking maps.

"What's that?"

"Nothing." She clicked her phone off and flipped it over, but less than a minute later, she had opened the same website again, reloaded it quickly.

"What are you checking? Is it something for the presentation? I can help."

Emmy sighed. “I get here early so I can check things. First off, it’s to make sure that I don’t get delayed during security, but then I prepare. These” — she indicated her phone — “are PIREPs, which are the reports of turbulence that pilots send in as they’re flying across the country. I tend to cross reference them with the planned flight path and then figure out how far along I should expect to feel any bumps.” She took a sip of her drink, then a gulp. “And I’ll also check general weather forecasts, delays from around the country, the type of plane I’m flying on, where it’s coming from, the average time of arrival and departure for the past few weeks. Sometimes, if I get here early enough, I can find out the last time the plane was serviced, but that depends on the airline and the airport.”

Not for the first time, Ryan’s heart ached when he thought about the weight of the anxiety that Emmy carried constantly. He knew she worked on it, knew she went to therapy every other week, knew what medications she took, knew she would claim that it was just part of who she was, but if he could wave some magical wand of serotonin, he’d take it all away in a second.

“But you already knew I was crazy,” she said softly into her drink.

“Don’t,” Ryan said, more sternly than he intended. “Don’t say that.” Emmy’s eyes raised up and met his, and he saw that same vulnerability and fear that had first caused him to draw her into his arms that one snowy night months ago, to find a way to give her pleasure. He hated the fact that he'd taken that away, hated how he had never let himself tell her how he felt.

"You know you can't really *do* anything about the plane once you're in the air, right?" Ryan said, immediately, once again, realizing the way he had said something that inadvertently caused Emmy pain.

"When has my anxiety ever made a lick of goddamn sense?" Emmy muttered, clenching her teeth around her straw. "It just *is*. It's a constant. I can prepare, and if I know to expect turbulence, I don't freak out as much when it happens." She shrugged again, finished her drink. "You, more than any person, should know that's how I operate. I prepare for the worst, and then I can expect it and be ready when it comes."

"The worst thing doesn't always happen," Ryan replied.

"Tell that to my recent history," she shot back, her eyes to his. "The last time I took a leap and expected the best, I had it thrown in my face."

"Em," he said, reaching out to touch her hand lightly.

"No," she said, pulling her hand away to her lap. "You can call me Emmy." She opened her mouth to say something else, then closed it and went back to her drink. It was mind-blowing the way Ryan missed her rage, missed the way she would rile him up constantly.

"Truce," he said, turning to her and using her words from months ago. "We have to work together this weekend. We have to figure out a way to do this presentation and get through the conference without everyone knowing that you hate me."

She looked at him, took a moment to think. "I don't hate you," she said quietly.

"Really?"

"I'm disappointed. You hurt me. You let me down – but I don't hate you," Emmy said sadly.

Ryan sighed, unable to find the words to say. This wasn't the place to apologize. This wasn't the way he was going to let Emmy know what she meant to him, though he almost threw all his plans to the wind and slid off his barstool to get on his knees and beg her to take him back.

But, thank god, he was prevented from doing that by an announcement over the airport PA that their flight was boarding. Emmy paid her tab quickly, and Ryan reached for his wallet to pay for his. The bartender gave a wink and slipped him a piece of paper that said *On me* with a phone number. Emmy made a disgruntled noise, and he looked up to see her with a straight face, frustration emanating from her skin.

Of all the fucking times to get hit on by a bartender, it had to be when I'm traveling with the woman I love who cannot stand to be in the same room with me.

Of course – of course – Ryan's seat was right next to Emmy's, which he should have thought about because the museum had booked their tickets. And, of course, because of the perennial struggles of the museum's budget, they were in coach. Again, a few weeks ago, he would have loved this arrangement. Probably tried to sneak his hand into her lap and between her legs during the flight. But now it was four hours of pure temptation.

But only if you're mine, too.

You don't get to tell me what it means for me to be successful.

We are only colleagues.

I don't hate you.

Not for the first time, shuffling down this too-small-airplane aisle, Ryan had the desire to smash his head into an overhead baggage compartment and maybe knock some sense into himself. Or go back in time and duct tape his mouth shut.

"We've got middle and window," Ryan said, checking his ticket. "Which one do you want?"

"You're the tall one. What works best for you?"

"Because you're pocket sized." He smirked back. "Ideally, my legs need the aisle seat, but here we are with these first-class accommodations." He tried something. "Does it help your anxiety to see out the window?"

"Not really. I watched too much *Twilight Zone* as a kid." A ghost of a grin then. "Is it too much to ask you to take the window? I'd rather work on focusing on my computer or book or whatever terrible show I downloaded last night."

"Still working through that survival show?" he asked, contorting his body to fit into the tiniest airplane seat. Ryan wasn't sure that Mountain Air was a reliable airline, but apparently it fit the museum's budget. He crunched his body into the window seat, knees knocking against the tray table in front of him. Ryan attempted to tuck his carry-on underneath his feet but had to settle for resting his feet on top of the bag. He slid out his iPad and AirPods and opened the screen to an article he had been working through last night.

Out of the corner of his eye, he watched Emmy slide into her seat and perform a similar maneuver, but in addition to a book and a computer, she had bulky noise-canceling headphones, earplugs, a face mask, and a small pillow.

"Don't say anything," she said, noticing him watching her. "The last thing I want to do in the air is have to contort my body under this seat to try to find something, so I'd rather have everything within arm's reach if I can." Her fingers ran lightly over all the items, checking that they were all there, and Ryan noticed her blue nail polish was chipped.

"Aren't there, like, meds you could take for when you fly?"

"They exist and they work for some people, but not me. Xanax and I are decidedly not friends. I get into a really bad 'who the fuck cares about anything' thought spiral, so I avoid that." Emmy's hands twitched, and Ryan resisted the urge to take her hands like he had gotten accustomed to, to slide his fingers through her own when she started to ball her fingers into fists. "Edibles make me either pass out or super anxious, so I don't do that either. So alcohol it is." She made a production of shrugging her shoulders, then let them fall, that look of vulnerable defeat on her face.

"I took an aerodynamics class in undergrad. Do you want me to explain the science of flight?" As usual, Ryan didn't know when to keep his mouth shut around Emmy.

Emmy sniffed. “I don’t need you to patronize me. Logically, I know it’s safe. Just like logically, I know that high ropes courses are safe or that ski lifts won’t fall apart. It doesn’t stop my brain from spiraling the minute I’m out of control.” She looked him straight in the eye, steel staring through him, and added, “If anyone should know that, it’s you.”

Her words hit him like a punch to the gut. Ryan nodded, then turned to the window and watched luggage be loaded onto the plane while Emmy continued to organize her belongings. He flipped through pages on his iPad, attempting to connect to the shoddy in-flight wi-fi. All things to busy his hands, busy his mind, busy his eyes.

“Cabin doors are checked and armed. Flight attendants, prepare for takeoff,” came the voice over the speaker. Emmy clenched and unclenched her hands, then realized she hadn’t buckled her seat belt.

“Sorry, I always avoid this until the last minute,” she said, fumbling near her hip for the belt and inadvertently brushing over Ryan’s as she found the clasp. He gritted his teeth to keep from grunting. Memories of all the times her painted fingernails had gripped his hips from the front or the back came rolling through his mind. Emmy, however, was clicking her seat belt together, tightening it, and checking the tray table in front of her.

“Em,” he said, turning toward her, trying to distract her. “Tell me about something.”

“What?”

He pulled his headphones out of his ears, pausing the music. “Tell me about what you studied in undergrad.”

“Why?”

“Because your brain is going. Tell me about your favorite class.”

She sighed and straightened her shoulders, still jiggling her left leg nervously. Occasionally, it brushed against his. “I once took a class on utopian experiments that I loved.”

“What are those?”

“Cities, towns where people tried to make an ideal or perfect society. Really big in the Midwest around the turn of the century.” She looked at him. “What kind of silverware do you have?”

“I have no idea,” he lied.

“Yes, you do,” she said, just a tiny hint that she had been in his house, had practically moved herself in.

“Oneida.”

“Thought so. Fun fact: that was a Christian socialist community in New York in the mid-1800s. They practiced free love and group marriage and” — she sassily flicked her eyes to him — “it was on the men to be responsible for birth control.”

“How?”

“Holding it.” She grinned, the first true Emmy grin he had seen in weeks. Figures it took talking about obscure sexual practices in history for her to smile. *What a wonderful, weird woman.* The engines roared to life, and Ryan kept Emmy talking about utopian experiments — she was adamant that Burning Man and Renaissance Faires be considered modern versions — until the wheels left the tarmac with a tiny bump.

"All good," he whispered, putting his headphones back in.

49

Emmy

All good, her ass. Ryan had distracted her through taxiing and takeoff; that much was true. So they had avoided a repeat of Tenerife (almost six hundred people died when two planes ran into each other on the runway on the Spanish Island in 1977), and she hadn't heard the plane's tail hit the runway (the cause for the largest single airplane disaster in Japan in 1985).

She could relax when the plane hit ten thousand feet, when she could put her tray table down. *Then* the plane would be out of the range where statistically most accidents occurred.

Looking for another distraction, she allowed herself to look at Ryan but not to acknowledge the way their thighs were pressed up against one another, courtesy of the tiny seats and their long legs. He was skimming through an article, the damn pencil twirling in his fingers in the same way it used to drive her up a wall in meetings before they had ever touched. He was totally unaffected by the fact that the plane lurched and drove forward, going what Emmy knew was at least one hundred and fifty miles an hour. Finally, there was the tiny bell that signaled ten thousand feet, and Emmy ripped her book out of the seat back, put her headphones on, and turned on a favorite playlist to drown out the whine of the engine.

She struggled to focus on her book, her eyes darting from the page to the drink cart making its way down the aisle, to Ryan, who had lain his head against the window. His glasses were slightly askew, and he had the tempered breathing that Emmy knew was the rhythm of his sleep. Not only was she pissed that he was able to sleep on the plane, but seeing him there, calm and content, reminded her of all the mornings she had woken up before him and watched him sleep. His curls were always messy in the morning, and he always slept with a small smile on his face. Emmy liked to think it was his purest state.

And the jerk could do it on a plane. Ugh.

Emmy's spiral of jealousy and rage and...something was paused as the beverage cart stopped by Emmy and Ryan's row. She removed her headphones and tried to control the way her pulse spiked when she heard the roar of the engines again. *Seriously, how could Ryan sleep through this?*

She ordered her standard airplane drink, then, rolling her eyes at her own hesitation, tapped Ryan on the shoulder.

"Hey." *Tap.* "Ryan." *Tap.* "Ry." *Tap, tap.* "Doc." The old — is three weeks old? — nickname woke him up suddenly, his eyes searching and finding hers.

"Em?" She nodded toward the cart.

"Get a drink," she said, holding out her credit card. "It's on me because you have to deal with all of my shit."

"You don't have to —"

"Sir? What would you like?" The flight attendant was clearly impatient with their bickering, and Emmy saw a slight blush cross his face. *He still cares so much about what people think about him.*

"Bourbon and coke, please." Ryan nodded at Emmy's drink. "Your standard G&T?"

"Nah, ever since I was a little girl, I only drink ginger ale while flying," Emmy said, taking a sip of her drink. "With gin now, though."

"Well, then change my order to a bourbon-ginger," he said to the flight attendant, giving her his standard grin that caused Emmy to either roll her eyes or simmer with jealousy when they had gone out. The flight attendant smiled at him and quickly changed the order, passing the drink to Emmy to hand to him, along with a small bag of pretzels. She shifted in her seat and rotated her torso to pass the drink, Ryan's fingers wrapping around hers as he took the small plastic cup from her, the bag of pretzels falling down below.

Ryan reached down and felt around on the floor for the snack package, inadvertently grazing the side of her foot with his hand. Emmy heard him suck in a sharp breath, noticed the way her own body reacted to the part of her that Ryan had explored and loved in a way no other man had ever done. He straightened up quickly, passing the pretzels to his left hand with a muttered "sorry."

This was the most they had touched, the most they had shared space and oxygen, since the morning she stormed out. Meetings had felt like torture, and Emmy avoided the office and the gym and the coffee shop – carving out a relief map of the places on campus she had known without him.

Thank god they had never pursued the fantasy she had about the library.

Emmy and Ryan made casual conversation over their drinks, talking about nothing in particular – how the weather had been in Vanberg, stale jokes about airplane food, the basic types of communication that two people who had once shared the most intimate moments could revert to. As the conversation awkwardly died down, Emmy put her headphones back over her ears in the universal sign for "I'm done talking to you." She didn't have it in her – not with flying, not with the conference – to put up with talking to Ryan, to pretend there wasn't this chasm between them. Better to listen to a playlist and pretend to read a book on the history of shopping malls.

That plan lasted for roughly a half an hour. Until Emmy – even through her noise-canceling headphones – heard a dim ping of the flight announcement. Her eyes flicked up, and she saw the fasten seat belt sign go on. She paused her music, removed one earpiece, and looked around the cabin.

"Flight attendants, please take your seats."

"Shit, shit, shit, shit," Emmy muttered to herself. She looked across, over Ryan, through the windows.

Dark thunderheads in the distance. She quickly checked their plane's position on the flight monitor, mentally comparing it to the weather and turbulence reports she had seen back in Denver. *There wasn't supposed to be anything here.*

Ryan, who, by this time, had noticed Emmy's movements, took out his AirPods. "What's up?"

"We're in the damn Midwest," she said to him, beginning her unconscious habit of clenching and unclenching her hands. "These storms pop up out of nowhere, and they're hard to avoid." Emmy rose up in her seat, scanned the cabin again, saw no flight attendants. "It's never a good sign when they ask flight attendants to sit down." Her chest began to rise and fall quickly, her breathing quickening as she fought with her anxiety and lost — as usual.

"Em," Ryan said. "It's going to be fine."

Just that moment, the plane dropped.

"Fuck!" Emmy yelped, her hands flailing, looking for something to hold on to, as if this was a roller coaster and she was looking for a lap bar to hold.

Ryan, damn him, reached his left hand over, across his body, and laid it over Emmy's shaking hands, stilling them with a calm pressure that he had used before on the ski lift. Without Emmy realizing it, he had slipped his right hand behind her and had begun making small circles on her lower back.

"Shh, Em," he whispered, his hand on her back continuing to soothe. "Breathe through it. Planes don't crash because of turbulence."

"I know, I know," she said, squeezing her eyes shut as the plane shook again and another spasm of terror racked her body. "I know, but –"

"You don't have to explain anything," he whispered, his breath tickling her ear. Ignoring the pit in her stomach, she kept her eyes closed and leaned against him, squeezing his hand in what she was sure was a painful grip. His hand on her back never stopped moving, and he began to whisper short affirmations to her.

You're doing fine.

You've got this.

It's good.

I'm here.

Gradually, she felt the muscles in her back relax, her quads release, her breathing calm ever so slightly. After what felt like seconds or hours, another 'ping' rang through the cabin, and the fasten seat belt sign turned off. Emmy blinked her eyes open, looked around again. Everyone had continued on like nothing happened, still watching movies, still playing stupid phone games. Everyone except her.

Tears pricked at her eyes and embarrassment shot through her body. "Shit, I'm so sorry," she said, trying to pull away from Ryan. Just for a second, he held on, perhaps even pulled her a few inches closer to him.

"Stop apologizing," he hissed. "You are *you*, and you should never apologize for that."

"I'm fine," she said, pulling away, building her walls up again. "I don't need you to take care of me."

"Emmy, I'm here for you," Ryan said, still soft, letting her hands go. "You know that. I care about you. That hasn't changed throughout all of this."

That felt dangerously close to the type of confession Emmy had dreamed about, had wondered if her anger and quick temper had put out of the realm of possibility. But thirty thousand feet in the sky, out of control, and three drinks in was not the time to be asking those questions or having those conversations.

"Thanks, Ry," she said quietly. "I appreciate it."

Fortunately for Emmy, the rest of the flight passed by without much consequence, and with only one awkward moment where both Ryan and Emmy had to squeeze out of the aisle so he could piss, they arrived safely. Emmy didn't fully relax until they had landed on the ground and she could use her cell again and send a text to Phoebe and June.

Emmy: Landed.

June: Hooray!

Phoebe: WHAT IS THE HOTEL SITUATION

Emmy: ???

June: She's convinced that the museum booked you in one hotel room.

Phoebe: With one bed!

Emmy: Fun night?

June: She's having feelings tonight and putting them on you.

Emmy: Who's all there?

June: Me and Jer. Colin's coming to pick us up. He just left a farmers' market meeting.

Emmy: Dork.

Separate thread

Emmy: Is she good?

June: She's fine. Just sad.

June: You know how she can get if she's been drinking and stoned.

Emmy: Don't I know it.

June: Colin's outside with her now. They're having a brother/sister heart-to-heart.

Emmy: Thanks for taking care of her.

June: I love you and I love her. You're my friend. She's basically my sister. No problem.

Emmy: Okay, we're trying to figure out the public transit situation now.

Emmy: Ryan can't read a map.

Emmy: We're fucked.

June: Hey — and one thing? Just remember to follow what feels right.

June: It worked for me.

June: And I'm both talking about my career.

June: And love.

Emmy successfully took over navigating the way to their hotel, which was where they would be presenting tomorrow. It was a fast turnaround. As much as she would have loved to be here for the entire week of smaller sessions and breakout groups, the museum (and her own budget) could really only afford the weekend of keynotes and important sessions. Which, she had to continually remind herself, was when she and Ryan were presenting. This was why she had started. This was her chance to make an impact. Change things, create a future for herself.

They had gotten a key spot — the final day of the conference, which began with a keynote about visitor experience. Their session was right before lunch, which gave her the entire afternoon to mingle during a poster session before the closing dinner and drinks.

Walking into the lobby, they quickly checked in, got their room keys. They rode the elevators in silence, both of them checking their phones to avoid looking at each other.

"Well," Ryan said lamely, lingering at his door. Their rooms were next to each other, the type that a family would rent. Emmy was sure there was a door between their rooms that a month ago would have been left wide open.

We could have saved the museum, like, four hundred dollars, she thought grimly.

"Thanks," she said quickly, waving her keycard over the door handle and unlocking it. "I appreciate what you did for me on the flight." He needed to know that, just like he needed to know that she didn't hate him. Ryan was still a good person, even if he maybe wasn't a good person for her. Or it wasn't a good time. Or maybe Emmy wasn't a good person. Fuck, she didn't know.

Emmy went to open her door but looked to her right, where Ryan was leaning against his own, bag in his hand.

"It's never a problem, Em." She didn't bother correcting him about the nickname.

"I know this week is awkward, but you know that presenting here means the world to me. Thank you."

"It's never a problem," he repeated, then nodded his head at her to communicate good night. Emmy opened her own door, heard the lock snick shut behind her. She set her suitcase down and busied herself with setting up the necessities. Toiletry bag, meds out, comfortable clothes to sleep in, phone charger, white noise machine.

Finally, with nothing else to do, she plugged her phone in and turned on the noise machine.

"Fuck," she said to the empty room.

The room didn't respond.

50

Ryan

RYAN WOKE UP HARD and alone, the way he had for the previous month. He stared at the shared door between their hotel rooms, the one he knew Emmy had deadbolted and probably put a chair in front of, and wished that he could rip the door off its hinges. He could go to her, find her in the blankets, her bun some kind of nest on top of her head, sleeping in an old shirt and boxers. She'd be the sexiest thing he'd ever seen, and he could crawl over her in the blankets. Or, better yet, crawl underneath them. Use his mouth to beg for forgiveness, among other things.

Knocking the back of his skull against the headboard, he swore. He couldn't do any of that. He could only wake up and see whether the hotel had a pool. Emmy would have known, would have found some type of pool-specific Yelp to see if he could do laps.

Luckily for him, he was able to do a half hour of swimming just to get some nervous tension out of his body. Grabbing a quick shower, resisting the urge to touch himself, Ryan got dressed in his conference wear.

It had been so long since he had to wear a suit. It felt a bit like a little kid playing dress-up. Was the last time the gala? The night he had given Emmy his scarf?

He put a tiny bit of gel in his hair, trying to tame it in some type of professional manner, then slipped on the light blue button-up, the sport coat with extra wide shoulders, the slacks, and belt. He double-checked that all of his notes and the presentation were downloaded on his iPad, sent an extra copy of the presentation to the coordinator and Emmy. He knew she would have emailed one, printed out a few copies, and probably had a thumb drive as a backup.

Slipping everything he needed into his bag, he took the elevator downstairs for the morning coffee session. A mentor of his in graduate school had given him the following advice on being successful at conferences – wake up early and stay up late. That was the way to meet everyone. Get a jump start on connections in the morning, then solidify them over drinks in the evening. It had always felt natural for Ryan, usually sharing drinks with other scientists late into the evening, but now he saw it as a way of managing the old boys' club. These sessions were for extroverts who felt comfortable mingling, who loved small talk, who already felt like they belonged at the conference. Thinking back to his last paleontology conference, he realized that the only people who had been at the bar during the last call had been white men who looked like him, had gone to the same schools.

All of this was on his mind as he turned the corner into the breakfast session, expecting a quiet repeat of that same conference. What he saw shocked him: Emmy at the center of the room, a cup of coffee in her left hand, smiling and sparkling with a ring of people surrounding her as she talked animatedly with her right hand.

That damn smile. It was the same one he had chased watching her videos from the collection tours during shutdown, the same one she had given him when their ideas flowed back and forth from each other, the same one he had gotten used to waking up next to.

Her hair was down, sleek and shiny, some of it pinned back so only her bangs brushed her face. She was in a loose white blouse that hugged her curves but covered up her arm muscles, paired with a dark green pencil skirt that fell to just below her knees. His eyes drifted lower, saw that her ensemble was paired with patent leather heels that had him imagining her talking about exhibition theory as he lay at her feet.

She scanned the room, and he saw the moment her eyes landed on him. Those gray circles widened, her eyebrows raised, and for a moment, an expression of relief glimmered across her face before it was replaced with the same charming public Emmy. Ryan filled a cup with coffee, tossed some cream into it haphazardly, then made his way over to where she was holding court.

"And here comes my colleague and co-curator now," Emmy said, stepping back slightly to make room for Ryan in the circle. "Everyone, this is Dr. Andersson,

Paleontological Curator at the Vanberg University Center for Science, Technology, and History."

"You can call me Ryan," he said, nodding to the gathered group, ignoring the way that Emmy saying his title made him feel. It made them sound like a team, like they hadn't been repelled by each other like two magnets over the past few weeks.

Maybe the magnetic poles were reversing. That would explain everything.

Ryan let Emmy take the lead in the conversation as it inevitably swerved from their backgrounds and research to their presentation. Not only was it on the busiest day of the conference, but their session, Fusing Curatorial Practices, was featured as a recommended session by the keynote speaker. Ryan was nervous, and he couldn't imagine what Emmy was feeling. His mind wandered to how he would have calmed their nerves just a few weeks ago. He also found that, contrary to what he would have expected, he was nervous as hell, but Emmy seemed self-assured, confident.

She was able to joke and charm, to poke and prod in the way that only she could, deftly avoiding the conversation that one fellow attendee tried to have about joining him for drinks after with a joke and a casual dismissal that emboldened Ryan for a second before he remembered that she had stormed out of *his* house.

But he had a plan. Contrary to what she had accused him of, Ryan could plan for something he cared about, and he had spent a lot of time putting this one together. But the conference had to come first. Nothing about this would be worth a damn if their presentation didn't go well. If Emmy couldn't show the entire museum world her brilliance.

He'd compliment her colors — the orange to her blue, the purple to her yellow, the green to her red. She was primary colors, bold and assured, and Ryan was there to support her. In whatever way she needed.

Breakfast began to peter out, and Emmy sipped the last of her coffee, tossed her cup in the trash, and turned and looked at him. "Ready, Doc?" A hint of a smile.

"Of course, Em," he replied and followed her into the large room where their session would be. Emmy fiddled with the projector, checked the slides, while Ryan double-checked his notes for their presentation on the iPad. People began to trickle in, and soon, the entire room was full of attendees, even some standing on the sides. He looked at Emmy, and she grinned, fully in her element. He was ready to bask in the glory of her brilliance.

51

Emmy

It had gone better than expected, better than those fantasies Emmy had allowed herself to indulge in when she couldn't sleep and her brain, contrary to its normal inclination, began to dream of the good outcomes. How the audience would erupt into a standing ovation, how she could consult with any museum around the country, how she could turn their tiny mountain town museum into a leader in their field.

How Ryan would realize that he was wrong about her.

And maybe she would admit that she was wrong about him.

Ha! Emmy laughed to herself as she ordered a gin and tonic from the after-dinner bar. *That's not likely to happen*. In conversations with her therapist, with Jeremy, with June and Colin, Emmy had gradually begun to realize she might have jumped to conclusions a bit quickly in her fight with Ryan. But he hadn't rushed to correct them, hadn't fought with her to show he cared.

Phoebe agreed with Emmy, but Phoebe would probably defend her no matter what.

Emmy stood awkwardly to the side of the room, looking around for familiar faces from old conferences or even graduate school. Katie had to be around here, right? But she saw a mass of unfamiliar faces, all holding drinks and mingling. *Ryan would know what to say*, she thought, and then she caught a glance of him, holding a neat bourbon (of course), chatting to another paleontologist who had come up to him after their presentation. Probably from the Science Museum of Minnesota or the American Museum of Natural History or somewhere else that was "better" than VU. He had probably packed up his house already. Emmy should check the VU job boards to see if his position was posted—

"Ms. Bonaire?" a voice to the left of her jolted her out of her spiral.

"Yes?"

"Hi, I'm Dulce Hernandez. I'm the cultural collections curator at Science Museum of Minnesota —"

"Oh, I've read your work!" Emmy said excitedly. "The way you totally publicized your NAGPRA process was astounding!"

The small woman with dark skin and a mane of gray hair smiled at Emmy. "I'm glad you think so. I was incredibly impressed with your presentation today."

"Thank you so much. It was really a combined effort —"

Emmy was cut off again by the woman slipping a business card into her hand. "I'd love to talk to you about curatorial opportunities in Minneapolis," she said with a nod of her head. "I think you could bring a fantastic perspective to our team. The breaking down of institutional silos is truly the next big thing in museums, especially as we decolonize…"

Emmy nodded, continued talking, sneaking glances at the business card in her hand. *This would be an amazing chance*, she thought, but she remembered all the plans she had in Vanberg. The flexibility with her research. The consults she had already scheduled with the local tribal representatives, how consistency would be important for her visitors and stakeholders.

"Thank you," Emmy said again. "I'll think about it."

The rest of the night passed in a blur of business cards, job offers, conversations about consultations, contracts, paper proposals, and more. Emmy was having a hard time keeping up with all the names and barely had time to get a second drink before someone else wanted to talk to her. Was this what it felt like to be popular? She felt like the debutante in a Regency film, her dance card full from the moment she stepped into the ballroom.

She looked around for Ryan, to see whether he was getting the variety of job offers that he so clearly wanted, but found that they had switched positions. She was in the center of every conversation, and he lingered around the outside, bourbon in hand the entire time. A few times, she caught him watching her, but she simply tossed her hair and tried to ignore it.

When the hotel staff had kicked out the last few drunk historians arguing with anthropologists over what the difference between their disciplines were, Emmy followed the crowd out, her feet aching, desperate to get to her hotel room and out of this high-waisted skirt (fuck

Spanx, seriously). She wanted comfortable clothes, an unsatisfying orgasm with her travel vibrator, and sleep.

Emmy had just thrown on an oversized T-shirt, brushed her teeth, popped her pills into her mouth, and was searching for the cup of water to throw back the meds when there was a knock at the door. She cupped her hands and gulped down a bit of water frantically. Looking through the peephole, she expected to see someone from the hotel, maybe to bring a towel or something she had forgotten she requested.

Instead, there was Ryan. Ryan with his hair a bit messy, his bow tie untied and hanging at the sides of his neck. The top few buttons of his dress shirt were undone, and his jacket was off, tossed over his arm. Emmy had orbited around Ryan the entire night and had always seen him with a glass of bourbon in his hand, but as she racked her brain, couldn't remember seeing him drink it. Her mind had been spinning after the successful presentation, compounded by the barrage of job offers and interviews that had fallen at her feet during the after-party.

"Em?" came his voice through the door, quiet, almost defeated. "Em, are you awake?" She had gotten lost in her recounting of the party and forgotten that she was looking through the door while Ryan was *there*, just a few inches away from her. Still quieter, "I know it takes a while for you to fall asleep, so I was hoping you would still be up."

"I'm here," she said, her voice sounding foreign to her own ears. She unlocked the deadbolt, the added lock she had bought from an Instagram ad, and finally the door lock, then opened the door just a crack. Ryan stayed where he was, his tall body collapsed against the frame, devoid of its usual strength and lightness, devoid of the smile and charm that usually emanated from his body.

"Hi," he whispered.

"Hey, Doc," she said, the nickname slipping from her lips without a second thought. Ryan clearly heard it, closed his eyes as if in momentary pain.

"Em," he said, the name coming out in a whisper. "I'm so fucking sorry."

"Are you drunk?" She had to know if he meant this. Whether the words he was saying were from the whiskey or his heart.

"I carried around the same damn glass all night," he said, looking up at her. "I didn't touch a fucking drop. I watched *you* all night."

"Me?"

"Yeah, Em. I watched you mingle and charm the pants off every director in that room. I watched the fucking director of the Science Museum of Minnesota beg you to be on their exhibits team. I saw the Exploratorium ask you how to integrate history into a new exhibition. Shit, I saw Williamsburg come over and ask you to interview for a curatorial position there." He ran a hand through his hair and sighed, looking at her with a pained expression on his face. "I watched these leaders of our field beg you to leave VU, and I watched you turn all of them down." He swallowed. "I think I know why, but I want to hear it from you, Em."

Emmy swallowed, nervous, still in her doorway. "Because those places aren't my home. My people are in Vanberg, my passion," she finally said. "Those museums don't need me to help tell their story. VU does. Sara needs me to help bring her story to light. And after that, there are a million other stories to tell. There will never be enough time."

"You want a place where you matter," he said.

"Yes. I want to be seen. I want to leave a legacy through my work." Emmy pulled herself up to her tallest height, broadened her muscles beneath the thin T-shirt. "My work doesn't matter less because it's at VU and not at the Smithsonian. My worth doesn't diminish because I don't have a PhD."

"I know. I *see* you. You matter."

"You know? You see?"

"Yes." A whisper. "I didn't, but now I do. Because that's what you do, you damned beautiful historian. You teach me things and make me rethink myself. You're the fucking living embodiment of the scientific method."

"Oh."

"That's a compliment."

"Oh."

"And I fucking love you for it." An ice-cold blast shot through Emmy's core.

"What?"

"I love you."

Emmy scrambled for words, found one. "Why?"

"Because you're *you*, you damn fool," he said, a glimmer of his old smile coming to his face. "And I know it's late and this is not well organized and — fuck, Emmy. I'm sorry and I love you."

"Ryan." Emmy opened the door an inch wider.

"Emmy."

"Doc."

"Em. Give me another chance. I swear I won't fuck it up. We're epic together. What we did here at the conference, what we're doing at the museum, it's —"

"Shh," Emmy said, closing her eyes for a second, focusing on regaining control of her breath. Wasn't this what she had wanted? Wasn't this what she had secretly hoped for, the one time her anxiety allowed her to think about making something right? *Remember why you started.* It was originally about her work, but somewhere along the line, it had become about building the life she wanted. And didn't she want Ryan as a part of that life?

"I care for you," she said quietly, a bit confused. "I knew it, but I buried it. And here you are, and—" His eyes blazed, his hands twitched, but he stayed still. Emmy was in the driver's seat now, and he was letting her control where they were going. "I'm still hurt, and we still have to talk about things, but today went so fucking well and —" She paused, looked at him, every emotion so plain on his handsome face. Gently, sweetly, she raised up just slightly on the balls of her feet and pressed her lips to his. She cupped his jaw in her hands and kissed him harder. Emmy kissed him in the way she had dreamed about for the past month, the way she had when they were together. She opened her mouth over his and groaned her affection, then immediately slid her tongue into his mouth, let it dance with his. Ryan's arms slid down to her waist, grabbed her ass underneath her T-shirt, pushing the fabric up.

She pulled back for a second to whisper, "*Come in, please*," tugging him into the room by the collar of his shirt. Ryan followed willingly, but when he kicked the door closed behind her, he held her at arm's length and looked up and down her body, taking her in.

"Em. Emmy," he began, then swallowed. "Emmeline Bonaire, you enticing witch. Promise me you'll spend the day with me tomorrow." Emmy went to kiss him, and he stiffened his arms to keep her away. "I have something I want to show you."

"Okay," she said, nodding her head.

"And we can talk. We should talk," he added.

"Fine." Emmy thought she would have agreed to anything at this point to feel Ryan's lips on hers again, but Ryan held her with those damn piercing green eyes. She steeled her face, tried to recall all the serious conversations she and Ryan had had under covers, between their pillows at three a.m. when neither of them could sleep. "Yes, Ryan." Now it was her turn to swallow. "Okay. I'll spend the morning with you." *I'll spend my life with you*, but she wasn't quite ready to admit that. He had said he loved her, but she should wait until morning to see if his emotions were true, to know whether it was safe to return them, past the words she had almost admitted already.

"I have plans," he said, leaning down to bite her earlobe.

"You know nothing about plans," she gasped.

"Says the woman with a fifteen-year plan sketched out in the back of her notebook," he whispered in her ear, sending shivers down her spine.

"You weren't supposed to see," she replied.

"I'm trying to make myself a part of that plan," Ryan said into her neck, finally connecting his lips to her skin. Emmy ignored the flip in her stomach, the way her brain raced to conclusions and glimpses of a future. All the things she had never allowed herself to dream of, that she had pushed down to focus on her career, came flooding to the surface. A partnership that would allow her to continue to grow as a person.

But, came the tiny Anxiety voice in the back of her brain, *didn't Ryan already once say that wasn't good enough? That she was settling?*

But he loved her. He had said that, too.

Emmy shut the voices up in her brain by pressing her lips to Ryan's neck, running her hands down the line of buttons at his front, and tugging his shirt from his waistband, her intentions clear. Ryan fisted a hand in her hair and pressed her into the wall at the doorway to her hotel room.

"Yes?" he asked.

"Yes," she breathed. "God damn, Doc, I missed you. I missed everything about you." It took a second, his brain seeming to process her consent, the fact that she hadn't thrown him out into the hallway, before he pressed his lips to hers and kissed her, licking into her mouth with an unrestrained passion. Emmy walked him backward, slipping her fingers into the belt loops of his pants and pulling him toward the bed. He kept his hands on her body, her T-shirt already above her hips.

"I missed you, too," he whispered into her stomach as he dropped to his knees.

"You and your foot thing," she said, pressing the ball of her foot into the muscle of his shoulder. He ran his hand up her leg, turned and kissed her ankle.

"It's more of a leg thing," he protested, but Emmy scoffed. Ryan rolled his eyes behind his glasses, then began to kiss up the inside of her thigh. "Okay, maybe it's a foot thing, but it's also a *you* thing. Every damn inch of your body drives me wild." He reached the top of her thigh with his lips, then, against the damp fabric covering her, said, "Especially this part." He mouthed her through the fabric, the extra scratch of her panties driving her wild. Ryan lifted a hand between her thighs, slid the fabric to the side, and pressed in, fucking her with his tongue, teasing her clit.

"Up," she said, tugging on his hair, tossing his glasses to the side.

"You need to come," he said against her belly button.

"I have a vibrator — never leave home without it," she quipped. "It's in my bag in the bathroom." Ryan was gone from her body in a second, tossing off his clothes as he walked. While he scrambled in the bathroom, Emmy took off her T-shirt, her nipples pebbling in an instant. When he came back, naked, he had the silver bullet in one hand and a condom in the other.

"Expecting big things from the conference, were we?" he said, tearing open the packet, sliding it on, and crawling onto the bed.

"It was for you," she confessed against his neck. "Even if it was just one drunken night, I missed you." He pressed his torso up, and his eyes roved her face, then locked in on hers. She felt drunk but hadn't sipped alcohol in three hours. It was from the sensation of Ryan here, close to her, his words and his body and everything in between.

"I'm sober," he said.

"Same," she replied.

"I love you," he said, sliding his hand between them.

"Ryan, I —" But he silenced her with a kiss at the same time the vibrator buzzed to life between her legs.

"Don't worry about saying anything," he whispered, his hand moving until Emmy gasped at the perfect placement. "Just worry about feeling good."

"You worry about feeling good," she muttered back, and the two of them shared a laugh as Emmy grew slick.

"Never a worry when I'm with you." He rolled slightly to the side, moving the toy in the way that he had learned, whispering confessions of love against her ear. With a held breath, she came. And Ryan wedged his large body between her legs as she was coming down, the press of his heat in her almost sending her sky high again.

"Ryan," she whispered as he fully seated himself.

"What do you need?"

"You." With that, he began to move slowly, cautiously. She wanted him unleashed again, so she wound her fingers into his hair, running her nails along his scalp.

"Really, Ry?" she murmured against his skin. "I know you've got more than this. It's been three weeks." She canted her hips, tugged his curls. "Show me what I missed."

"Three weeks," he grunted, pulling her hands from his hair and pinning them down. "Three weeks and four fucking days." *Thrust*. "Too long." *Thrust*. "Not again."

"No," Emmy confessed, wrapping her long legs around his hips.

"Never."

"Never." A groan from Ryan, and he was pressing himself as deep as he could go, muttering *I love you* against her jaw. Pulling him to her, enjoying the weight of him collapsed on top of her, she kissed his forehead. "Sleep here," she whispered.

"Did you take your meds?" he asked drowsily as she went to the bathroom, cleaning herself up with tissues from the countertop.

"Yeah, Ry. Thanks for checking." How normal this felt.

"Come back to bed." And she did.

52

Ryan

Ryan woke up feeling content and warm and unaware of his surroundings until he went to move his arm and found that Emmy was sprawled over it. She always slept like the dead, and Ryan grunted as he slid his arm out from underneath her, then ran his hand slowly down the side of her body, the curve of her hip, before curling it around her and tugging her body toward him.

“Em,” he whispered in her ear.

“No,” she grunted.

“Em, wake up,” he said, pressing a light kiss to the back of her neck. “Em, the conference is over, and I have plans for us today.” She adjusted her pillow and flopped back down, and he decided to use his trump card. “I found a coffee shop that makes their chai from scratch. Yelp says it’s the best dirty chai in Boston,” he whispered, blowing a light stream of air across her neck.

“You’re buying?” she said, blinking her eyes open.

“Yes, you mooch.” He smiled at her and gave her a light kiss on the lips.

“Mmm, you make more money. Science.”

"We have the same job," he replied. "Get out of bed, get dressed. I've got plans."

"We'll see," she muttered, but Emmy got out of bed and rifled through her suitcase. Ryan grew immediately hard at Emmy's unabashed nakedness this early in the morning, the way she didn't move to cover her body as she pulled out jeans and a shirt. He willed his dick to calm down, to remember that he had plans, that he needed to convince Emmy that he loved her — all of her. Her prickliness, her creativity, her sass, her friendship, *and* her body. He needed to convince her that the connection between them — their different approaches to curation, their respective backgrounds, and yeah, their passion — made them a team that would be unstoppable.

Ryan had developed his first Plan to Win Emmy Back roughly twelve hours after he had found the bottom of a whiskey bottle after Foster and Jeremy had left, their advice still ringing in his ears. He had spent that night researching and thinking and planning, and finally came upon the idea of showing Emmy examples from the history of couples that had worked. He had gone down a thousand rabbit holes, trying to find an example of a couple that had worked together successfully.

Unfortunately, all he found that night were examples of how men in academic couples had taken advantage of the women in the relationship. How many wives actually wrote and edited their husbands' academic papers. How many men took credit for discoveries done by their wives. How many had fucked secretaries while their wives held down careers and parenting. How many women had been denied opportunities because of their gender.

Which caused him to wake up with a massive hangover.

With a determination he hadn't found since he started grad school, he downed a triple-shot latte the next morning and went back to researching, finally stumbling on something that mirrored how he saw himself and Emmy. It wasn't a perfect historical comparison, but he thought Emmy would appreciate the connection. After more research and a few new books downloaded to his Kindle, he found the perfect exhibition to take her to.

And it was here in Boston.

All he had to do now was get Emmy caffeine, get her to the museum, and hope to god he guessed right about this interpretation.

"I'm going to my room to change clothes," he said, gathering up his suit that had crumpled to the floor by the doorway during last night's activities. "I'll meet you at the elevator in ten minutes?" Emmy nodded as she brushed her teeth, walking over to the coffee maker to start the tiny pot. She had thrown on a light gray tank top that brought out her eyes, paired with a pair of high-rise jeans and boots. "You look really nice today," he said softly as he walked to the door.

"Hurry up, Doc," she said, smiling. "I want to see what this chai and the whole adventure are all about."

His heart hammering in his chest, Ryan went to his room to change, throwing on a pair of jeans, his boots, and a light green sweater his mom had bought him for

Christmas. He brushed his teeth, ran fingers through his hair, and went to meet Emmy at the elevator.

53

Emmy

Ryan knew she didn't like surprises. He knew this. Emmy had been open with him about it since the first day they worked together, so he did give her a tiny hint as to what he had planned for the day. While in his room, he had texted her the name of the coffee store so she could begin organizing her order, and he had added a cryptic clue.

Ryan: After coffee, we're going to take the subway to a museum.

Ryan: And no, I'm not telling you which one, because you'll spend all of breakfast looking up their exhibits.

Emmy: Fine.

Emmy: I hope it's not the children's museum.

Emmy: Though it was the first children's museum in the US.

Emmy: So that's interesting from a historical perspective.

Ryan: It's not. And I'm not going to tell you. I'll see you in two minutes.

Emmy left after that and was waiting by the elevators when Ryan sauntered out of his room wearing one of Emmy's favorite sweaters. She recalled a very specific night that he had worn it, and the two of them had finished a bottle of wine while discussing the relative merits of keeping older, scientifically inaccurate animal dioramas on his deck before his sweater and her dress had ended up tossed on the ground.

"Hey," she said, waving awkwardly, and he slipped his hand into hers, lifted it to his mouth, and placed a gentle kiss on her knuckles.

"Ms. Bonaire."

"Dr. Andersson," she teased, her eyes flashing as they waited for the elevator.

"Not now, you infernal woman," he growled as the doors opened. "We have things to do today."

"I can think of plenty of things to do in that hotel room," Emmy said as he tugged her inside the elevator. There was a part of her — a not insignificant part — that wanted to hide in the hotel room all day, fuck Ryan, and not think about what any of this meant. Not think about what he had said to her last night, not think about whether she had made the right choice turning down those job offers, and not think about what would happen when she and Ryan got back to Vanberg.

"Emmy," he said, breaking her out of her thoughts. "Give me today, and if you decide that we're back to colleagues at the end of it, I'll understand." Ryan's face was deadly serious, devoid of the grins and the cheer he usually brought to their conversations. "I've been thinking a lot over the past few weeks and reading a lot, and well — I think you'll understand today. I hope you'll understand what I mean."

Again, cryptic. But Emmy appreciated the effort. Things came easily to Ryan, but she could tell that he had worked on something today. Using his phone, he navigated them to a tiny coffee shop called Jude's, where a gruff barista made Emmy the spiciest dirty chai she had ever had. It burned her throat in all the best ways, and the shot of espresso added complemented the flavors perfectly. She and Ryan split a bagel sandwich while Emmy pointed out the Freedom Trail that ran underneath their feet as they passed by the Old North Church.

"One if by land, all that shit?" Ryan asked, pointing to the window.

Emmy nodded, then sighed. "You know that Paul Revere, while important, wasn't the only rider? He was chosen to be featured in the poem because his name rhymed best." She laughed. "History is funny like that." They casually meandered to the subway stop, with Emmy only stopping five or six times to read historical markers. Honestly, in a city like Boston, Ryan should be lucky she wasn't taking over the day and dragging him to as many museums and sites as she wanted to.

Ryan took over directions again when they made it to the subway, with Emmy only reminding him three different times that it was the oldest subway system in the United States.

"Em, I know," he said as they got off at the Science Park exit. "You've explained the miracles of nineteenth-century civil engineering to me more times than I can count."

"Where are we going, Ryan?" she asked, looking around until her eyes landed on the sign and her heart sank slightly. A brick building sat on the river with large sans serif letters that read: MUSEUM OF SCIENCE.

"Dinosaurs, Ryan?" she said. "I mean, they're cool, but you've already taken me to the Denver Museum of Nature and Science, like, thirty times."

"We went twice, Em," Ryan said, opening the door to the museum for her and ushering her in. "And we're not here for dinosaurs."

"I don't believe you," she said. They flashed their American Museum Association membership cards for discounted admission, then Emmy grabbed a map, trying to quickly study the exhibitions to guess where Ryan was taking her. Standard natural history museum stuff, some hands-on science exhibitions – and then Ryan tugged the map out of her hands, folded it, and put it in his jeans pocket.

"Follow me," he said, lacing his fingers through hers and walking her in a very determined and specific direction. Emmy was shocked that Ryan actually walked past the prehistoric life exhibit without a second glance, not even using the wayfinding signs to see where he was going.

They turned a corner, and Emmy was greeted with an exhibition she recognized but knew she had never seen in person. She racked her brain trying to figure it out, then saw the entrance sign as soon as Ryan started to speak.

"This is Mathematica. First opened in 1961 at the California Museum of Science and Industry in Los Angeles. It was commissioned by IBM for the new museum, and it was designed by Ray and Charles Eames. It's this amazing blend of mathematics, history, and design, and it was so popular that they made three versions of it. This one was originally in Chicago before being moved here." Emmy slowly walked into the exhibition, starting to recognize specific elements from her textbooks, from her early days of studying exhibition design and museum theory. Ryan kept speaking behind her, and she peeked over her shoulder to see that he was reading from a series of note cards he had made, shuffling through them every time he recited a new fact about the exhibition. "The Eameses also made science education videos. There's a cool one I watched called 'Powers of 10' that is really trippy, and they apparently designed some of the most important furniture of the 1960s." Ryan cleared his throat again, and Emmy turned around.

He had shoved the notecards in his pocket and was looking at her intensely, his hands twitching. "The reason I wanted to bring you here, Em, is that Ray and Charles were married for thirty-seven years, and that's only when he died. They worked together the entire time. They created this." Ryan gestured around him. "And they stayed in love, and they brought history and science together." He looked at the ground, then up at her, his eyes shining. "I love you, Emmy, and I think we could do this."

She looked around at the exhibition, took in the dated design and the interpretation of the out-of-date information. “What’s *this*?”

“Make exhibitions. Curate together. Build a life and careers. Together.”

“Where?” This was the sticking point, wasn’t it?

“Vanberg,” he said simply. “Where else are we going to be able to do exhibitions in this way?” That charming, boyish grin that she had come to love.

She eyed him warily. “It’s just because that one barista gives you lattes and charges you for black coffee.”

“You’ve nailed it.”

“It’s because you can’t get enough of working in a drafty historic house full of asbestos.”

“Exactly.”

“It’s because —”

“It’s because of you, Emmy.” He took her hands, pulled her close. “And not just *you*, though I love you wildly. It’s because of your friends, of the life you’ve created there. And how you’ve let me in.”

“Okay, fine, it’s a little bit because of me.” She laughed, then lifted up onto her toes and kissed him. “But if it’s because of me, it’s also because of you.”

“Me?”

“You listen and think and reflect and push me to be better.” A kiss. “And that’s why I love you,” she whispered against his lips.

“You love me?”

“Yes, you infuriating paleontologist. I love you. I love your insistence that pterodactyls aren’t dinosaurs —”

"They aren't."

"I love your research skills, how you apply them to any problems in your life. I love how you love your sisters. I love how you welcomed me into your professional and personal life with all of my baggage." He kissed her, and she melted, his lips opening and his tongue sliding and his hands roaming in ways that were, frankly, wildly inappropriate for a public museum at ten thirty in the morning. At some point, Ryan pulled back, and Emmy immediately looked around.

He chuckled. "You want to check out the exhibition, don't you?"

"Of course!" She ran over to the introductory panel, already pulling up the Wikipedia page about Charles and Ray Eames on her phone to double-check the facts. But something was missing. Some*one*.

She turned around, went back, grabbed his hand. "But you're coming with me."

Epilogue

Ryan rolled over to where Emmy was already awake, scrolling through her phone. She looked especially gorgeous in the morning, softer than she was during the day, with her hair in a bun and her face screwed up in concentration as she read an article. The sheets were slung low over her hips, revealing her bare chest, and Ryan was overcome with love for this woman, the knowledge that she was it for him.

"Em?"

"Mmm?"

"Marry me."

Emmy hit him in the face with a pillow. He grinned at her, and she rolled her eyes, which were their standard facial expressions of love at this point. They had their rhythms: Emmy pretended like she still couldn't tolerate him, and Ryan asked Emmy once a week if she would marry him. Especially after he found out she didn't want to get married at all.

That fact had come out one Wednesday, a few weeks after they had gotten home from Boston, with the entire group out at Mountain Friend for trivia. At this point, their trivia gang had gotten so big they had to split into three different teams. Emmy and Ryan had gotten paired up with Phoebe and Declan, while June and Colin were partnered with her old teaching partner and his husband. Satya and the collections managers rounded out the third team. Jeremy usually attended but was out in the National Forest working on a new project for the museum he was being cagey about.

“Next question,” Foster said over the noise of the crowd, which had gotten rowdier in recent months as the brewery continued to grow in popularity. “What year were women able to apply for credit cards without permission from their husbands?”

Phoebe and Dec looked at each other and shrugged. “Uh, 1940?” Dec offered.

Emmy had snorted. “The credit card wasn’t even invented until the 1950s.”

Ryan shrugged his shoulders, and Emmy bobbed her head from side to side, thinking. “I’m thinking it was around 1973.”

“That late?” he asked, the words spilling out of his mouth.

Emmy grimaced. “Yeah.”

“Wait, you’re telling me that women could vote and have an abortion before they could get a credit card without their husband?” Ryan’s journey through history still shocked him.

"Yeah, that's why marriage is stupid and not worth it," Emmy said. She looked at the other teams and sighed. "Well, it might be different for Kevin and John because they fought for that right." She looked at June and Colin. "And, of course, if people want it, great for them. It just has never felt like something I wanted, you know?" Ryan had nodded, considering a new perspective on something he had always assumed to be the next step.

They had discussed it later that night in Emmy's bed, and Ryan had nodded, listening, as Emmy listed all the ways that marriage had hurt women. Ryan asked multiple questions, hypothetical and practical, to understand Emmy's perspective, then had to ask a lingering one.

"But you're committed?" he asked, his voice shaky.

"You're mine." She grinned.

"You're mine, too."

"I trust you," Emmy whispered. "With my thoughts and my heart."

"I don't take that lightly," he responded. "I'll always listen." And somehow, that was better than a ceremony for Ryan, this set of whispered promises between pillows.

Eventually, their conversation shifted to nothing in particular, and Emmy had brought up the fact that the root beer float had been invented in Colorado, which led to an entire conversation about sodas and Prohibition. By the end of it, Ryan was so turned on, as he usually was when she talked history, that he was nearly cross-eyed with need.

"Ugh, I have to go home and get stuff." Emmy groaned, rolling out of bed and stealing a pair of Ryan's shorts.

"You don't have to," he said, his stomach flopping like a fish on land. He had wanted to have this conversation with Emmy for weeks now, but anytime he began it, she distracted him. Either she was asking a question about how something scientific worked, sharing a piece of history she learned, or giving him *that* look and clothes miraculously fell off both of their bodies. But now? Unbrushed teeth and messy hair? This was when they were their most unassuming, their most malleable. When they joked and whispered, brainstormed and bickered, and always ended it with a kiss.

"Huh?" she asked, pulling a tank top on. He loved it when she didn't wear a bra in the mornings.

"You don't have to go home and get stuff," he said, rolling over onto his stomach and propping his chin in his hands. "Not if you moved in here."

"Doctor Ryan Andersson," she said, spinning around and looking at him.

"Yes, beautiful?"

"Do not distract me with your flattery," she said, but he knew she loved those tiny nicknames of affection, the ways they were both able to show their love in sarcastic jabs and snark. Hell, he still lost focus in meetings when she called him by his academic title, and it had been months since she had first used "Doctor Andersson" in bed. "What are you actually asking me?"

"Fine, you obstinate woman," he replied. "Move in with me." Her jaw dropped open and, she struggled for words, so Ryan supplied more. "Don't say anything yet. Just come downstairs and let me give you a presentation."

"What?"

He squeezed his eyes shut and admitted in a low voice. "I made a PowerPoint."

He was so damn precious at times like this, Emmy reflected as she watched him move around his living room and connect his laptop to the television. When he put his mind to something and pursued it, whether it was research for work or for their relationship.

Ryan had attended a few of Emmy's therapy sessions when they had first started dating, and he'd thrown himself into reading studies about the approach her therapist used. He was also at a session where Emmy, with the encouragement of her therapist, had brought up eventually trying to find a doctor who would tie her tubes. The look of joy and relief on Ryan's face when they both acknowledged to each other they didn't want to be parents made her fall in love with him all over again. Ryan had been ready to call the university's insurance provider the next day, though Emmy let him know her IUD was fine for a few more years.

She quirked a smile at him from the couch, curling her hands around a cup of coffee, as he stood next to the TV, balancing his laptop on one forearm.

"Em," he began and clicked open the slide show. "I think you should move in with me here."

"Okay, but —" she began, and he playfully shushed her.

"Do not interrupt the presenter when he is speaking." He clicked to another slide. "I know you value your independence and your own space, but I have prepared a series of reasons, supported with evidence, of why this is the best option for us."

The next slide popped on the screen, with the heading: Fiscal Responsibility

"Housing prices and rent have continued to rise over the past year, and if we both share the mortgage here, it allows more wiggle room for money for ski trips, travel, and nights out dancing." A graph of Colorado rent prices accompanied this.

Environmental Impact

"We can save on the electricity and heating impact if we're sharing one location, in addition to using body heat at night to minimize the gas we use during the winter. Also, commuting together means we lessen our use of gasoline."

"I take the bus from my house, so actually, I'm more sustainable," Emmy argued.

"Please save comments and questions for the end of the presentation," Ryan said briskly. *Oh*, he was in stern professor mode. Emmy felt a spike of heat between her legs.

More slides were presented: workplace collaboration, bulk purchasing from Costco, potential to adopt a dog, proximity to the highway for skiing. At one point, he had even looked up the historic sites in his neighborhood and mapped their distance from his house. Emmy felt her heart grow and warm with each click of his track pad and each readjustment of Ryan's glasses as he talked through graphs and data.

"And that," he said, pushing his glasses into his hair and clicking the laptop one last time, "is why you, Emmy Bonaire, should move in with me, Ryan Andersson."

"Doc," she said, standing and setting her now-empty coffee cup down. "That was a wonderful presentation. I appreciated the use of statistics and an emotional call. Really appreciated the historic context of the neighborhood." He bit his lip, was looking at her nervously. "But you missed the most important point."

"Which is?" He had started to fiddle with his shorts.

"I love you," she said. "And, while I appreciated your research skills on display, I was ready to say yes back in your bedroom."

"You were?"

"Yeah, and we should go back there immediately, because your research and argumentative skills are sexy as fuck."

"So you're moving in here?" That classic, all-American grin that used to drive her up a wall. "We live together?"

"Yeah, Doc." Emmy's cheeks hurt from smiling. Ryan walked over to her and delicately pulled her up from the couch. Emmy only had time to say "*What are you—*" before Ryan had picked her up and tossed her over his shoulder. "Put me down!" Emmy was giggling, though, as Ryan spun her around in circles, their laughs mingling in what was now their house.

Acknowledgments

There are what seems like a thousand people to thank for this book, so I'll do my best.

First off, to my team of beta readers and support crew as I drafted this book. S'mores was a solo adventure, this was a team mission. Ellen, Jilian, Emma, Kelsey, Laura, Meg, Andi – you helped me to bring the best version of Emmy and Ryan to life.

Hannah and Dani – thank you for making me feel like a real author and dealing with all the ups and downs and crises that we all constantly deal with. I love you both so much.

Brittani – my business brilliance! I am so happy we met back in my yoga days and we are both taking the world by storm,. Give Burger an apple for me.

Sam – I still don't know how you take my rambles and turn it into the perfect cover. Also I love our shared love of Scraggly Doggies.

Beth – For helping me pare down 600 (!) em dashes and pulling out all my unnecessary words. You're stuck with me.

Allie and Mackenzie – my real-life smut reading friends that I can always count on to swap book recs.

Angela - You're the best friend I could have ever asked for and your support through this wild last year has meant the world to me. I owe you a guava margarita from Baja Betty's.

Brady – You mean more to me than I can even say. Your support and love is unmatched and I love **us**.

To me – For finding joy and your true self in 2022.

Also By

Need S'more Time (June & Colin)

Coming Soon...

Educated (Phoebe & Declan)

Exhibited (Jeremy & ???)

About Author

Nellie Wilson is the pen name of a historian in her 30s who has an impossible-to-spell real name. Originally from western Pennsylvania, Nellie spent time in Ohio and Colorado before settling in San Diego with her partner, dog, and cat. She enjoys drinking beer, talking about true crime and medical history, listening to emo music from the 2000s, and exploring the outdoors. When not writing books, she works as an architectural historian and reads Wikipedia entries for fun. You can find her on Instagram and TikTok at @woahnelliewrites.

www.ingramcontent.com/pod-product-compliance
Ingram Content Group UK Ltd.
Pitfield, Milton Keynes, MK11 3LW, UK
UKHW031315090125
4035UKWH00033B/273

9 781088 109595